Saving the Market from Itself

The 2007–2009 financial crisis threatened economic disaster on a scale not seen since the Great Depression, but rapid state action prevented the widely feared devastation. The German response was considerably more generous to banks than the American or British bailouts were. Drawing on author interviews and primary sources in government, private firms, and media, Mitchell explains how the structure of national financial systems and interbank relationships produced extensive private rescues and pressure on different states. Mitchell explores the different responses and results in Germany, the United Kingdom, and the United States using a combination of detailed case-study analyses of the three countries' responses to the crisis and a quantitative analysis of patterns of state responses to financial crises. This book will be essential reading for scholars and advanced students of political economy, comparative politics, economic sociology, economics, and public policy.

Christopher Mitchell is a visiting assistant professor of International Affairs and Director of the International Trade and Investment Policy program at the George Washington University.

Saving the Market from Itself

The Politics of Financial Intervention

Christopher Mitchell
George Washington University, Washington, DC

CAMBRIDGE
UNIVERSITY PRESS

CAMBRIDGE
UNIVERSITY PRESS

University Printing House, Cambridge CB2 8BS, United Kingdom

Cambridge University Press is part of the University of Cambridge.

It furthers the University's mission by disseminating knowledge in the pursuit of education, learning, and research at the highest international levels of excellence.

www.cambridge.org
Information on this title: www.cambridge.org/9781107159235

First published 2016

A catalogue record for this publication is available from the British Library.

Library of Congress Cataloging-in-Publication Data
Names: Mitchell, Christopher (Political scientist), author.
Title: Saving the market from itself: the politics of financial intervention / Christopher Mitchell, George Washington University, Washington DC.
Description: Cambridge, UK: Cambridge University Press, 2016. | Includes bibliographical references and index.
Identifiers: LCCN 2016028918| ISBN 9781107159235 (hardback) |
Subjects: LCSH: Financial crises – Government policy. | Monetary policy. | Economic policy.
Classification: LCC HB3722.M58 2016 | DDC 339.5–dc23
LC record available at https://lccn.loc.gov/2016028918

ISBN 978-1-107-15923-5 Hardback

To my wife Elizabeth, without whom I never would have made it this far.

To Henry Stender, who so wanted to see this book in print.

To my mother, for her love and support.

Contents

Figures and Tables

Figures

Tables

Preface

The 2007–2009 financial crisis demonstrated once again the potential for enormous devastation in a capitalist system, and that even the most advanced economies are not immune to potentially catastrophic crises. It also demonstrated how states are willing to spend massive sums of money to contain financial crises. Given the potential devastation from an uncontained financial crisis, spending even billions of dollars, euros, or pounds may be justified. However, while the public will be universally hostile to such bank bailouts, not all bailouts are created equal. Some states, such as the United States, constructed their rescues in such a way that the state recouped the vast majority of taxpayer money invested in saving the banks. Others, such as Germany, adopted policies that were much more generous to bankers and were never designed to, nor in fact did, recover a significant portion of taxpayer funds.

This project had its genesis in the very heart of the financial crisis, as I closely followed the development of rescue plans in the United States and Europe. Although much of the business literature and academic literature had emphasized an increasing convergence in global business and regulatory practices, the affected states adopted at times strikingly different policies. This project, therefore, was devoted to explaining why such divergent policies came about and whether they could be explained simply as a product of individual leaders in power or driven by deeper structural forces. What eventually became clear is that the extent of convergence has been overstated. Even if divergent financial systems have moved closer to each other, they retain key differences, especially in the political clout of banks and bankers in times of crisis. As such, financial crises, rather than deepening convergence, in fact reinforce diversity in national financial systems. Moreover, they do so in a way that has significant impact on the long-term costs to the state. Although the public is universally hostile to bailouts regardless of the specific forms, and although all affected states can be expected to invest significant public money in containing the crisis, the nature of the national financial system will play a key role in determining the shape of the rescue, the costs to shareholders, and the likelihood of the state recovering its funds.

This book would not have been possible without the support of a great many individuals. I would like to thank, first and foremost, my wife Elizabeth and the rest of my family for their constant support. Thanks to the following people as well who provided valuable input on the book and its earlier drafts: Harvey Feigenbaum, Susan Sell, Emmanuel Teitelbaum, Jeffrey Anderson, Henry Farrell, Cornelia Woll, Jason Sorens, Eric N. Budd, Azzedine Layachi, Jane Gingrich, Pascal Petit, Phil Cerny, Geoffrey Underhill, Lucia Quaglia, Stefano Pagliari, Kevin Young, Cornel Ban, Orfeo Fioretos, Martin Rhodes, Rachel Epstein, Andrew Kerner, Jonathan Hanson, and David Earnest. My apologies to anyone who I have omitted; I assure you it does not reflect my lack of gratitude. My thanks also to the following organizations for their support: the German Academic Exchange Service; the Horowitz Foundation for Social Policy; the Institute for European, Russian, and Eurasian Studies at the George Washington University; and the Collaborative Research Center at Freie Universität Berlin.

Abbreviations

ABA	American Banking Association
AIG	American International Group
APS	Asset Purchase Scheme
BaFin	*Bundesanstalt für Finanzdienstleistungsaufsicht* (Federal Financial Supervisory Authority)
BdB	*Bundesverband deutscher Banken* (Federal Association of German Banks)
BVR	*Bundesverband der Deutschen Volksbanken und Raiffeisenbanken* (National Association of German Cooperative Banks)
CDO	Collateralized Debt Obligation
CDS	Credit Default Swap
CDU/CSU	Christian Democratic Union/Christian Social Union
DSGV	*Deutscher Sparkassen- und Giroverband* (German Savings Banks Association)
DSW	*Deutsche Schutzvereinigung für Wertpapierbesitz*
ECB	European Central Bank
FDIC	Federal Deposit Insurance Corporation
FHFA	Federal Housing Finance Agency
FSA	Financial Services Authority
GSE	Government-Sponsored Enterprises
HBOS	Halifax Bank of Scotland
HSBC	Hong Kong and Shanghai Banking Corporation
IKB	*Industrialkreditbank*
KfW	*Kreditanstalt für Wiederaufbau*
LBBW	*Landesbank Baden-Württemberg*
LTCM	Long-Term Capital Management
OCC	Office of Comptroller of the Currency
OFHEO	Office of Federal Housing Enterprise Oversight
OTS	Office of Thrift Supervision
RBS	Royal Bank of Scotland

SDP	Social Democratic Party
SEC	Securities and Exchange Commission
SLS	Special Liquidity Scheme
SoFFin	*Sonderfonds Finanzmarktstabilisierung* (Special Financial Market Stabilization Funds)
TARP	Troubled Asset Relief Program
UKSA	UK Shareholder Association
WaMu	Washington Mutual

1 Introduction

Beginning in 2007, the largest financial crisis since 1929 hit Europe and the United States. As the value of mortgage-backed securities collapsed, worry turned to panic as more and larger banks began to fail. By fall of 2008, some of the largest banks in the world were under threat. If the financial system collapsed, the damage to the real economy could have rivaled the Great Depression. Therefore, despite public hostility toward bailing out the banks, virtually every state hit by the 2007–2009 financial crisis committed substantial resources to contain the crisis. Some would spend as much as a trillion dollars to rescue banks and limit fallout.

However, the ways in which these states spent their money differed. Although in the popular imagination, all state bailouts of banks were giveaways from taxpayers to financial interests, the actual terms and effects differed substantially. The United States showed great willingness to impose terms on banks, wiping out shareholders of smaller banks and forcing large banks to accept part-nationalizations through capital injections on state-dictated terms. Because of this, the United States actually turned a small profit on its bank rescues after only a few years. The United Kingdom similarly relied on nationalizations and compulsory state aid, imposing even harsher terms on its banks with an eye toward recovering state funds at a profit. Germany, on the other hand, spent a comparable sum on its bailouts but favored generous aid that minimized state ownership, generally being much more willing to shield shareholders from losses. This, in turn, meant that the German plan neither recovered state funds nor was intended to do so.

This fits in a general historical pattern of consistently divergent responses to financial crises across advanced capitalist economies. Contrary to what may be expected, state intervention in systems with a liberal, laissez-faire tradition in economic policy is generally much more compulsory and on harsher terms than in states with a tradition of state-managed, organized, or corporatist capitalism. Those states with liberal financial systems, in which the stock market is a primary source of capital and interbank relationships are generally thin and arm's-length, favor state intervention on fairly stringent terms. State aid is generally compulsory and terms are relatively harsh, involving punitive rates of repayment or compulsory nationalization. By contrast, in states with corporatist economies, private banks dominate the provision of capital, and those banks have much tighter interbank relationships, including greater interdependence and stronger private governance associations. Because of this, healthy banks play a much greater role in shaping state responses in the corporatist systems. This means that private banks are willing to shoulder a greater burden of the costs of crisis containment, but also that they will influence the state to offer public assistance on more generous and less invasive terms than in states with liberal financial systems.

Remarkably, the politics surrounding immediate state responses to financial crises have been largely unexplored, with far more attention paid to either debates over financial policies in good times or the longer-term postcrisis reform process. Exploring the dynamics of immediate crisis response is obviously important from a public policy perspective. The nature of bank bailout policies shapes not only the degree of damage financial crises do to the broader economy but also the direct costs to the state. Given the immense upfront costs that states pay, whether the state recovers its money could have a major impact on state finances going forward. Additionally, the terms of response shape the likelihood of future crises: generous rescues that insulate shareholders from losses risk encouraging further reckless actions in the future, while punitive responses that push costs onto shareholders encourage banks to avoid needing such rescues in the future.

Additionally, this research provides insight into the comparative capitalisms literature. The literatures on convergence and comparative capitalisms have long been in tension with one another over whether national diversity in economic systems will persist or collapse into a single "best practices" model under the pressure of increased global interconnectedness. Financial crises provide a crucial test of the stability of financial systems, when major actors are weakened and assumptions about the strengths of the financial system model may be questioned. The ability of national financial systems to self-replicate in these moments of crisis will be crucial to determining whether national diversity persists.

A Primer on Financial Crises and Policy Responses

The literature on financial crises and their responses is vast, spreading across multiple disciplines and with significant divisions over the causes of, culpability for, and best practices in responding to financial crises. This diversity, however, rests on a common fundamental understanding of the basic technical issues of financial crises, which are worth exploring in some depth to provide a basic lexicon to discuss state responses. This is even more valuable given how different authors may use the same terms in somewhat different fashions. This is most apparent in the case of "bailouts," which for some authors refers to all state aid but for others refers only to state aid that substantially insulates private actors from losses, with the attendant moral hazard and perverse redistribution issues.

Financial crises are an aggregate of multiple events, filtered into a single event as a cognitive construct (Mayntz, 2012a, p. 7). Therefore, there may be many different causes and forms of financial crises. Here we are concerned with banking crises, where a large number of banks run into distress, as well as market crashes, when the value of a state's stock market drops dramatically. The term "financial crisis" may also encompass sovereign debt or fiscal crises, where the state's ability to pay its debts comes into doubt. Financial crises may also refer to currency crises, when currency traders question the state's ability to maintain a set value for its currency. Both these sovereign financial crises are outside of the scope of this book, although an expensive bailout may lead to a sovereign crisis by straining a state's finances or ability to defend its currency.

Banks may fail because they are either insolvent or illiquid. Insolvency is a simpler problem to grasp, though more difficult to fix. If a bank owes more money to investors or depositors than it holds in assets (loans and investments), then the bank will fail simply because it will not be able to pay its obligations unless it somehow increases the value of its assets, typically through an injection of fresh capital from a new investor. Insolvency typically occurs because a bank invests in assets that fail to perform as expected and lose value. In the 2007–2009 crisis, the collapse in value of mortgage-backed securities was a chief driver of bank insolvency. Such a collapse may affect many banks at once, if they are all exposed to the same collapsing assets, as was the case with banks holding mortgage-backed securities in 2007–2009.

Banks may also fail because they run short of liquidity. Banks operate by funding long-term investments with short-term credit. Customers of both commercial and investment banks provide the banks money on a short-term basis, meaning they can withdraw their money at any time. That money, however, is used to fund investments that may not be rapidly converted into cash, such as loans with long periods of repayment or assets that are difficult to sell quickly. Because of this, banks hold some cash back as a "liquid" capital reserve. However, no bank has enough cash on hand to repay all or a significant portion of its creditors. Since the capital reserve earns no profit, banks have an incentive to make it as small as possible while still preserving enough of a liquidity cushion to pay back those customers demanding repayment. However, no bank holds enough of a capital reserve to repay all of its customers. If many demand repayment, the bank may be forced to close because it has run short of liquidity, even if it has valuable assets that it simply cannot convert to cash in time. Unless some form of deposit insurance program is in place, everyone who had not already withdrawn their money will lose it when the bank closes. This means that bank runs are rational even if the bank is otherwise healthy: once enough people start withdrawing their money from the banks, the remaining depositors or creditors should also withdraw their funds to avoid losing out when the bank closes, deepening the crisis. This principle holds whether the initial run was sparked by legitimate concerns over the bank or a baseless panic.

This opens up multiple channels of contagion. Since banks frequently engage in interbank lending, other banks may be among the customers wiped out by another bank's failure, especially if loans are inadequately collateralized. Therefore, a single bank's failure may drive other banks into insolvency or illiquidity as well. Additionally, once a high-profile run on one bank occurs, investors in other banks may begin to fear a run on their own banks. Once started, such runs become self-fulfilling prophecies, and otherwise healthy banks can be driven to failure by a contagion panic. This is especially likely if the second bank bears a resemblance to the failing one, such as by holding a similar investment portfolio.

If a bank is illiquid but not insolvent, it can potentially be saved by loans from a third party. So long as the bank is solvent, it has assets that will, in time, pay enough to repay those loans. However, in a banking crisis, lenders may be in scarce supply, either because they are unwilling to risk lending to an illiquid bank or because they are afraid they will need to shepherd their own liquidity reserves should they be subject to a bank run. An insolvent bank, however, can only be saved by making its assets once again greater than its liabilities, either by an infusion of capital, thereby increasing the value of its assets, or by somehow reducing the value of its liabilities.

As Goodhart (2009) notes, in modern financial systems, liquidity and solvency issues may blur together. Banks typically are highly reliant on liquidity from access to interbank lending, collateralized by a claim on the bank's financial assets. If the bank has valuable assets, it should be able to avoid liquidity problems through interbank lending unless a general panic causes other banks to hoard their own liquid reserves. Even then, however, central banks are typically willing to play lender of last resort and provide liquidity to any bank capable of posting adequate collateral. If collateral assets fall in value, banks may face both solvency issues, as their asset portfolio loses value, and liquidity issues, as other banks demand more collateral to make up for drop in value of collateral assets or higher interest rates to offset the greater risk of default.

Separating liquidity and solvency issues is increasingly difficult, but it remains a matter of great concern to both banks and the state. Other banks may be interested in buying an illiquid bank and, in doing so, may be able to get a good deal on the bank's solvent assets. Buying an insolvent bank, however, would produce a net loss to the purchaser, and therefore banks may buy assets but not an entire insolvent bank. The state may be more willing to provide support to an illiquid but solvent bank. Liquidity crises may be externally caused by a baseless panic rather than by internal mismanagement, meaning there may not be substantial moral hazard in aiding an illiquid but insolvent bank. It is harder to avoid moral hazard issues in providing state aid to an insolvent bank, which is more clearly culpable for its own bad asset purchases.

Further complicating matters are "toxic assets," which may have been overvalued by speculators in the run-up to the crisis but are likely undervalued in the immediate aftermath, as investors shun the formerly popular assets. This makes it virtually impossible to accurately estimate how much value the asset will recover over time. Toxic assets complicate evaluations of both solvency and liquidity. Toxic assets can precipitate a liquidity crisis by limiting access to interbank lending. If toxic assets were used as collateral, the lending bank will favor a low estimation of their current value, decreasing the liquidity available to the borrowing bank. Toxic assets also make it harder to evaluate solvency. The "book value," or precrisis price, is clearly no longer accurate. Valuing toxic assets at current market value may make asset holders insolvent. Valuing at some estimated future price may make the holder solvent, at least on paper, depending on the credibility of the methodology used to make such a valuation. The current asset holder has strong incentives to overestimate that future value, meaning that others may reasonably question the credibility of that estimation.

Responses to Banking Crises

The failure of a bank can easily precipitate the failure of other banks. Failure in the financial sector generally is also more likely to cause harm to the broader economy than in other sectors. Without a steady access to credit, many businesses in the "real" economy would be forced to suspend or contract operations, meaning that a banking crisis can have far wider collateral impact than a comparably sized crisis in, for instance, manufacturing sectors. Therefore, both other banks and the state will have clear interests in taking action to contain banking crises so as to limit damage to the broader economy. Responses to financial crises come in many varieties, but can all be evaluated on two dimensions: effectiveness at containing the crisis and the degree of moral hazard created by the intervention (Wright, 2010b, p. 18). At one extreme, relying only on private market solutions creates no moral hazard issues but may prove ineffective at containing the crisis. At the other extreme, using state funds to completely insulate market actors from losses contains the crisis but with severe distortions of incentives and massive redistribution of wealth. Responses may be broadly categorized into three groups: private solutions, liquidity solutions, and capital solutions (Rosas and Jensen, 2010, p. 108). Within each category, a number of policies may be implemented, and their effectiveness in containing the crisis and diminishing moral hazard concerns will vary substantially based on their implementation. Without understanding their goals and methods, policy options cannot be easily compared in their moral hazard implications. Therefore, it is important to understand how the policies work and what separates a "good" moral hazard–limiting version of a policy from a "bad" moral hazard–creating one.

Private Solutions

Private solutions, in which no public money is used, are most in keeping with the logic of orthodox classical economics. Any injection of state funds in markets distorts prices, creating inefficient outcomes by encouraging inefficient patterns of behavior (Bagehot, 1892; Wright, 2010b, p. 18). Letting private actors sort out market problems themselves eliminates distortion and generally purges inefficient or unstable firms in favor of the stronger and more prudent. This not only eliminates market distortions but also the problem of moral hazard. If firms know no public rescue is coming and that they will be held accountable for their bad decisions, they will act in a more prudent manner. Because of this, financial crises should be rarer if a laissez-faire state response is expected (Rosas, 2006, 2009; Schneider and Tornell, 2004).[1] Furthermore, the direct cost to states is minimal, as no expensive outlay is required to finance a private response. The indirect effect on the real economy, however, can be immense, dragging GDP down for years. This cost gives policymakers an incentive to intervene despite market distortion and moral hazard problems and gives firms reason to anticipate state intervention if their fall will precipitate a broader economic disaster.

[1] A corollary to this is that speculative booms should also be smaller, as firms are more reluctant to lend.

Do Nothing

The prima facie simplest option for policymakers is to not involve the state in a financial crisis, letting market forces and the actions of private actors separate those firms capable of withstanding a crisis from those that cannot. Doing so avoids direct costs to the state and prevents moral hazard. It also most clearly reflects the private risk/private reward logic of free market capitalism.

There are several reasons, however, why this is not the best option for policymakers. Most prominent is the problem of contagion, when the distress or failure of a single firm, or small number of firms, causes a loss of confidence in the sector in general. The financial sector's susceptibility to bank runs makes it uniquely vulnerable to contagion effects. A firm may face failure not through its own actions but because a rival's collapse causes a general lack of faith in the sector. Aid to an otherwise healthy firm suffering from another's poor decisions may be justifiable, especially given the costs to the broader economy of allowing contagion to overrun the sector. Once healthy firms become caught in the panic, only action by the state, with its significantly greater reserves, may serve to stem the panic.

Firm collapse in the financial sector is devastating to an advanced economy, given the sector's central role in allocating capital to the real economy. The resulting broader recession would likely both activate automatic stabilizer welfare programs and create demand for a state economic stimulus package, indirectly causing the state to increase spending even in the absence of a financial rescue. Therefore, there are good reasons to expect significant costs to both the state and the real economy from simply letting a crisis "burn itself out." Furthermore, an action bias will likely prevail among policymakers. The public may not want to spend public funds on the financial sector, but neither will they want a broad economic crisis. Electorally sensitive policymakers will want to appear to be acting to solve the crisis, even if they are skeptical that government intervention will be effective. Voters more readily forgive unsuccessful action than no action at all, which may be perceived as "fiddling while Rome burns."

Nevertheless, states will let even large and important firms fail, for a number of reasons. They may lack the legal or fiscal resources necessary to save the firm or have philosophical or practical objections to state aid. Policymakers may conclude that state aid will create too great market distortions or encourage other firms to engage in risky behavior since they have confidence that they will receive support if they run into trouble. Alternatively, policymakers may conclude that the firm is small enough or its troubles have been broadly known long enough that its failure will not cause disastrous repercussions. All of these reasons were cited by people close to the decision by the US government not to save Lehman Brothers in 2008, by far the most prominent recent example of a state letting a firm fail. This action was not unprecedented, however. The Hoover administration chose not to intervene following the Great Crash of 1929, believing that state intervention would ultimately cause more problems than it solved.

Private Rescues

The state does have options to save banks without committing funds directly. States will frequently attempt to broker a rescue of the distressed firm by private actors. Private market solutions, in which other firms act to contain the crisis, are optimal from a policymaker's perspective in a number of ways. If effective, the crisis is contained and damage to the broader economy prevented. Using private funds instead of public monies eliminates redistributive consequences, which should limit negative public fallout. Finally, as bargains between private actors, moral hazard issues in private rescues are limited.

Because of these advantages, policymakers frequently seek to broker private market solutions. A healthy firm may purchase a distressed firm, either in full or by making an investment that increases the distressed firm's capital reserves and makes the healthy one a part owner. Two distressed firms with complementary strengths and weaknesses may merge, such that the merged firm is capable of surviving even if the constituent firms would fail on their own. Finally, healthy firms may provide lending to distressed firms, a solution that addresses liquidity issues but not solvency issues.

Private rescues may also take the form of consortium rescues, in which a group of firms pools their resources to assist distressed firms, either by issuing joint loans or, more rarely, by making a pooled capital injection. Such consortiums may be standing facilities, preexisting institutions ready to provide private funding to firms that require it and meet their qualifications. The German LIKO Bank facility provides an example of such a privately funded facility (Roth, 1994, p. 43). Alternatively, consortium rescues may be conducted on an ad hoc basis. The 1998 rescue of Long-Term Capital Management is an example of the latter. The US Federal Reserve organized a consortium of US financial institutions to provide liquidity assistance to the failing hedge fund. Such rescues distribute the burden of assistance across financial firms but require greater organizational effort than a relatively simple individual bank-to-bank rescue.

State involvement in brokering such private rescues may be politically problematic. By actively brokering mergers, policymakers risk accusations of undue meddling in markets. They may be seen as cajoling less-than-willing firms to take actions they otherwise would not or as showing favoritism by either acting to preserve favored weak firms or providing advantages for favored strong firms. Policymakers may also be tempted to encourage private solutions by including "sweeteners": public funds to absorb debts, guarantee loans, or otherwise incentivize the merger. The use of such publically funded sweeteners, however, should be considered a form of public rescue.

Public Rescues

Public assistance in financial crises can be classified into two approaches: liquidity assistance and solvency assistance. Liquidity assistance helps firms meet their immediate cash needs with loans or guarantees, but does not affect the underlying balance sheet of the firm. Liquidity support may buy time for an insolvent firm to find a private solvency solution, but cannot itself solve problems of solvency. Solving solvency issues requires the state to directly address a firm's capital ratio, generally by taking full or partial ownership of a firm or its assets. Both approaches vary in their moral hazard implications, depending on how state aid is priced and the terms attached to such aid.

Liquidity Approaches

Regulatory Favoritism

The state may assist a firm by altering its regulatory restraints, either temporarily or permanently. Temporary regulatory relief typically removes or relaxes capital reserve requirements. This allows the firm to address liquidity needs without falling below the minimum capital reserves necessary to remain open. Permanent relief involves changing the firm's legal status. This may be a change in the regulations governing a type of firm, or it may allow the firm to adopt a different legal status that provides certain advantages. For instance, in 2008, US regulators accepted applications from investment banks Morgan Stanley and Goldman Sachs to reclassify themselves as bank holding companies. This put them under increased regulatory supervision, but expanded their ability to borrow from the Federal Reserve. Regulatory favoritism may alter a firm's legal capital requirements, but, unless accompanied by a capital injection, can only affect a firm's liquidity. A change in the legal minimum capital requirements may change the point at which regulators force a bank to close. This may free up capital to address liquidity concerns and, in doing so, allow a firm more time, but will not actually change the ratio of assets to liabilities, and so this cannot make an insolvent firm solvent again.

Regulatory favoritism does not directly involve state funds, so may introduce fewer moral hazard issues than other state aid approaches. Typically, it is used to allow firms to access state liquidity reserves available to other kinds of firms and thus indirectly puts more state funds in play. The effects, however, are relatively small if the change merely provides the at-risk firm access on the same terms as other, healthy firms. Morgan Stanley and Goldman Sachs' shift to bank holding company status, for instance, was an option available to them in good times as well as bad, at the discretion of the Federal Reserve, so it did not provide them with significant extraordinary access. It merely gave them the same status as existing bank holding companies, granting them certain advantages but also the disadvantage of increased regulatory oversight. Relaxation of capital requirements and other temporary relief are more problematic from a moral hazard standpoint, but still do not directly involve public finances in extraordinary spending. Therefore, the distorting effects are present, but smaller than in rescues involving direct state aid, as the firm is allowed greater lenience than it is entitled to under the existing legal framework.

Guarantees

States may attempt to solve liquidity problems by guaranteeing repayment to creditors or depositors, reducing or eliminating the pressure to withdraw funds and the reluctance to make new loans. State-backed guarantees remove doubts over repayment in the event of firm collapse, making lending to the firm as safe as lending to the state. As such, if guarantees work as intended, the provision of the guarantee itself solves the crisis of confidence, and state funds need never actually be used. If the firm's crisis is purely one of confidence, guarantees can solve the crisis at no direct cost to the state.

Guarantees do create moral hazard issues with both the firms themselves and depositors and creditors. The firm gets to substitute the state's superior creditworthiness for its own, escaping market judgment of its likelihood to honor its obligations. Therefore, the provision of guarantees creates moral hazard by insulating firms from losses, if only prospective ones. Typically states address this concern by charging a fee for the provision of guarantees, even if they are not used. If guarantees are standing facilities, as in the typical case of deposit insurance, firm fees may be collected into a standby reserve, such that the state incurs no direct costs even if guarantees are paid out. The US Federal Deposit Insurance Corporation (FDIC), for instance, pays its deposit guarantees out of the Deposit Insurance Fund, an FDIC-managed pool of money funded by an annual levy on FDIC-insured institutions. For emergency guarantees, the state may charge the firm a fee based on the amount covered, regardless of whether the guarantee is called on or not.

Guarantees also create moral hazard problems for depositors and creditors, who can disregard a firm's failure risk when making guaranteed deposits or loans. States generally address this problem by imposing some limit on the guarantee protection provided. States may provide depositors a limit on the amount covered, either by a cap on coverage or by only protecting a percentage of assets. In the United States, deposit insurance only covers a depositor's first $250,000, and nothing above that amount. Deposit insurance in the United Kingdom covers 100 percent of the first £50,000 and then only 90 percent of deposits over that amount. States may provide creditors only a "backstop" against losses, with guarantees kicking in only after a lender has lost a certain amount of the value of the loan.

Lender of Last Resort

The state may also address liquidity issues more directly, by lending to a firm when no other institutions will. This is known as the "lender of last resort" role. The classic guide for a lender of last resort, per nineteenth-century journalist Walter Bagehot, is to lend freely on good collateral at a high, or penalty, rate of interest. This formula would ensure that solvent banks do not fail from lack of liquidity, but at a high enough cost to make it an undesirable option. Modern central banks, however, have frequently forgone a penalty rate of interest, fearing that a penalty rate would discourage firms from taking advantage of such funds. Firms may instead "gamble for resurrection" rather than pay a penalty rate, engaging in extremely risky behavior in a last-ditch effort to save the firm, then turning to the lender of last resort when the need has become much greater (Rosas, 2009). In addition, in times of crisis, central bankers may loosen their definitions of "good collateral" in order to more easily facilitate lending. Without a penalty rate of interest, or without requiring good collateral, state liquidity provisions can provide firms with "free money," or below-market-rate access to liquidity, and thus introduce moral hazard problems, endangering public money in loans to firms that the market regards as too risky to lend to.

Even at penalty rates, however, the state is still supplying loans that private lenders are either unable or unwilling to provide. If other firms are unable, because they cannot spare their own liquidity, such loans may introduce few moral hazard problems, by providing only the access that the private market would normally provide in a nonpanic environment. If, however, sources of liquidity exist but are unwilling to lend, for fear that they will not get their money back or will not get their money back in a timely fashion, then moral hazard problems are inevitably created, as the state is giving failing firms an opportunity that private interests deem to be a poor investment. A high rate and good collateral mitigates, but does not eliminate, these problems.

Solvency Approaches

Liquidity approaches may vary in the degree of moral hazard created, but can only address problems of liquidity. Liquidity provision can delay the failure of an insolvent firm and, in doing so, perhaps give a firm time to solve its solvency problems by finding a new source of private capital, but liquidity alone cannot prevent the failure of an insolvent firm. Therefore, the state may adopt policies to repair a firm's solvency position. As with liquidity provisions, the price a firm charges for solvency assistance determines the degree of moral hazard created.

Cash Grant

The simplest form of solvency assistance is for a state to simply give funds to troubled firms without expectation of repayment or conditions attached. When weighed against the immense costs of a financial crisis, such a transfer may be a relative bargain. However, cash grants nakedly create moral hazard, by directly subsidizing firms' losses. As such, cash grants are rare, although not unheard of. The US aid to failing airlines in the 2001 Air Transportation Safety and System Stabilization Act included a direct grant of $5 billion without an attendant ownership stake (Gup, 2010, p. 48). Such an aid was justified in that instance by arguing that state action, the grounding of all commercial aircraft for several days after the September 11 attacks, is what caused the losses to the airlines.

State-Subsidized Private Purchase

The state may provide incentives for a private firm to purchase a failing firm. The state may take ownership of less desirable parts of a firm's assets, as a form of "bad bank" discussed below. The state may also involve a guarantee of losses for the acquiring firm. Such a guarantee would work similarly to loan guarantees, with the state agreeing to absorb some amount of prospective losses. This may be a "backstop," with the state agreeing to cover any losses above a set amount, or the state may first take losses up to a set amount on an asset, with the acquiring firm taking losses above that amount. Such purchases inevitably introduce moral hazard issues, as the state is subsidizing a private sale. This inevitably benefits the purchasing firm, but may or may not benefit the failing one, depending on how the deal is structured.

Partial Nationalization/Capital Injection

The state may provide capital directly by purchasing stock in a distressed firm. Doing so not only provides additional funds to deal with solvency issues but may also indirectly solve liquidity issues by restoring the confidence of would-be lenders and providing additional collateral to access interbank lending. The moral hazard from capital injections depends chiefly on the price the state pays for its ownership stake. State ownership shares dilute existing shareholders, therefore diminishing the returns of those shareholders. If the state pays at or below market rate for those shares, the moral hazard effect is negligible, as state aid is equivalent in price to private assistance. If, however, the state pays above-market rates, this creates moral hazard, as the state will have a smaller ownership stake, and a smaller share of future profits, than if it had purchased shares at market rates. Below-market share purchases, therefore, reduce future losses to existing shareholders, as the value of their shares are less diluted and they retain a greater share of future profits.

Capital injections may take the form of ordinary shares, with the same dividend and voting rights as other investors. States frequently instead opt to use forms of stock that do not include voting rights, but pay a higher, generally fixed dividend, variously called "preferred shares" or "silent partnerships." Without voting rights attached, control by ordinary shareholders is not diluted, though typically the state claims a greater share of the profit than with ordinary shares. Preferred shares are generally "senior," meaning their dividends are paid in full before ordinary shareholders see any return, and preferred shareholders will recover more of their money in any bankruptcy proceeding. Preferred stock may in some cases be convertible to common stock or come with warrants giving the state the option of purchasing stock at a preset price at a later date. The moral hazard of preferred stock is determined chiefly by the level of the fixed dividend. A higher dividend lowers the moral hazard created, by reducing the money left over to pay out to ordinary shareholders.

With their fixed rate of return and lack of control, preferred stock injections resemble in some ways loans more than ownership stakes and are frequently referred to as hybrid capital. As such, their legal standing counting toward core capital may vary depending on the exact form of the capital and the regulatory regime under which the firm operates. Under Basel II capital guidelines, most hybrid capital is generally counted as Tier 1 core capital and therefore could be counted toward a bank's capital reserves.[2] The revised Basel III standards, however, classified most kinds of hybrid capital as a form of loan, and not eligible to count toward capital reserves. Preferred stock injections, therefore, fall somewhere between liquidity and solvency as a form of aid, depending on the specific legal form of the injection used and the accounting standards in the relevant country.

Full Nationalization

The most radical step a state can take to address solvency issues is to take full ownership of a failing firm. In some cases, the state will purchase existing owners' shares, but in others, the state may seize the firm by fiat, at a level of compensation determined by law or policymakers' discretion. Once acquired, the firm may then be sold in full or in part to other firms or held by the state as a state-owned enterprise. A temporary nationalization with intent to reprivatize the firm essentially intact is conservatorship, while a temporary nationalization with intent to sell off the firm in separate parts is receivership. Once the state completely owns a firm, it may inject capital into that firm without redistributive consequences, as this is a transfer of funds from taxpayers to a state agency, and not from taxpayers to a private firm. Although it may distort competition, such a move does not create moral hazard for private actors that are no longer in control of the firm. It may, however, create moral hazard for state-owned firms, encouraging them to take risks that private firms would not.

Toxic Asset Purchase/Bad Bank

States may also provide solvency assistance by buying bad assets from a firm. Such assets may simply have lost value, in which case

[2] The Basel Accords are a series of agreements among the world's leading central banks (initially the G-10 plus Luxembourg and Spain, but as of 2009 the G-20) to set common minimum capital and other operational requirements for their banks. Basel I (1988) set minimum capital requirements that were seen by the 2000s as outdated and not reflecting the current state of financial innovation and consolidation, and so was replaced by the Basel II in 2004. Basel II redefined and lowered capital requirements, reflecting current thinking the ability of financial innovations to allow superior risk management. Basel II, in turn, was seen as too lax in the wake of the 2007–2009 crisis, and so was replaced in 2009 by the more stringent Basel III requirements. Note, however, that all of the Basel Accords are non-binding recommendations, and thus have been unevenly adopted internationally as the basis of domestic banking regulation.

the state may purchase assets at an above-market rate to minimize losses to the firm by having the state take losses instead. They may alternatively be toxic assets, which will likely recover some of their value but over too long a time horizon for a bank already struggling to avoid failure. Such a state asset purchase is generally referred to as a "bad bank." Removing toxic assets reduces uncertainty about a firm's solvency and, if the price is high enough, can help restore the firm's capital. The state, meanwhile, holds the assets, which may potentially regain some of their value. The state may purchase the assets outright or merely hold them for a period of time, after which the firm agrees to buy them back. In either form, the key question when evaluating both the efficacy and moral hazard consequences of a bad bank is the price the state pays for the toxic asset. A low purchase price imposes a penalty on the firm, reducing the moral hazard problem of a state-funded "cleanup" of the firm's balance sheet, but this limits the degree to which the operation helps the firm. Conversely, a high purchase price provides substantial assistance to the firm, but creates significant moral hazard issues. In short, bad banks work by *creating* moral hazard, by insulating firms from the costs of having bad assets on their balance sheets. Bad banks must pay above-market rates for bad assets, if they are to be more effective than having the firm simply write off the value of assets and take the loss.

Nevertheless, bad banks have been a popular tool of financial intervention, because they address the core problem of solvency crises: the drop in value of assets on a firm's balance sheet. Despite the moral hazard problems, bad banks provide a highly effective way of preserving firms as solvent and privately held institutions. State asset purchases avoid the creation of "zombie banks," in which underlying problems remain but are made manageable by state subsidies. Instead, the bank's balance sheet is cleaned up and lingering questions about toxic assets removed. Asset purchases also avoid extensive state ownership of banks, which may be regarded as undesirable by both ideological opponents of state ownership and rival banks not eager to face state-subsidized competition.

Mandatory and Voluntary Assistance

One final key consideration in the implementation of state policy is whether state aid is mandatory or voluntary. Voluntary state aid gives the firm significant advantages in negotiations with the state. Firms may gamble for resurrection, resisting accepting state aid until they have no choice other than bankruptcy. State aid may be undesirable either because of the direct costs or because accepting state aid stigmatizes the bank in the eyes of investors. Banks may therefore refuse state aid early in the crisis, when such assistance might save the firm at a relatively low cost to the state. They may instead wait until all other options are exhausted and the cost of saving the firm has grown substantially. Since waiting to accept aid increases costs to the state, firms have leverage in negotiations with the state. If the firm refuses to accept state aid unless it is issued on favorable terms, state policymakers may find it cheaper to offer a smaller amount of aid on generous terms early in the crisis rather than offer harsher terms on a larger amount of aid later when the firm's greater need compels it to accept those harsher terms. Because of this, voluntary state aid will generally be cheaper for banks than mandatory state aid. However, the state may be constrained from being able to force mandatory assistance, and the time required to legislate mandatory assistance may itself raise the cost of aid enough that voluntary aid on generous terms may ultimately be less costly to the state, even if it does increase moral hazard problems.

Evaluating Responses to Financial Crises

States will frequently use several of the above methods in a given crisis, sometimes even with regard to a single distressed bank. Both liquidity support and capital support may be generous or harsh, depending on the terms offered. The key standard in evaluating the stringency of terms is whether the state charges more or less than a hypothetical private actor would in the same circumstances.[3] If shareholders of failing firms receive market rate or worse terms for state assistance, they are still required to shoulder a substantial burden for their rescue, and this will present less of a moral hazard problem than if state aid is generous and better than could be expected from a private savior. A key determinant of this may be whether state aid is mandatory or voluntary, as mandatory aid limits the space for firms to negotiate more favorable terms. Whether the state offers generous or harsh terms will be determined in large part by the structure of the national financial system and the willingness and ability of healthier banks to pressure the state into offering more generous terms of assistance.

[3] Note that, especially in large cases, there may be no private actors able to provide assistance on the scale needed, while in other cases, the issue may be that private actors are simply unwilling to take on ambitious expansions of their portfolios in a time of high uncertainty.

Outline of the Book

Chapter 2 introduces a theory of how different patterns of interbank relationships and private governance produce state responses in financial crises, drawing on and building on the comparative capitalisms literature. The economics and public policy literatures are briefly touched on, but are of relatively little utility, as the policy prescriptions that follow depend highly on which model of financial crises dominates. That question, in turn, is determined by the political strength of the relevant actors and the ability of the banks to promote a frame of understanding financial crises that casts their actions in a favorable light, maximizes the case for state assistance, and minimizes the negative consequences of such action.

While much attention has been given to the political clout of individual banks and the widespread adoption of a profinance neoliberal ideology, neither individual bank strength nor ideology provides a satisfactory account of state divergence in bank bailouts. The widespread acceptance of the profinance ideology limits its explanatory power, as there is little variance across cases. Similarly, banks have tremendous access to the advanced capitalist world, and at any rate, failing banks' political clout should be at a low point as they seek to avoid collapse. Therefore, a focus on the comparative financial systems literature offers considerably greater traction. Chapter 2 outlines how the nature of the national financial system shapes interbank relationships and how that, in turn, affects the capacity of banks to both respond to crises directly and help shape state responses. The atomized nature of interbank relationships and the lack of private governance structures in liberal, capital market–based systems leave failing banks without allies, allowing the state to adopt policies that minimize moral hazard and perverse redistribution from taxpayers to financiers while maximizing the likelihood of the state recovering its funds. By contrast, in states with organized private bank–based financial systems, greater interbank interdependence and stronger banking private governance associations give failing banks allies with both the incentive and means to shape policy responses on more favorable terms. This produces more generous state aid provision, but also increases the likelihood and size of privately funded rescues. Chapter 2 concludes with a brief quantitative analysis of state responses to financial crises in advanced capitalist states since 1974. It demonstrates a significantly greater likelihood for states with capital market systems to both favor nationalization and other forms of state ownership and to recover their money when they do engage in recapitalizations or partial nationalizations.

Chapters 3, 4, and 5 explore the dynamics of responses to the 2007–2009 crisis in Germany, the United Kingdom, and the United States. These three cases provide a useful basis of comparison, all being leading economies and exemplars of the two chief models of national financial systems, with the United States and United Kingdom often cited as the model liberal capital market systems, and Germany the exemplar of a corporatist private bank system. Moreover, Germany and the United States both have a federal system versus the British unitary state, and both Germany and the United Kingdom are EU members while the United States is not, allowing an exploration of potential alternative hypotheses related to the importance of the European Union or state structure. All three were also hit by a common financial crisis with broadly similar causes: the rapid devaluation of subprime mortgage assets beginning in 2007. All three responded with rescue plans of comparable size, though they differed substantially in the details. The German plan was voluntary in nature and considerably more generous to banks than the UK or US plans, which were frequently mandatory and relatively punitive and relied far more on nationalization and part nationalization than the German equivalent. However, German banks organized and contributed to private and public–private rescues, which were all but unknown in the US and UK cases. Case study analysis traces how these patterns can be traced to the nature of the interbank relationships and the presence or absence of strong private governance associations.

Finally, Chapter 6 summarizes the findings and examines what can be concluded about the role of divergent national systems in state responses to financial crises. It also connects specific findings with broader theoretical implications, especially those pertaining to the resilience of divergent national capitalist systems and the study of governance and multilevel governance. Potential policy implications of a comparison of state responses to banking crises will also be considered.

2 A Theory of Responses to Financial Crises

State responses to banking crises can vary substantially, with significant differences in the costs imposed on banks and bank shareholders and in the gross and net cost or gain to the state. These responses can vary both in process and in outcome. In some cases, such as the German response to the 2007–2009 crisis, representatives of both failing and healthy banks may play an integral role in shaping policy responses. They may serve as advisors, but also contribute funds directly through private or joint public–private rescues. In other cases, such as the United States and United Kingdom in the 2007–2009 crisis, banks may be shut out of policy deliberations, with state–firm relations taking on a much more adversarial cast, as the state dictates terms to failing banks. As might well be expected, the nature of the process helps shape the form and cost of crisis responses as well. Responses built from public–private cooperation, which Woll describes as "balanced" rescues, may feature greater private contributions, but also will generally produce more generous terms from the state to the failing banks (Woll, 2014). Responses in which the state dictates terms to the banks in a more adversarial fashion produce more limited private rescues, but also may mean the state imposes harsher terms on failing firms. Not only the costs but also the form of bank rescues may also vary substantially. Responses may differ not only by the presence or absence of a private component but also by the tools and institutions used to intervene. As discussed in Chapter 1, states may rely on a wide variety of policy options to provide both capital and liquidity support. State support may be directed through existing state agencies, such as the US Treasury and Federal Reserve, or through a newly created institution, such as the French *Société de Prise de Participation de l'Etat*.

To some degree, of course, the nature of the state's response to a given crisis will be determined by the specific form of the crisis. The size of the crisis, the specific financial instruments under stress, the nature of the specific banks involved, whether the crisis originated domestically or was "imported" from abroad, and other factors will color policymakers' choice as to the most appropriate tools to respond to the crisis. That is not, however, the whole story. As demonstrated empirically later in this chapter, state responses follow generally consistent patterns, with certain states favoring different tools and different cost-sharing consistently over time. Moreover, these patterns are not necessarily consistent with what might otherwise be expected. The United States, commonly seen as being dominated by Wall Street interests, has demonstrated a consistent pattern of either letting the firms fail and suffer the effects of market discipline, or engaging in temporary nationalizations that decimate shareholder value. The latter happens most commonly under the auspices of the Federal Deposit Insurance Corporation (FDIC), which has resolved over 3,000 banks since its creation by nationalization and reprivatizing them in a manner that wipes out shareholder value (Federal Deposit Insurance Corporation, 2013a). The United Kingdom, similarly seen as being dominated by the financial interests of the City of London, has a comparable history of relying on market discipline or punitive nationalizations. Germany, by contrast, despite a history of the state taking a strong hand in the economy, has avoided both nationalizing banks and letting them fail, preferring to either rely on private rescues or support banks and their shareholders through state aid.

Explaining this variance requires looking past some of the less sophisticated narratives offered in the wake of the 2007–2009 crisis, which generally do a poor job of accounting for the significant cross-country variations seen in state responses. A common explanation for bank bailouts, especially among those who see all bailouts as overly generous to financial interests, is that they illustrate the dominant lobbying power of the financial industry. In this narrative, banks use their influence to secure generous "golden parachutes" for themselves. This narrative misses that many bank shareholders, especially in the United States and the United Kingdom, were wiped out either by decisions to let banks fail or through state operations that wiped out or severely diluted shareholder value. More importantly, this narrative cannot adequately account for transnational variance. Woll (2014) is certainly right that individual banks command comparable and significant levels of access in all of the major advanced capitalist states. Explaining variance, therefore, requires looking at ways in which states differ, either in the structure of their financial industries, as argued here, or along some other dimension. A similar but more subtle argument is an ideological one: that the neoliberal consensus has shaped how policymakers respond to crises, understanding the interest of the state as in line with that of the financial industry. US President Calvin Coolidge once remarked that "the business of America is business," and surely many of his successors across the advanced capitalist world have come to hold that the business of the modern state is finance.

However, as with the simple lobbying story, ideological capture cannot explain divergent response patterns. Perhaps before the 1990s such an argument would have carried more clout, when the French state nationalized its banks and the British Labour Party actively called for nationalizing British banks. In the twenty-first century, however, the neoliberal ideology seems too pervasive across Europe and North America for ideological arguments to offer too much explanatory traction. Similarly, party politics explanations offer relatively little explanatory power, when the right-wing Republican Bush administration and the center-left Labour Brown government adopt substantially similar policies, while the center-left/center-right Merkel Grand Coalition in Germany is the outliner among the three. Therefore, it is necessary to look at alternate explanations that can account for the variance across states in their responses to the 2007–2009 crisis, and to crises more generally.

This chapter lays out such an argument, focusing on how the nature of the financial system determines the form of interbank relationships and thus the interests and capacity for action of both failing and healthy banks in times of crisis. In short, failing banks in liberal financial systems, dominated by capital markets and with limited bank interdependence, lose their influence in times of crisis and have few allies. This gives policymakers a free hand to set policies that will serve the interests of other actors more concerned with limiting the costs to the state and limiting the moral hazard of bank bailouts. In private bank–based systems, by contrast, interbank relationships are marked by interdependence and the presence of private governance associations to solve collective action problems. Because of this, healthy banks have both the incentive and means to intervene on behalf of failing ones, pushing policymakers to enact bailouts that are more favorable to the financial industry. They are much more likely to organize private rescues than their liberal counterparts.

This chapter begins by laying out the existing literature on financial crises in both the economics and political economy literatures. The former's focus on technical questions limits its ability to explain the political dynamics driving bank bailout policy choices, while much of the latter is limited by either not directly addressing crisis responses or failing to address bailouts in comparative perspective. I then lay out the foundations of my argument in the comparative financial systems literature, as well as highlight how a focus on financial systems in crisis can illuminate theories of change for the Varieties of Capitalism framework. Having demonstrated how the structure of financial markets shapes the interests of financial actors in times of crisis, I explore how differences in structural power of financial actors in different systems can limit the options available to policymakers. After laying out a series of hypotheses and alternate arguments, I demonstrate clear patterns of state responses to financial crises through a quantitative analysis of state responses from 1974 to 2009. I close with a discussion of case selection and methodology.

The Economics Literature on Financial Crises

Policymakers confronting financial crises face a wide range of technical choices in how they respond to financial crises. State responses to financial crises, however, cannot be understood simply in technical or functionalist terms. The economics and public policy literatures offer tremendous detail in modeling financial crises and policy responses, but are of regrettably little utility in explaining divergent national patterns of response to financial crises.[1] Both can offer "best practices" for response to financial crises within the parameters of the models upon which they are based, but the choice of model is itself a contentious, political, and potentially self-interested choice. Different models of financial crises offer substantially different accounts of the culpability of bankers, the necessary and optimal terms of state intervention, and the likely dangers and benefits of state intervention to rescue failing financial firms. In the absence of a clear consensus as to which model is dominant, self-interested actors will have an interest in promoting a model that casts them in the most favorable light. Bankers will prefer narratives that cast their own firm in the most positive light and ensure them the most favorable terms from the state. Because of this, state responses to financial crises cannot simply be understood as applying "best practices" to accomplish a generally agreed-upon goal. Rather the very terms of the policy debate and thus the definition of "best practices" will be subject to a debate that must be understood in terms of the strength of the actors promoting models that favor their own interests. In other words, since the choice of response policies is in part a choice of model, and the choice of model is not a technical one, state responses to financial crises must be understood as *political* – and determined by the clout and self-interest of relevant actors – rather than *functional*, and a simple matter of finding a Pareto-optimal policy solution. It is for this reason that economics and public policy literatures on financial crises are inadequate. They can provide a framework for understanding crises and identify the space for action and best practices within that framework, but cannot explain why a given framework dominates.

[1] For a review of the current economics literature, see Claessens et al. (2014).

Because the best practices in response to financial crises flows relatively unproblematically from the choice of model, economics work on state responses to banking crises tends to treat state intervention as yes/no question: either the state intervenes or it does not. Within a given framework of financial crises, the nature of the problem will be understood a certain way, and thus the best way to respond will be clear. State intervention may be treated as binary because the state can be assumed to either respond in the best conceivable way or not at all. The model defines not only the short-term effectiveness of a policy but also the causes of the problem being addressed and the longer-term likelihood of problems down the line. The choice of economic model, and thus the best response policy, is itself a political one and outside of the scope of economic modeling (Rosa and Pérard, 2010). In the context of a financial crisis, for instance, the culpability of banks and the effect a policy will have on the likelihood of future crises varies substantially between models used to explain the origins of the crisis. Therefore, self-interested groups will have reason to favor one model over another. This occurs even in contexts where interests are problematized, as the choice of model shapes the terms of debate. Some terms will be more favorable to different groups than others, by offering an understanding that paints the group as a villain or victim, prioritizing or diminishing the importance of a group and its preferences, and by suggesting policy remedies that assign costs or benefits accordingly.

Competing Models of Financial Crises

Two competing models of financial crises dominate the modern debate in economics, dividing chiefly over whether financial crises are a product of random exogenous shocks or an endogenous result of firm actions and the business cycle (Allen and Gale, 2000; Boyd, Kwak, and Smith, 2005). Under an exogenous shock, or "sunspot," model, financial crises are essentially random in nature, as firms are targeted for panics regardless of their actual fundamental solvency. Under a business cycle model, however, firms engage in speculative practices that leave them more vulnerable to bank runs, and financial crises can be understood as a deviation by firms from prudential practices. These two models produce sharply different understandings of the culpability of firms and thus the danger of state intervention creating "moral hazard" and increasing the danger of future financial crises. A narrative in which firms are the victims of exogenous shocks is one in which state aid can be justified as helping innocent firms recover from forces beyond their control. On the other hand, a narrative that sees financial crises as of the firms' own making makes state aid both harder to justify on fairness grounds and more dangerous, as it increases the willingness of firms to make the same mistakes going forward. In the business cycle model, the very acts of preventing or containing a financial crisis can create the roots of the next crisis.

The sunspot model is so named because it is rooted in a nineteenth-century explanation of how purely exogenous events unconnected to financial markets, such as solar flares, could produce financial panics with severe consequences (Kindleberger and Aliber, 2011). Diamond and Dybvig offer a modern formulation, focusing on how the time inconsistency of banks' short-term lending and long-term borrowing, together with information asymmetries that enable banks to conceal their true health, leave even healthy banks susceptible to bank runs driven by the rational behavior of depositors and creditors (Bryant, 1980; Diamond and Dybvig, 1983; Kindleberger and Aliber, 2011). Because the sunspot model frames financial crises as the product of random shocks, it eliminates or reduces culpability of firms affected by a bank run. If banks can credibly argue that the crisis is not of their making, it is easier to justify a generous provision of liquidity support by the state. Early work in this tradition emphasized the desirability of separating insolvent firms, which were unworthy of state assistance, from merely illiquid ones, which were fundamentally sound and should receive generous state aid (Bagehot, 1892). Modern theorists dismiss the importance of determining solvency. Goodhart argues that, because illiquidity creates insolvency problems, it is both impossible and unnecessary to separate the insolvent from the merely illiquid, and both should be provided liquidity on generous terms (Goodhart, 2009).

The chief rival to the sunspot model, the business cycle model, is derived from Minsky's financial instability hypothesis and sees financial crises as the culmination of long-term cyclical dynamics in financial markets (Allen and Gale, 2000; Bhattacharya and Gale, 1987, p. 69; Champ, Smith, and Williamson, 1996; Chari, 1989; Minsky, 1982). In the aftermath of a financial crisis, firms and regulators both embrace prudential practices to avoid a future crisis. This crisis aversion leads to prudential investing and state fiscal policies focused on maximizing stability, producing both stability and moderate growth. This stability, however, becomes its own undoing. A long period of stability reduces the fear of future crises. There may be a general feeling that financial crises have been "solved" and that new financial instruments or policies can increase growth without threatening stability (Kindleberger and Aliber, 2011; Reinhart and Rogoff, 2009). Reinhart and Rogoff (2009) trace numerous instances prior to financial crises through the history of capitalism of economic actors and policymakers espousing the belief that "this time it's different." Firms begin to seek riskier investments and states relax prudential regulations, both in the name of increasing growth.

This expansion makes the financial system vulnerable again. Firms increase their exposure to risky investments and decrease their liquidity cushion. As a consequence, losses become more likely as well as more likely to create significant problems, as banks are much more highly leveraged. This increased leverage makes financial systems highly vulnerable to crises from events that would be only minor disturbances in earlier times. Actors becoming aware of this vulnerability only increases the danger of crises at this late point. Awareness that the market is highly vulnerable to only minor disturbances increases investors' willingness to react quickly and severely to any such disturbance.

Unlike in the sunspot model, firms create the circumstances of their own undoing. These problems are exacerbated if firms believe that a state-backed rescue is likely. In this model, moral hazard from the precedent of state intervention becomes a very real concern. How the state responded in the last crisis will provide a guide as to how it can be expected to respond in the next one. If that earlier precedent either let firms fail or imposed harsh terms, then the firms that can expect to survive a crisis in the best shape will be the ones with more conservative and less short-term profitable risk portfolios. If that earlier precedent insulated shareholders from losses, then the state can be expected to do so in the future. This makes risky investments more attractive, as some of the downside may be passed from private owners to the public.

Therefore, under a business cycle model, state aid to banks should be on stringent terms to discourage such risky behavior in the future. Under a business cycle model, it is even more important than in a sunspot model to separate banks with solvency problems from those that are merely illiquid. Illiquid banks, caught in the contagion from the fall of their less prudent brethren, are not clearly culpable and may be supported with liquidity supports without significant moral hazard dangers. Insolvent banks, which for business cycle models are the ones at the core of the crisis, require either capital injections to recover their balance sheets or an orderly wind-down, and any aid to them carries severe moral hazard dangers.

Empirically, there is little consensus as to which model is more valid. Boyd, Kwak, and Smith (2005) provide evidence in support of the sunspots model, in that they cannot find statistically significant macroeconomic indicators of crises. Gorton (1988), however, comes to the opposite conclusion, finding stronger support for the business cycle model, as financial crises follow asset price bubbles. Undeniably, however, the models produce different interpretations of the causes of crises, the culpability of banks, and the moral hazard of state aid to banks. Therefore, it should not be surprising that materially interested parties adopt the model that best suits their interest. Proponents of financial liberalization in the run-up to the 2007–2009 crisis seized upon the Efficient Markets Hypothesis out of the neoclassical tradition to deflect blame from firms for earlier financial crises, shifting blame onto state regulations and justifying financial liberalization. Similarly, managers and owners of failing banks would favor sunspot explanations of why their bank was suffering while others survived. Dick Fuld, CEO of Lehman Brothers, was highly vocal that his bank was fundamentally solvent and healthy and that the only real problem it faced was that short-sellers had targeted his bank unfairly (Sorkin, 2009, p. 507). In this argument, therefore, Lehman Brothers was fundamentally sound and should be given unlimited liquidity until such time as the panic passed.

If there is a lack of consensus on which model is dominant, there is also a lack of consensus on the efficacy of policies to contain financial crises. Several studies find little or no macroeconomic effect from spending on financial rescues, that even substantial spending to contain financial crises has little effect on containing damage to the real economy (Granlund, 2004; Rosas and Jensen, 2010). Such studies, however, are frequently flawed, in how they conceptualize or measure the effects of policy action (Rosas and Jensen, 2010). Policymakers in financial crises have a strong political incentive to act, regardless of the economic efficacy of a policy, just to appear to be doing something instead of nothing. Outside of the smallest of financial failure, there is almost always some form of state intervention. Therefore, few cases exist from which to model the effects of no support. Empirical work may also not examine if or how state intervention affects the potential for future financial crises. Potentially as damaging, such empirical work frequently does not differentiate between forms of state intervention (Teteryatnikova, 2009). In part, this failure to differentiate is a function of the models themselves. As discussed earlier, the models not only determine the origins of the crisis but also imply the optimal policy approach to address it. As such, policy choice is not problematic and can be assumed to follow best practices under the model used to examine crises.

Political Science and Financial Crises

This lack of consensus in the economics literature means that policymakers must make a choice as to which model of financial crises, and thus which policy choices, they wish to adopt. This is a choice that cannot be understood in purely economic or functional terms, as it is prior to the application of economic models. It therefore must be understood in political terms, as a product of the interests and ideologies of the relevant actors. As Moran and Payne discuss, this is problematic for much of mainstream political science, which has sought to carve out a distinctive identity for itself by examining specifically questions of state power, leaving market power to the attention of economists (Teteryatnikova, 2009). As such, much of mainstream political science has not developed adequate tools to examine the role of market power and how the constitution of market actors may shape the model choices – and thus policy choices – of policymakers in response to crises. McCarty, Pool, and Rosenthal attempted to adapt their tools of general interest group influence developed in the study of the US Congress to model how Wall Street interests were able to promote the policies that ultimately sowed the seeds of the 2007–2009 crisis. Their analysis, however innovative in its application, fails to delve into deeper questions of how Wall Street interests were able to organize internally to promote such policies and at any rate were limited in applicability specifically to the US Congress (McCarty, Poole, and Rosenthal, 2013). More generally, most existing theories of the power of interest groups rest on the notion of "regulatory capture," which as Carpenter and Moss (2013) rightly highlight is often theoretically underdeveloped and difficult to prove in the best of circumstances.

Fortunately, the political economy literature has been better equipped to engage with questions of financial power and the politics of financial regulation and deregulation, financial crises, and postcrisis financial reforms. However, even here much of the literature is less than ideally suited toward explaining divergence in state policy choices, as it focuses on either explaining financial crises as global events or explaining crisis responses in a single country. Global approaches may be immensely valuable in explaining how the crisis occurred and in prescribing or predicting future reforms for the global financial architecture, but generally give relatively little attention to national divergence in crisis responses. Single-country responses, meanwhile, can offer a superior level of detail in addressing crisis management in a single case, but in the absence of comparative cases, it can be difficult to establish a baseline from which to evaluate how effective policies were, let alone evaluate the relative strength of various causal arguments. Ultimately, therefore, the best way to evaluate responses to financial crises is through comparative analysis, when differences between states in both policies and outcomes become clear.

Several of the most high-profile works on the 2007–2009 crisis have focused on the global crisis, most notably Blyth and Wolf (Blyth, 2013; Wolf, 2014). Much work using this approach focuses on how the seeds of the crisis were sown, tracing the rise of financial interests, and of a general financial ideology of deregulation and sophisticated risk management (Helleiner, Pagliari, and Zimmermann, 2010). In this they dovetail well with the more generally focused convergence literature, which examines how increased global integration creates functional pressures for both firms and states to converge on a single common standard of institutional design and "best practices" (Burnham, 2010; Boyer, 1996; Callaghan, 2010; Callaghan and Höpner, 2012; Cerny, 2005; Coates, 2005b; Katzenstein, 1978; Loriaux, 1997; Menz, 2005; Panitch and Gindin, 2005; Tsingou, 2010; Zimmermann, 2010). Wolf especially fits well with this approach, examining how states were increasingly pressured to promote a fusion of American-style light-touch regulation with German-style universal banking. Such work is valuable in setting up expectations for a common response among states to the financial crisis. Whether the mechanism of convergence is the pressure to conform to best practices for functional reasons, the rise of a dominant neoliberal ideology, or the pressure to adapt to the dominant American financial system, the expectation of the convergence literature would be for states to converge in their responses to financial crises just as they had converged during economic good times. If anything, the impulse to converge might be stronger in times of crisis, when the status quo is weakened, and reformist actors presumably would have an advantage in pushing their agendas. Wolf (2014) here is especially useful, demonstrating how the run-up to the financial crisis was dominated by common pressures and, to a significant degree, common policies as well.

However, the empirical evidence for convergence is mixed. Moreover, even if real, convergence remains incomplete, especially in regard to variance in private governance structures and political influence of financial actors (Lütz, 2004, 2005). As such, the dynamics of state responses to crises continue to vary substantially from case to case. That significant variance was seen in state responses to the crisis does not necessarily invalidate the convergence thesis, which may simply be more valid in good times than bad, but does suggest that a moment of true convergence has not yet arrived, if indeed it ever would.

Wolf and Blyth both engage in discussion of global responses to the crisis as well, though both focus more on the global response than on state-level variance. Wolf (2014) focuses both on attempts by the key central banks to coordinate efforts and on the G-20 to establish a common response framework. Blyth (2013) focuses on how the powerful states, especially Germany, used their political clout to attempt to force their preferred policy choices on other states. Neither, however, gave significant attention to state-level variation, and instead directed their attention to attempts at international coordination of responses. To that end, a significant portion of both Blyth and Wolf's work is devoted to exploring the postcrisis political economy, especially with an eye toward how, in Blyth's case, power politics and dominant ideologies of austerity have driven states to press for their favored response policies and, in Wolf's case, an exploration of potential channels for both minor and substantial reform of the global financial system. Such work, of course, may be useful in exploring the postcrisis environment, but does little to illuminate the observed state-level variation in crisis responses.

A number of scholars have also attempted to analyze both the run-up to and management of financial crises in single-country case studies. For obvious reasons, much of this attention within American political science has focused on the United States (Johnson and Kwak, 2010; McCarty, Poole, and Rosenthal, 2013; Stiglitz, 2010). Significant scholars have also focused on other single-country responses, especially the larger European states (Bonatti and Fracasso, 2015; Hardie and Howarth, 2013; Jabko and Massoc, 2012; Johal, Moran, and Williams, 2014; Royo, 2013). As is common in comparative politics, a tension exists here between the specificity possible from a single-country case study and the advantages of comparative case studies. This problem is perhaps especially acute in the study of financial crises, where the literature is less well developed than in other issue areas, and it is therefore harder to establish a baseline of expected pressures and responses from which to examine how countries depart from expectations. Because of this, the measurement of both independent and dependent variables may be obscured.

This may be most apparent in evaluating the severity of terms offered in bank bailouts. Some follow Rosas' lead in dividing state responses between "Bagehot" (letting market discipline work by allowing institutions to fail) and "bailout" (state policies to save the banks regardless of terms) (Rosas, 2006, 2009). This has the advantage of parsimony, but it misses substantial variance within the "bailout" category. Looking at just the United States or United Kingdom in the 2007–2009 crisis, analysts such as Krugman and Wolf can easily conclude that state bailouts create a situation in which private actors profit in good times, but the public picks up the costs in bad times (Krugman, 2009; Wolf, 2010). However, this analysis misses both the degree to which both these states imposed costs on bank shareholders and, perhaps more importantly, the fact that other states, such as Germany, offered far more generous terms to their bank shareholders. While there are inevitable moral hazard and perverse redistribution problems in any bank rescue, the degree to which states attempt to minimize these problems may only become clear in comparison to other states.

At the same time, evaluating how generous or punitive the terms of a given bailout are is hard enough in comparative perspective. Culpepper and Reinke, for instance, disagree with Woll as to whether to classify the American response to the 2007–2009 crisis as costly or generous, and as discussed later on, I disagree with both Culpepper and Reinke and Woll as to the evaluation of the German response (Culpepper and Reinke, 2014; Woll, 2014). Without comparisons from other cases, at different times or in different countries, it becomes even more difficult to evaluate bailout terms. Such bailouts, after all, almost by definition involve the state making investments that no private actor is willing or able to make at that time, or else the state would let private actors handle crisis management. Moreover, regardless of terms, bailouts are always received hostilely by the general public, which understandably resents taxpayer money going to fund the very actors that caused the crisis just as the public begins to feel the real economic effects of that crisis. Therefore, regardless of how terms look in contrast to other rescues, single-country studies almost always cast financial bailouts as generous to the banks.

Single-country studies also have difficulty evaluating the relative importance of different independent causal variables. McCarty, Poole, and Rosenthal emphasize the importance of the unwieldy US political structure, which provides numerous veto points where special interests may block undesirable legislation (McCarty, Poole, and Rosenthal, 2013). However, the much more streamlined British system produced a rescue plan that looked substantially similar, while the French system, which like the United States has numerous veto points, produced a substantially different response plan. Similarly, some approaches emphasize the role of a deregulatory neoliberal ideology or which emphasize the importance of a "revolving door," in which regulators frequently go to work in finance and financiers take jobs as regulators (Johnson and Kwak, 2010; Stiglitz, 2010). These arguments may seem plausible in a single-case study, but comparative analysis reveals their relatively weak explanatory power, given the near-universal dominance of neoliberalism and comparable revolving door phenomena across the advanced capitalist states.

There is, of course, a body of literature focusing on comparative responses to financial crises, though the actual examination of crisis response policies is somewhat underdeveloped. In part this – no doubt – is a product of the relative scarcity of developed world financial crises since the Second World War. In the Bretton Woods period from the late

1940s to the early 1970s, controls on movement of capital across borders prevented international financial crises by blocking the channels of contagion. Even after the removal of controls in the 1970s, there were not any significant international crises in the advanced capitalist states before 2007. Individual banks certainly failed, and some states even saw multiple financial firm crises, such as the British secondary banking crisis in the mid-1970s, the American savings and loan crisis of the late 1980s, and the Japanese crisis of the 1990s. But apart from a handful of relatively small incidents, such as the failure of the German bank Herstatt in connection to a panic in UK markets, the advanced capitalist states experienced virtually no large international financial crises for decades. This period of relative calm, since dubbed the Great Moderation, led to a general belief among financial actors, regulators, and academics that financial crises had been "solved." No less prominent an actor than Ben Bernanke, then a Federal Reserve Governor, reflected these views in 2002. In toasting Milton Friedman, Bernanke praised the nonagenarian economist, saying "I would like to say to Milton and Anna: Regarding the Great Depression. You're right, we did it. We're very sorry. But thanks to you, we won't do it again" (Bernanke, 2002). Given this consensus that financial crises were "solved," responses to financial crises, especially in the advanced capitalist states, attracted relatively little academic interest.

Much more attention was instead paid to longer-term financial reforms, both in the aftermath of crises and in debates over financial reform in good times. Prior to 2007, this appeared to be a more relevant question, as the chief focus of financial politics was not the terms of bailouts but rather how to reform financial regulation to best take advantage of the Great Moderation. Although it does not directly concern itself with questions of bank bailouts, this literature is nevertheless useful by demonstrating the power of the financial sector in normal times. This allows for an exploration of how that power manifests itself in several different forms. Perhaps most obvious is a focus on the direct lobbying capacity of firms, as well as how parties will seek to shape regulations to appeal to financial actors for electoral reasons (Allen, 2006; Becker, 2009; Beyer and Höpner, 2003; Deeg, 1999; Hall and Soskice, 2001; Martin, 2005; Roe, 2003). Additionally, it demonstrates the structural power of firms, in that states must shape regulation to maintain healthy domestic markets, wanting neither to diminish financial productivity nor to encourage banks to relocate to other financial markets (Becker, 2009; Beyer and Höpner, 2003; Gourevitch and Shinn, 2005; Hall and Soskice, 2001; Martin, 2005). Finally, a considerable amount of work has been done exploring how financial reforms, and especially deregulation, have been shaped by the rise of a deregulatory neoliberal ideology

(Abdelal, 2007; Becker, 2009; Callaghan, 2009; Callaghan and Höpner, 2012; Cioffi and Höpner, 2006; Langley, 2005). Additionally, this literature helps explain how the regulatory structures prior to the crisis were constructed and how banks may play differing roles in the regulatory process.

Ultimately, however, this literature is limited in its power to explain crisis responses. Implicit in this literature is that banks are generally in good health. This may paradoxically be especially the case in postcrisis financial reforms, when the weakest banks have been culled through collapse, merger, or state ownership, leaving only the healthiest banks to shape the policy process. Therefore, there is little attention to how policymaking dynamics may shift in moments of crisis. The political clout of banks may shift dramatically, as they go from being important sources of campaign contributions and economic growth to desperately seeking support to avoid failure. As will be discussed later, the nature of the drop in the power of banks in time of crisis is not consistent across countries and needs additional attention.

Comparative studies of state responses to financial crises have been somewhat limited. As discussed earlier, this reflects the paucity of cases of international crises in the advanced capitalist states to examine. The terms of response to financial crises may vary considerably based on the source of the crisis. Crises based on a collapse in value of a specific class of assets, such as subprime assets in the 2007–2009 crisis, may necessitate different responses than the collapse in value of sovereign bonds, or crises from general capital flight. Therefore, it is difficult to control for these variances in state responses across crises. This has necessarily limited the scope of comparative research to international crises, most of which have been found in the developing world since the 1940s. Therefore, most comparative research on financial crises has focused on either the Latin American debt crisis of the 1980s or the East Asian financial crisis of 1997–1998 (Bello, 1999; Devlin and Ffrench-Davis, 1995; Felix, 1990; Haggard, 2000a, 2000b; Kaminsky and Pereira, 1996; Radelet and Sachs, 1998; Remmer, 1990, 1991; Satyanath, 2006; Tabb, 1998; Woo, Sachs, and Klaus, 2000). This research is valuable, but of relatively limited utility as a guide for exploring the dynamics of advanced capitalist states, for both economic and political reasons. Economically the less developed state of Latin American and East Asian markets both created a greater space for foreign banks to play a central role and created a greater danger of capital flight from advanced capitalist investors "flying to safety." In contrast, European and North American financial markets are typically dominated by domestic banks, and the likelihood of capital flight is diminished because those very American and European markets have generally been seen as the safest markets, leaving capital relatively few places to go.

The 2007–2009 American/European crisis also differed from the Latin American and East Asian cases in that it occurred almost exclusively in consolidated democracies. The earlier crises affected an assortment of authoritarian regimes and fledgling democracies, with only a handful of consolidated democracies in either crisis. The role of financial crises in influencing political transformations and the difference in response from authoritarian and democratic states have both been key focuses of the literature on earlier crises (Haggard, 2000a, 2000b; Remmer, 1990; Satyanath, 2006). While this is obviously of great importance in those crises, it is a dimension simply lacking in the 2007–2009 crisis

Therefore, the 2007–2009 crisis produced the first major case for comparative studies of banking crisis response in the advanced capitalist states since the Great Depression. While there has certainly been a substantial explosion in research on the topic, the relative recency of the crisis means that most of this scholarship has been confined to articles, with relatively few book-level treatments of the crisis in comparative perspective. Some of this research, such as Weber and Schmitz, has focused on applying the Varieties of Capitalism framework to crisis responses, relying on the focus on institutional complementarities from Hall and Soskice's original articulation of the framework to explain divergence (Hall and Soskice, 2001; Weber and Schmitz, 2011). Others have suggested a story of regulatory capture, but as Carpenter and Moss (2013) note, this can be extremely difficult to demonstrate. Weber and Schmitz's research, while somewhat weak on mechanism, has an admirable scope, attempting to comparatively evaluate all of the responses of the EU states (Weber and Schmitz, 2011). Others such as Culpepper and Reinke or Hardie and Howarth focus more narrowly on country dyads of the United States and the United Kingdom or Germany and France, respectively (Culpepper and Reinke, 2014; Hardie and Howarth, 2009). Of these, Culpepper and Reinke are more relevant to the question of the terms of bank bailouts. Hardie and Howarth are ultimately more concerned with explaining why the German crisis was more severe than the French rather than explaining the terms of the two countries' responses. Culpepper and Reinke, like Weber and Schmitz, focus on how the structure of national financial systems shapes outcomes. While Weber and Schmitz focus on the Varieties of Capitalism division between liberal and coordinated economies, Culpepper and Reinke examine variation within liberal economies' responses. Culpepper and Reinke focus on explaining why the US terms were harsher than the UK's, by focusing on how the more internationalized UK banks could more credibly threaten exit if they disliked the terms of the state rescue plan. This focus on financial structure is useful, as is the discussion of operationalizing financial power. Ultimately, however, the constraints of an article limit Culpepper and Reinke to only two cases, both of which are liberal financial markets.

Woll (2014) similarly focuses on the structure of national financial systems, examining how the lack of organization of a financial sector creates space for "collective inaction." In brief, Woll argues that financial sectors with strong mechanisms to solve collective action problems actually find themselves in a disadvantage in state–firm negotiations over crisis responses, as the state can credibly lean on private actors to contribute to financial rescues. By contrast, in disorganized sectors, firms can credibly claim to be blocked from participating in public–private rescues because they cannot overcome collective action problems. Woll has a much broader approach, examining six cases varying in the nature of their financial systems and the size of their economies. Her cases – the United States, the United Kingdom, France, Germany, Iceland, and Denmark – overlap with those considered here, although she lacks a quantitative component. In part, this is because her dependent variable is somewhat different. While Weber and Schmitz, Culpepper and Reinke, and this book focus on how generous or punitive terms offered by the states were to banks and shareholders, Woll is more concerned with whether responses were "balanced" or "unbalanced," which is to say whether responses involved public–private cooperation or not. As Woll herself notes, balanced or unbalanced rescues may be unrelated to the generosity of state aid or the likelihood of the state recovering its investment. Ireland, for instance, had a balanced rescue, but is regarded as among the most generous to its banks and the most costly to the state. Germany and the United States are both described as having unbalanced rescues, though the United States recovered its rescue funds with a small profit while Germany took substantial losses. Moreover, there is significant debate in the literature on responses to financial crises over how to classify the generosity of responses, especially the US response. Woll, as with many of the single-case analysts of the United States, finds the US response to be relatively generous. Others, including Culpepper and Reinke and myself, find the US response to be among the most effective in terms of pushing costs onto the banks and recovering state funds. For Culpepper and Reinke, this is because they focus primarily on how the United States structured its plan in a way that maximized its ability to recover its funds and ultimately turn a profit. I focus on this as well, but also give greater attention to bank resolutions carried out under existing statutory authority, especially the FDIC resolution process and the resolution of Fannie Mae and Freddie Mac, which did not involve creating new regulatory authorities but did enable the United States to resolve a significant number of financial institutions, including some of the biggest ones involved in the crisis, at a minimal cost to the taxpayer and at a significant cost to bank shareholders, most of whom were wiped out in the state resolutions. Woll, by contrast, is more concerned with the participation of private actors rather than the terms of state involvement and gives little attention to resolutions through the FDIC or other pre-existing resolution authorities.

A Theory of Divergent Responses to Financial Crises

Identifying the sources of variance in responses to financial crises requires identifying first the ways in which different states face common or divergent pressures. As will be argued later, the key difference lies in the differing structural advantages of financial actors across different financial systems. Obviously, given the centrality of finance to the operation of modern capitalist economies, there are a wide range of actors with an interest in the terms of resolution of financial crises. The majority of these actors, however, will have common interests across countries, meaning that they offer little leverage to explain cross-country variation. Nonfinancial firms, for instance, will always want the crisis contained with minimal disruption to their own access to credit and capital. Similarly, the general public will also want the crisis contained in a way that minimizes disruption to the real economy. Moreover, as taxpayers, they will want the crisis contained at a minimal cost to the state and thus to themselves. This combination of a fear of real economic losses and resentment over the perverse redistribution of state funds to the very actors that caused the crisis fuels a substantial hostility to bailouts from the general public. Bailouts, regardless of the specific terms, are nearly always received with great public anger at both the banks for requiring them and state officials for providing them. Moreover, this anti-bailout attitude is generally consistent across other ideological divisions. Some libertarians may be more concerned about avoiding expansion of state ownership than avoiding real economic costs, but partisans of both the left and right share a hostility toward state largess going to the financial sector in times of crisis. Foreign firm and states may also have an interest in how states respond to financial crises, with foreign firms wanting the crisis contained without needing to compete in the future with a state-subsidized competitor, and foreign states wanting their own citizens protected from losses. In some cases, the foreign state itself may want to be protected from losses, as was the case of China in 2008, when it was a significant holder of Fannie Mae and Freddie Mac bonds.

All of these actors should have similar interests across states. Moreover, in all cases, these interests are generally similar: nonfinancial and international actors want the crisis contained, and at a minimal cost to themselves. This means that, leaving aside the financial sector, policymakers face a common set of preferences from a common set of actors. Some actors may be of greater strength in certain cases, especially foreign actors, and some interests may be contradictory, such as the desire for both effective crisis containment and minimal cost. However, overall, these interests present a relatively coherent set of preferences: for the state to contain the crisis in a way that avoids subsidizing financial sector actors and contains the costs to the state. Therefore, explaining why states have not converged on a common set of responses to financial crises requires examining those actors and structures that differ across states. The organization of financial actors is the most important of these. Other variations across states, such as state institutional design and party in power, may conceivably account for different outcomes. However, as demonstrated later, these do not have a statistically significant impact.

The crux of my argument is that the healthy banks play a key role in determining both public and private responses to financial crises, and that the nature of interbank relationships is what determines the incentives and ability to act of banks to provide private rescues and shape public ones. The key distinction in national financial systems, long recognized in the comparative financial systems literature, is between private bank–based and capital market–based systems. A closer examination of the underlying forces driving the different systems, especially the nature of interbank relationships and the resulting difference in levels of private governance, demonstrates substantially different power resources for failing firms in the two kinds of systems, with attendant differences in the ability of state policymakers to address the concerns of nonfinancial actors versus financial ones.

Comparative Financial System

The comparative political economy literature on finance has long recognized the diversity in the organization of national financial systems. While a comparative study of capitalist systems can be found as far back as Weber's *The Protestant Ethic and the Spirit of Capitalism* and Shonfield's *Modern Capitalism*, John Zysman's 1983 work on comparative financial systems, *Governments, Markets, and Growth*, has been the bedrock of much of the analysis of comparative financial systems that has followed (Fioretos, 2011; Hardie et al., 2011; Shonfield, 1965; Streeck, 2010; Weber and Karberg, 1930 [2001]; Zysman, 1983). Much of that subsequent literature has followed Zysman in identifying three varieties of financial systems within capitalist states: the liberal capital market–based system of the Anglo-American world, the corporatist private bank–based system of Germany, and the state bank–based system of *dirigiste* France. Each offers a distinct way of solving the political and economic problems of growth.

In states with liberal financial market–based systems, firms chiefly obtain funding through sale of stocks and bonds on capital markets. This focuses firms on short-term objectives, limiting the capacity of firms to engage in projects that may not be profitable for some time. Only firms with a long and successful track record can access long-term funding from the bond market without paying a high-risk premium. In capital market systems, investors have very little control over firms, being generally small minority shareholders, but can easily unload their shares if a firm's performance declines. This makes lack of control less of a problem for investors, but means that firms must consistently show short-term positive returns or lose the ability to access capital markets.

In systems where banks provide the bulk of firm capital, a longer-term focus is possible, though there must be some mechanism to guarantee investors' stake. This mechanism is generally for banks to take large enough ownership stakes in firms to influence firm decisions. In statist bank–based systems, the state controls the flow of capital to firms and can direct credit to those sectors it wishes to promote and away from those it wishes to deemphasize. This enables the state to promote new industries with greater ease than in liberal systems, but allows unprofitable firms to survive because of their political influence rather than economic performance. Alternately, in private bank–based systems, banks solve this dilemma by taking an active role in managing investments than the essentially passive role of capital investors in capital market systems. Unlike the many small investors in a capital market system, the bank will be one of only a few major owners and, therefore, will have much greater say in how the firm is run. This enables the bank to more confidently provide long-term financing, as the bank will have greater influence over the operation of the firm and greater access to private information, such as the firm's internal accounts and strategies. The state in such a system plays a smaller role than in statist systems. However, the state can more easily shape industrial policy than in a capital market system, where it has relatively few levers to shape firms' incentives. The state does not have direct influence over firms, but because it is dealing with a handful of banks rather than a large number of small investors, the state can find the banks to be useful allies in accomplishing shared objectives. Conversely, the banks may more easily promote their interests to the state than investors can in a capital market system.

Zysman pays relatively scant attention to the organization of capitalist systems beyond the realm of finance, except insofar as firms respond to long- or short-term funding incentives. However, the ability of bank-based systems to function depends in part on the structure of the industry. Capital market systems can function with any form of industrial organization, since they ultimately are only concerned with short-term growth prospects. This in turn favors firms that can rapidly adapt to maximize short-term potential. Bank-based systems, however, because they involve long-term funding, operate better in more stable environments. In the absence of stability, long-term funding is extremely risky, given the greater potential for future disturbances and thus losses. Therefore, banks will require some manner of assurance of stability. In part, this can be provided by greater control, but even complete control cannot prevent disruptions from labor strife or other market disruptions. In state–bank systems, state ownership can solve this problem through implicit or explicit state guarantees, such that state–bank systems can weather some degree of instability. Private bank systems lack that clear state guarantee. Therefore, they must provide some form of private guarantee of stability. To that end, corporatist arrangements are both enabled by bank finance, which allows a longer-term view and thus easier coordination, and enable private bank finance to survive, by guaranteeing a measure of stability absent in capital market systems. This greater stability makes longer-term investment possible and that longer-term investment reinforces corporatism as well, because firms are in less direct competition for fickle capital market investors.

The division between corporatist, bank finance systems exemplified by Germany and liberal, market finance systems of the Anglo-American states would be central to later work on comparative capitalisms, while the literature abandoned interest in statist systems after France abandoned *dirigisme* and privatized its banks (Albert, 1993; Deeg, 1999). Some scholars would add in their own alternate varieties of financial systems, such as Becker, who focused on East Asian finance as distinct from European bank–based finance (Becker, 2009). Most, however, followed the lead of Albert, who dropped French statism to focus more narrowly on comparing German and Anglo-American models (Albert, 1993).

Perhaps the most prominent work to follow from the work on comparative financial systems is Hall and Soskice's *Varieties of Capitalism*, which also drew on the literature on industrial organization to identify two major types of modern capitalist systems (Hall and Soskice, 2001). The first – Liberal Market Economies – is associated with capital market–based financial systems, while the second – Coordinated Market Economies – is associated with bank-based financial systems. Hall and Soskice's aim is broader than the comparative financial systems literature, emphasizing the importance of institutional complementarities in developing stable equilibria around divergent models of modern capitalism. Although capitalist systems may theoretically vary on several dimensions, including financial systems, efficiency gains from orienting all four of Hall and Soskice's core dimensions in the same direction produce a lock-in effect through institutional complementarity (Hall and Soskice, 2001). Therefore, liberal, capital market financial systems will generally be found with liberal orientations along other dimensions, and coordinated, bank-based financial systems will generally be found as part of a more generally coordinated market economy. "Mixed" national systems, without a common logic across dimensions, will produce inefficiencies and thus should feel pressure to converge to either a liberal or a coordinated model.[2] Implicitly, therefore, even in times of financial crisis, states will be reluctant to substantially reorient their financial systems, as such a move would be inefficient unless the broader economy were also to be overhauled.

A great deal of the subsequent work in the Varieties of Capitalism literature has focused on exploring the microfoundations and mechanisms of the model. Doing so addresses questions regarding the number of varieties of capitalism, theories of change and continuity, and the economism of underlying mechanisms. To a significant degree, this has resulted in a refocusing more narrowly back onto varieties of financial systems, not only as important in its own right but also as a driver of the broader orientation of capitalist economies.

Hall and Soskice identify two models of capitalism based on four dimensions on which an economy can vary: financial systems, labor markets, education and training systems, and research and development systems (Hall and Soskice, 2001). This produces a binary division because their causal mechanism, institutional complementarity, makes it more economically efficient to orient all four dimensions in the same way. However, both the number and the relative importance of these dimensions may be debated. Weber and more modern scholars following from Weber emphasize the importance of culture and norms

[2] This has been identified as one of the chief empirical weaknesses of the Varieties of Capitalism framework. Hall and Soskice themselves identify a "Mediterranean" cluster of mixed economies, of which France is the most prominent, which have largely resisted pressure to move more strongly toward either a liberal or a coordinated orientation. Additionally, *dirigiste* France did not clearly fit into either a liberal or a coordinated model and was a stable and successful economy into the 1970s.

as an independent force shaping institutional choices (Burnham, 2010; Cerny, 2005; Coates, 2005b; Tsingou, 2010; Zimmermann, 2010). Other authors point to the importance of political structures, especially the electoral system rules, dynamics of party competition, and the federal or unitary nature of the political system (Callaghan, 2009; Cioffi and Höpner, 2006; Cusack, Iversen, and Soskice, 2007; Gourevitch and Shinn, 2005; Iversen, 2005; Martin Höpner, 2005; Martin, 2006; Pagano and Volpin, 2005; Perotti and von Thadden, 2006; Roe, 2003). Deeg and Jackson provide an extensive list of the criteria used by various comparative capitalism approaches, including financial systems, corporate governance systems, industrial relation systems, skill creation systems, production models, welfare states, and innovation systems (Deeg and Jackson, 2007). However, these various typologies frequently arrive at essentially the same set of categories. It is desirable, therefore, to build a common typology, ideally rooted in a parsimonious definition.

Despite other variances, a general consensus exists on the importance of financial systems. Virtually all of the comparative capitalism typologies use financial system as one of the defining characteristics or, failing that, some category that correlates very closely with financial system. This suggests, therefore, that a framework based on Zysman's liberal capital market/private bank/public bank system offers significant advantages, not least in terms of parsimony (Becker, 2009; Fioretos, 2011; Kalinowski, 2011; Zysman, 1983). Whether a financial system has a short-term orientation of a capital market system or a long-term, "patient capital" focus of a bank capital–based system determines the time horizon for firms and thus their tolerance for short-term losses in pursuit of long-term gains from investments in worker training, research and development, and long-term labor contracts.

Moreover, the orientation of the financial sector may more plausibly drive the orientation of other sectors than vice versa. In a bank-based system, funding is determined on the basis of a long-term bank–firm relationship, which both creates an incentive for the bank to support the firm and vice versa. This frees firms to focus on long-term goals, rather than the quarter-to-quarter performance necessary to secure capital in a capital market–based system. Extensive worker training regimes, for example, collapse without a way to prevent parasitic firms from poaching trained workers once the expense of that training is paid. Norms of coordination, however, are unlikely to be self-generating. A financial system emphasizing long-term financing both has an incentive to promote those norms and a means to encourage those norms to dominate. Banks that may own stakes in multiple competing firms will discourage actions that are short-term profitable but long-term costly. Identifying additional variables as following from an essential financial system variable allows a much more parsimonious theory. It also suggests an entry point to explain theories of change in capitalist systems, especially as, empirically, change in the financial system can be seen as the driving force in changes elsewhere, as outlined below.

Finance is also a crucial sector in that it is the one most likely to be vulnerable to change, given that finance has more fungible assets and lower sunk costs than other dimensions of an economy. Therefore, especially since the liberalization of capital movement in the 1970s and 1980s, finance will be more vulnerable to international pressures. This perceived vulnerability to change has been a major focus of the convergence literature, which sees pressure from global financial integration driving financial firms to converge on a single set of best practices and institutional design. Advocates of the convergence thesis see a combination of global integration of financial markets, increasing trade integration, and the rise of international flexible production regimes in the real economy as pressing for a convergence on Anglo-American liberal capitalism, albeit a variant that incorporates the universal banks of the German model (Boyer, 1996; Callaghan and Höpner, 2012; Cerny, 2005). As economies become more integrated, firms and states must adopt "best practices," or fall behind economically (Boyer, 1996; Callaghan and Höpner, 2012). Others within the convergence school take a less functionalist line, emphasizing not adaptation to economically rational "best practices" but rather convergence as a result of the ascendency of neoliberal ideas (Cerny, 2005; Coates, 2005b; Tsingou, 2010; Zimmermann, 2010). Some scholars suggest that the end-point will be a "hybrid" model, combining elements of both systems (Callaghan, 2010; Deeg and Lütz, 2000). Theories that can be dubbed "hegemonic-convergence" approaches see convergence as a result of incentives to conform to the politically and economically dominant power in the international system (Burnham, 2010; Katzenstein, 1978; Loriaux, 1997; Menz, 2005; Panitch and Gindin, 2005). In this later view, neoliberal economic practices are not necessarily uniformly advantageous in all times and places, but are optimal contextually. The economic centrality of the United States, which has only increased with global integration, means that states have an incentive to adopt economic systems most compatible with American neoliberalism.

Although much of the convergence literature focuses on external pressures to converge, there is also a strand that focuses on endogenous pressures by domestic financial actors to converge to international systems, as banks see advantages from adapting to the practices of other financial systems (Beyer and Höpner, 2003; Callaghan and Höpner, 2012; Deeg,

1999). These advantages may be fiscal, seeking higher returns from adopting the financial practices of other systems, or tactical. Deeg and Beyer and Höpner, for instance, argue that German commercial banks pushed for liberalization in part as a way to attack the traditional state aid protections enjoyed by their savings bank competitors (Beyer and Höpner, 2003; Deeg, 1999).

A final approach to convergence worth noting is that of Hardie et al. They argue that banks may continue to diverge in their provision of capital, with banks in private bank systems providing direct capital and loans in large volumes, while banks in capital market systems provide underwriting for stock and bond raises (Hardie and Howarth, 2013; Hardie, Howarth, Maxfield, and Verdun, 2011, 2013). However, the underlying method of how banks fund themselves has converged, as banks in private bank–based systems have shifted away from a reliance primarily on depositors and large creditors and toward a reliance on market-based overnight funding, ultimately making them as vulnerable to short-term market pressures as their capital market bank peers. Hardie et al. argue that this convergence has been largely overlooked in the literature, which therefore missed how private bank systems had become as vulnerable to market disruptions as their liberal market peers.

If Hardie et al. are correct, this shift would cost private bank systems their chief competitive advantage. The most significant quantitative research on the performance of comparative financial systems found that capital market– and bank-based systems had different but broadly equivalent strengths, primarily in how they responded to financial crises. Allen and Gale find that capital market systems allow for greater innovation, improving growth in good times, but that bank-based systems provide more steady access to credit and that such intertemporal smoothing enables bank-based systems to do better in weathering financial crises (Allen and Gale, 2000). If bank-based systems are now as vulnerable to crises as capital market systems, these banks will be less capable of providing this intertemporal smoothing.

Despite the predictions of the convergence literature, significant divergence in national financial systems remains, perhaps most importantly in the political organization of financial systems and their private governance structures. Distinctive national financial systems have displayed stubborn persistence through not only the recent decades of financial integration but also the historic upheavals of the Great Depression, Second World War, and the collapse of the Bretton Woods system. Furthermore, much of the momentum toward liberalization has been endogenous, with financial integration a project promoted by the banks themselves. Dynamics of change and continuity in financial systems, and by extension broader national capitalist systems, cannot therefore be captured in purely economic terms as a product of increased global financial interconnectedness. Given the prominent role that banks play in shaping the regulatory regime, both internationally and domestically, financial actors' political clout plays at least as prominent a role in the persistence or evolution of a financial system as economic factors. The democracy and Varieties of Capitalism literature reinforces this, by emphasizing how financial interests, and political parties attempting to appeal to financial interests, will drive movements to reform or reinforce existing corporate governance regimes (Callaghan, 2009; Cioffi and Höpner, 2006; Gourevitch and Shinn, 2005; Höpner, 2005; Iversen, 2005; Martin, 2006; Pagano and Volpin, 2005; Perotti and von Thadden, 2006; Roe, 2003).

Here, a focus on the differences in interbank relationships and the resulting variance in capacity for collective action helps flesh out the microfoundations of comparative capitalisms, by providing a framework for evaluating the relative political clout and interest of financial firms in liberal and organized capitalist systems. In part due to the long-term nature of firm–client relationships, firms in private bank capital–based systems have greater space to form private and public–private governance structures. These governance structures enhance the political clout of the financial actors to perpetuate their systems. Their capacity for influence is increased by enabling them to speak with a single voice on issues and they can better resist state regulation through a greater capacity for self-regulation (Olson, 1982). These governance structures help determine the influence of the financial sector in good times, but in times of crisis, the presence or absence of private governance structures will play a crucial role in determining the state's response patterns as well as the ability of national financial systems to self-replicate in their times of greatest stress.

In capital market–based systems, firms sell stock directly to investors to raise capital (Allen and Gale, 2000, pp. 46–48). Banks may serve as investment managers and are also a source of loans, or liquidity, to firms. Because stock can rapidly be bought and sold, relationships between firms and investors are necessarily shallow and short term. Firms will be reluctant to share private information with investors that can easily sell their stock and share that information with competitors. Investors must therefore rely on publically provided information on firms, such as public earnings reports or stock price. That both firms and investors can easily end their relationship affects the relationship between banks. Easily severed firm–bank ties make it relatively easy for banks to poach each other's clients, and they will expend considerable energy attempting to do so. The zero-sum relationship between banks means that any measure that aids one bank harms its competitors. Little space for cooperation exists, unless the relative gains are in the bank's favor or dwarfed by the absolute gains. Interbank relationships in capital market systems, therefore, tend to be extremely limited. Banks will still lend to each other and engage in other cross-bank activities, but always from an arm's length. Interbank lending will only occur at rates favorable to the lending bank and on good collateral. Far from being interested in supporting an ailing peer, healthy banks will see opportunities in the collapse of a rival, as that failing bank's clients will be up for grabs. In such an environment, banks will collaborate only rarely, and little space will exist for the emergence of private governance institutions.

Private bank–based systems, however, have different relationships between firms and banks and thus different relationships among the banks. While relationships between banks and firms in capital market systems are short-term and shallow, in private bank systems relationships are long-term and difficult to break. Individual investors provide money to banks, which in turn are the chief investors in firms. In such systems, the private information problem is solved by making banks intimate confidants of firms. Because the bank cannot easily sever its connection with the firm, their fortunes are bound together, and the bank will not risk harm to itself by releasing private information. This has advantages for both firms and investors, as a long-term relationship enables more long-term planning. It also alters the relationship among banks. Because the relationship between bank and firm is hard for either one to break, it is extremely difficult for banks to poach each other's clients. Therefore, the direct competition between banks is diminished (Allen and Gale, 2000, p. 235). With less to gain by undermining one's banking peers, the importance of absolute gains increases and greater space exists for cooperation and private governance. Interbank linkages will be thicker and may even take the form of cross-shareholding between banks. This in turn means that while bank failures in capital market systems create opportunities for rivals, bank failures in private bank systems can do more harm than good for other banks, by bringing them down along with the initially distressed peer.

This space for cooperation allows for the formation of private governance networks to advance banks' common interest. Private governance offers several substantial benefits for banks over public governance that must manage zero-sum competition in capital market systems, both in interbank relationships and in relationships with the state. Private governance allows banks to compete as a group against rival banking groups both domestically and internationally. This is the basis of the *Gruppenwettbewerb*, the "group competition" in German banking, wherein the private banks work together to compete against the Landesbanken, and each is able to respond as a group to international pressures (Deeg, 1999). Members of each banking group can, through such networks, gain the advantage of being a large bank without sacrificing their individual autonomy.

Being less focused on relative advantage over rivals, cooperative banks can better organize self-regulation. This enables them to provide collective goods for themselves, such as deposit insurance and limited regulation, instead of relying on state regulators. Self-regulation enables banks to construct terms more in line with their own preferences than they would get from state regulators, increasing their autonomy. This has advantages for the state as well, costing regulators some control but shifting some of the burden of regulation onto private actors. Additionally, there are political advantages to an increased capacity for collective action. By acting in concert, banks gain greater clout in negotiations with the state. Because of private governance associations' role in the regulatory structure, they will have regular and, in some cases, formal access to state regulators and the state policymaking process.

These advantages are to some degree robust to changes in the underlying economic orientation of the financial system. The advantages of private governance exist across different financial systems; the difference is that the greater focus on interbank competition in liberal systems means that private governance is less likely to form. Once formed, however, private governance structures should be robust to significant shifts in the underlying dynamics of interbank relationships. Thus, even if the banks in a private bank system shift toward a greater focus on capital market finance, the institutions of corporatism will remain in place, and useful to the banks, barring a substantial shock to reorient banks' interests. Because of this, even more significant movement toward convergence than has been empirically documented may be insufficient to alter the differing political strength of private governance associations across financial systems. Convergence may prevent the emergence of new private governance systems by altering the nature of bank–firm relationships, and thus interbank relationships, but need not challenge the effectiveness of existing relationships. In other words, the circumstances that maintain the existence of private governance institutions need not be the same as those that created them. Because private governance institutions serve valuable functions for banks, by resisting state regulatory burdens and enabling collective action, they will continue to be valuable to banks even as interbank relationships may become more antagonistic.

Moreover, private governance institutions may themselves be resources to resist convergence. As noted previously, private governance institutions give banks a role in the policymaking process; as such they will be more active participants in decisions to alter the regulatory environment to encourage or discourage convergence. This in itself may not be a safeguard against convergence, however, as the banks themselves may be among the advocates for convergence, especially liberalizing convergence. It may more likely produce a two-tier response to convergence, as identified by Deeg and Lütz (2000), where some banks advocate liberalization while others use their existing power resources to deepen state protections. Crucially, this means decisions over convergence may be driven as much by political strength as economic functionalism. It also helps explain why, absent a significant shock, convergence to date has been relatively limited.

Financial crises, which dramatically weaken both the legitimacy of the normative underpinnings of a financial system and the strength of the status quo actors, may be expected to provide such shocks. However, as will be demonstrated below, rather than providing a window to substantially reform national financial systems, financial crises in practice deepen distinctiveness in national financial systems. Private governance institutions play a central role in shaping responses to the crisis, strengthening rather than flattening national diversity in financial systems.

Theorizing Capture and Financial Power

Crucial to exploring that central role of private governance institutions, of course, is focusing on how private actors can shape state policies. The literature on financial power has increasingly focused on how the financial industry may press its influence in ways other than simply crude lobbying. Much of this literature has drawn on Lukes' (1974) pathbreaking theorizing of power, in which he identified three distinct types, or "faces," of power: agency power, agenda control, and hegemonic ideational power. Subsequent scholars have added a focus on structural power. These various understandings of power are useful guides in thinking about how to explain diverging policy responses. Theories that focus primarily on agency or agenda control, and theories of hegemonic ideology, however, offer relatively little traction in explaining divergence in bailout policies, given the similarities across cases. It is only in examining structural power and how that changes the interests and ability of financial actors that compelling theories to explain policy divergence appear.

Agency power and agenda control are closely related, in that both involve actors more or less directly influencing policy debate. Agenda control is a bit subtler, as it involves controlling whether the debate occurs or not in the first place, but both involve financial actors making concrete steps to shape the policy process outcome. These may be operationalized in the capture literature as, respectively, simple direct lobbying stories and capture stories focusing on the "revolving door" phenomenon, wherein regulators frequently go to work in finance and financiers take jobs as regulators.

Obviously, the financial sector has tremendous economic resources to expend on lobbying, though this may be a less effective channel of influence than some other methods. Lobbying is most likely to be effective in areas of "quiet politics," outside of the attention of the general public (Culpepper, 2010). This may be the case for financial regulation in ordinary times, when the public's lack of understanding of the nuances of modern finance prevents most people from actively participating in or even following debates over financial regulation. In times of crisis, however, bailout politics become intensely visible and financial regulation moves from being an obscure and technocratic policy area to front-page news. Even if the debates themselves occur behind closed doors, the public will demand an accounting post hoc of what happened, making it extremely difficult to influence policy choices directly through crude lobbying. As such, lobbying strength may enable financial actors to gain favorable regulation in good times, but will be less effective in determining the outcome of bailout decisions.

The same technical challenges that make lobbying potentially more viable for finance in good times also increase the likelihood of a revolving door of regulators and regulated. In order to adequately understand the issues involved, regulators must rely on the specialized expertise of practitioners, who are most commonly found working in the regulated industry. Revolving door explanations, however, are problematic in two ways. First, the impact of the revolving door may be overstated. Gormley (1979), for instance, found no variation in the behavior of FCC regulators with a background in the relevant private sector from those without. Moreover, some evidence suggests that prior experience in the financial sector may actually leave regulators with a greater faith in market discipline and willingness to impose a burden on banks and shareholders. In the US response in 2007–2009, Treasury Secretary Henry Paulson, a former Goldman Sachs CEO, was among the strongest advocates of avoiding moral hazard, while President of the New York Federal Reserve Timothy Geithner, a career civil servant, was among those most willing to disregard moral hazard concerns in the interest of restoring overall financial stability. The second, more trenchant problem, however, is that the revolving door is unlikely to be a useful tool to explain variation in state responses to crises, given how much overlap between regulators and regulated generally exists in financial policy. French regulators and bankers have, if anything, an even closer relationship than their American counterparts, a product of their common education in *les grandes écoles* (Jabko and Massoc, 2012). Representatives of the German banking associations have both a formal and an informal role in managing bank failures, with formal private deposit insurance as well as a tradition of working with public regulators to identify and manage troubled banks (Author interviews, 2011). Even the United Kingdom, which has a greater tradition of independent regulators, turned to high-profile advisors with a professional financial background in managing the 2007–2009 crisis, appointing fund manager Paul Myners as Financial Services Secretary and bringing in investment banker Shriti Vadera as a key advisor to Prime Minister Gordon Brown (Culpepper and Reinke, 2014).

The larger problem with explanations that rely on either agency or agenda control is a lack of variation across the advanced capitalist states. Certainly, especially in good times, the power of individual banks and financial actors can be immense. However, as this is true across cases, explaining variation in state responses must explain why the power of financial actors in crises changes in different fashion from case to case.

Similar problems emerge when focusing on hegemonic ideology, or cultural capture, where the ideology or view of the regulated industry becomes accepted by regulators as well. In these accounts, there need not be any direct influence from financial actors, as regulators will independently adopt the position that their job is to facilitate the policies the industry will favor. Many accounts of regulatory politics in the run-up to the crisis have focused on the growth of a profinancial deregulation neoliberal ideology, both generally across the advanced capitalist states and especially in the United States (Johnson and Kwak, 2010; Stiglitz, 2010; Wolf, 2014).

Such accounts have some difficulties explaining crisis responses, however. Culture is a big concept, and cultural prescriptions may take in a range of policies. Both US Treasury Secretary Henry Paulson and German Finance Minister Peer Steinbrück followed one strand of neoliberal thought by focusing on the importance of market discipline and advocating letting banks fail, while others in their inner circles, such as New York Fed President Timothy Geithner, advocated the importance of stability and of preserving the financial system above all else. Either may be a defensible position based on neoliberal ideology. This limits ideology's explanatory power, though it may do much to inform global debates. Moreover, in both the United States and the United Kingdom, the heads of the central banks, Ben Bernanke and Mervyn King, respectively, at times took decidedly heterodox positions, with Bernanke willing to contemplate significant nationalizations and King holding a much firmer line on moral hazard than other UK policymakers. That these prominent financial regulators held such relatively divergent views indicates that the triumph of ideology may not be as complete as some of its advocates have claimed.

Finally, such explanations have little causal traction in examining comparative bailout responses. Neoliberalism has been widely accepted across the advanced capitalist states, especially since the 1990s, when even French and German leaders have extolled the virtues of laissez-faire and deregulation. This can be seen in international financial regulation, where internationally negotiated standards such as Basel II increasingly reflect a global consensus on the ability of banks to manage their own risks. It can also be seen in the domestic financial politics of states, where convergence has been driven not only by external competitive pressures but also by domestic actors. In Germany, private banks were among the strongest advocates for liberalization (Deeg and Lütz, 2000; Dyson and Padgett, 2005; Lütz, 2004, 2005). It can further be seen politically, as parties of both the center-left and center-right have adopted a new support for liberalization as a means of both promoting the economic well-being of their core constituencies and appealing to the votes and deep pockets of financial actors (Callaghan, 2009; Cioffi and Höpner, 2006; Martin, 2006; Roe, 2003). This is perhaps especially remarkable among the parties of the center-left, which have responded to the decline of their traditional working-class base by both attempting to expand their appeal to financial actors and by offering their working-class base easy credit in lieu of a traditional prolabor agenda. This has occurred not only in the United Kingdom, under New Labour, and the United States, under the New Democrats, but also in less liberally minded polities such as France and Germany. The very success of neoliberalism therefore is what limits its explanatory power regarding policy divergence in the 2007–2009 crisis. Ideology may be a powerful tool to explain why almost all of the advanced capitalist states left themselves dangerously exposed to crises, as Wolf argues, and why austerity has emerged as the dominant postcrisis paradigm, as Blyth argues, or why a "new Bretton Woods" overhaul of the global financial system toward less risk has not been forthcoming. However, it is a poor tool to explain divergence between states.

Recent literature has focused on other forms of power, especially structural power. Scholars of structural power have directed their attention to how policymakers desire to avoid causing damage to the economy. Because finance has become increasingly central to the operation of advanced capitalist economies, policymakers have strong incentives to maintain the good health of the industry, not because of direct pressure from industry actors or even because they necessarily regard the modern financial system as an ideological good but simply because a crisis in the financial sector will quickly spread to the real economy. Avoiding the resulting massive economic damage from an uncontained crisis would be enough to motivate policymakers to act even if financial firms did nothing to advocate on their own behalf. This attitude can be seen in New York Federal Reserve President Timothy Geithner's defense of the US bailout:

> People on the right and the left both believe that there was a way to save the country from disaster and still let the system all apart, impose losses on creditors. But in a financial panic, as we saw in '08, it's the opposite of what makes sense to protect people. In some sense, the paradox of this is the only way to reduce damage to the innocent victims of a crisis is to make sure you keep the lights on. Because if you don't keep the lights on in a financial system, then you're going to face depression level unemployment. That's the paradox of it. (Block, 2014)

Much of the literature on structural power has focused on what Culpepper and Reinke (2014) dub "passive" structural power, in which it is enough that the incentive structure for policymakers clearly makes some policy options more or less favorable. Culpepper and Reinke, however, go beyond this by focusing on "active" structural power, in which actors have greater influence and greater ability to make credible threats or promises based on their structural position in the economy. Culpepper and Reinke explore this in focusing on how internationally diversified UK banks can and did make more credible threats to relocate in the face of unfavorable state policies than their more domestically focused US equivalents, which could not make such a move without enduring much higher costs. Woll makes a similar argument by focusing on "collective inaction" (2014). In Woll's account, banks that could plausibly claim to lack the ability to overcome collective action problems were better able to resist state pressures for privately funded rescues because of the structure of their national financial systems. It is structural power that offers the best traction in explaining policy divergence in state responses to crises.

Examining the role of structural power reveals more telling differences between states. Culpepper and Reinke touch on this by exploring how internationalized UK banks are better able to resist state pressure than primarily domestically focused US banks. Important structural differences go deeper than that, however, most prominently in the differences between bank-based and capital market–based financial systems. Bank-based financial systems build stronger private governance associations, increasing their ability to respond collectively. While Woll recounts how this enables the state to potentially push more costs onto banking associations, it more importantly gives failing banks important allies among the healthy banks, the better to push the state toward bank-friendly bailout terms. Thus, the organization of private interests and their capacity for collective action gives banks in different financial systems dramatically different structural power resources, which in turn alter the dynamics of policymaking.

These structural differences across financial systems in turn greatly affect the politics of negotiating bank bailouts. Financial actors are tremendously influential everywhere, *when they are healthy*. However, in times of crisis, the degree of power lost by failing banks varies substantially based on the structure of their national financial systems. When banks fail in liberal systems, they lose their own ability to influence policymakers, because their strength has failed them, and have no allies willing to lend them support. By contrast, in private bank–based systems, healthy banks are interdependent with failing ones and their private governance institutions give them the capacity to act collectively to help their failing peer banks. Therefore, failing banks have allies with both the means and the incentive to assist them, either through direct assistance or by lobbying policymakers for more favorable terms in state rescues.

In liberal systems, the power of banks shifts dramatically in times of crisis. Failing banks lack significant power, as they lack the ability to mobilize other financial actors on their behalf. While they may have been tremendously influential before the crisis, their strength was chiefly dependent on their own economic resources. As those resources dissipate, failing banks cannot expect support from their peer institutions, which have no interest in supporting a rival. Moreover, not wanting to compete against a state-subsidized rival, the healthy banks if anything want the terms of state aid to be as harsh as possible while still containing the crisis. Failing banks may still be systemically important, but that only encourages states to save them in a way that contains the crisis and not necessarily in a way that insulates shareholders and management from losses. Therefore, state policymakers will have relatively little pressure from financial actors, and the interests of nonfinancial firms and the general public will come to the fore. Since these actors share an interest in containing financial crises in a way that minimizes costs to them, policymakers will press for bailout policies that contain the crisis at a minimum cost to the state or that have a reasonable chance of recouping state support.

In private bank–based systems, with private governance networks, banks will be peers more than rivals and are more likely to see dangers rather than opportunities from a peer's fall. Interdependence between banks, because of both direct cross-ownership and joint ownership in other firms, means that healthy banks will feel costs directly if a peer fails. Less intense interbank competition means that the costs of another bank's failure, chiefly general loss of faith in the financial sector, likely outweigh the benefits from gaining market share left open by a bank failure. Moreover, the private governance network can rapidly organize a joint private rescue, distributing the burden of rescuing the bank across the sector, providing a solution to collective action problems of private rescues. Such rescues may be more desirable than state-funded rescues, because they avoid an expansion of state control into the interdependent networks of banks. This provides benefit to the state as well. Rather than negotiating with all major banks as individuals, the state can negotiate with a single representative of an organization with the ability to speak for and make commitments on behalf of a wide range of banks.

The prospect of private rescues produces a higher threshold before state assistance is required for banks. However, when state aid is required, it should generally be on less favorable terms for the state than in the more atomized capital market systems. In capital market systems, failing banks have few allies in times of distress and are forced to accept whatever terms the state offers. Failing banks in networked, private bank systems, however, will retain allies through the private governance network. Although the bank itself may lose political clout along with its economic strength, the private governance network will remain a highly influential player. Indeed, because of its role in self-regulation, the private governance institution may already have substantial political clout, including a formal role in the financial policymaking process (BdB representatives, interview by author, 2011; Börzel and Heard-Lauréote, 2009). It will serve as an ally to the bank in negotiating the terms of any state rescue, lobbying for more favorable terms from the state. The state, which is primarily concerned with preventing broader economic damage, will accept these terms in order to prevent a broader crisis, even if it increases the costs to the state.

Predictions

This understanding of the different interests of financial actors across different capitalist systems predicts different dynamics for the policy responses across those systems. In capital market systems, atomized financial systems and weak or nonexistent private governance networks leave the state as the primary source of emergency assistance, but free of influence from the banking sector. In private bank systems, greater bank interdependence and stronger private governance creates a more complicated, two-stage pattern of responses. Interdependence and private governance create an incentive and a means for healthy banks to support failing ones. Therefore, for relatively minor incidents, private bank–based systems resolve crises with minimal state involvement or investment, relative to liberal systems where the state is not only the last resort but frequently the first resort for a distressed bank. When the state does get involved, however, banks and private governance institutions will press for terms more favorable to the failing banks and more expensive for taxpayers.

These dynamics can be modeled to create two testable hypotheses:

> *H1 – Private rescues will be easier to organize, and therefore more common, in states with private bank–based financial systems than in states with liberal capital market–based financial systems.*
>
> *H1A – With private rescues less forthcoming, state intervention will be more common in states with liberal, capital market–based financial systems.*

Across financial systems, policymakers will feel pressure from taxpayers and nonfinancial firms to contain the crisis in a way that minimizes damage to the real economy and minimizes long-term costs to the taxpayer, either by providing minimal support or through policies that will allow the state to recover its bailout funds, ideally with a profit. In liberal systems, healthy firms will share these preferences. Not wanting to compete against a state-subsidized rival, they may even be more concerned about generous aid to distressed firms. Policymakers will, therefore, favor terms that contain moral hazard and limit the politically damaging transfer of taxpayer wealth to shareholders. In networked, private bank–based systems, high interdependence means that healthy firms will have a clear interest in supporting distressed firms. Insulating their partners from losses will help the healthy firms themselves. Moreover, because they have less to fear from state subsidies of other firms, the advantage in establishing an above-market precedent over avoiding subsidy of the competition will be greater for coordinated firms than liberal ones. Stronger private governance institutions will give those firms the ability to act collectively to shape state policy responses. Therefore, states will be under greater pressure to provide aid on generous terms.

As a result of these factors, while the private sector may be called upon to invest their own funds in a rescue effort, for reasons outlined in H1, the terms of state assistance will be more generous in coordinated systems than in liberal ones. Liquidity aid and direct capital injections will be on more favorable terms in private bank–based systems than in liberal ones. Healthy firms will have a greater interest in pressuring the state to pay above-market rates. Healthy firms will also oppose state ownership stakes, which may entangle the state in their own private networks. Instead, they will pressure the state to solve capital injections through bad banks, rather than through direct injections. Doing so both supports the failing firm and avoids state ownership of an ongoing financial concern. Rather, the state will simply take possession of bad assets and hold them until they either lose their value or are sold back.

> *H2 – When states intervene with public funds, the terms will be more generous to firms in private bank–based financial systems than firms in liberal systems. The precise terms will manifest themselves in several ways:*
>
> a. *Liquidity support, including loans, loan guarantees, and regulatory relief, will be provided at lower rates and/or on more generous collateral in private bank–based systems. Regulatory relief will be more common in states with private bank–based systems.*
> b. *Capital injections will be more likely to take the form of toxic asset purchases in private bank–based systems and more likely to take the form of full or partial nationalizations in liberal systems.*
> c. *The pricing of capital injections, whether through toxic asset purchase, capital injection, or full nationalization, will be closer to market rates in liberal systems than in private bank–based systems.*

General Trends

The trends predicted above can be illustrated through quantitative analysis. Private aid, which should be more common in bank-based systems, is unfortunately difficult to measure systematically, given the difficulty in distinguishing between mergers of equals and fire sale purchases and the incentives for banks to keep assistance secret, to avoid advertising that an ailing peer is in distress. However, state aid is generally subject to public disclosure requirements and is considerably easier to measure. Here a clear trend toward more generous aid in states with bank-based systems can be seen.

The database used is based on Laeven and Valencia's 2012 Systemic Banking Crises Database, expanded by including those crises listed in Caprio et al.'s 2005 Banking Crisis Database and Reinhart and Rogoff's 2009 Historical Summaries of Banking Crises for the relevant time and income levels (Caprio, Klingebiel, and Noguera, 2005; Laeven and Valencia, 2012; Reinhart and Rogoff, 2009). The unit of analysis is country-crisis, examining the responses used by a state in any given banking crisis. It covers upper-income countries from 1974 to 2009, with "upper income" defined as countries deemed "Upper Middle Income" or "High Income" by the World Bank's World Development Indicators (Beck, Demirgüç-Kunt, and Levine, 2009). These parameters exclude cases in the pre-1972 Bretton Woods system, when widespread capital controls created different dynamics in crises, and exclude less developed states, where underdeveloped and fragile capital markets similarly alter the nature of banking crises. States are classified as "capital market–based" or "bank-based" depending on whether their ratio of capital market activity to capital from private banks is above or below the median for countries in their income category. Following Demirgüç-Kunt and Levine, I calculate a separate dummy for high-income states and for upper-middle-income states, reflecting the different levels of financial market development in the respective income levels (Demirgüç-Kunt and Levine, 1999). The resulting classification of states is found in Table 2.1.

Controls for trade as a percentage of GDP, GDP per capita, central bank independence, and the presence of an IMF assistance program are included to capture broad structural dynamics of the national economy.[3] Trade as a percentage of GDP is a standard control in the financial crisis literature, capturing how international interconnectedness creates pressures toward action to limit broader international crises. GDP per capita provides a measure of a country's wealth and thus its ability to afford an expensive bank rescue. Since central banks are a major source of liquidity support, the degree of central bank independence, and insulation from outside pressures, will shape a state's response patterns. Similarly, the presence of the IMF may have an important role in shaping state response policies, both directly, through conditions placed on states receiving IMF support, and indirectly, in its capacity as a source of technical advice for states experiencing crises.

Additionally, controls are included to test for alternate hypotheses. Party ideology could obviously play a role, as left parties should be more comfortable both with an expansion of state ownership and a greater role for the state in managing the economy. Therefore, controls are included for party control of both the executive and the legislature, to test for the impact of party ideology. Controls for political structure are also

[3] Measures of trade and GDP per capita are from the World Bank's World Development Indicators (World Bank 2012b). The measure of Central Bank Independence is from Cukierman (2008), as updated to 2000 by Polillo and Guillén (2005) and to 2003 by Crowe and Meade (2007).

Table 2.1 *Classification of National Financial Systems*

Upper-Middle Income	High Income
Bank-based financial systems	
Argentina (pres.)	Austria (parl.)
Botswana (parl.)	Belgium (parl.)
Bulgaria (mixed)	Canada (parl.)
Chile (pres.)	Croatia (mixed)
Colombia (pres.)	Czech Republic (parl.)
Costa Rica (pres.)	Denmark (parl.)
Jamaica (parl.)	Estonia (mixed)
Kazakhstan (pres.)	France (parl.)
Lithuania (pres.)	Germany (parl.)
Macedonia, FYR (parl.)	Greece (mixed)
Mauritius (parl.)	Hungary (parl.)
Panama (pres.)	Iceland (parl.)
Peru (pres.)	Ireland (parl.)
Uruguay (pres.)	Israel (mixed)
Venezuela (pres.)	Italy (parl.)
	Japan (parl.)
	Latvia (parl.)
	Luxembourg (parl.)
	New Zealand (parl.)
	Norway (parl.)
	Poland (pres.)
	Portugal (mixed)
	Slovakia (parl.)
	Slovenia (parl.)
	Trinidad And Tobago (parl.)
Capital market–based financial systems	
Brazil (pres.)	Australia (parl.)
Malaysia (parl.)	Finland (parl.)
Mexico (pres.)	Korea, Republic Of (mixed)
Russian Federation (pres.)	Kuwait (pres.)
South Africa (mixed)	Netherlands (parl.)
Turkey (mixed)	Singapore (parl.)
	Spain (parl.)
	Sweden (parl.)
	Switzerland (parl.)
	United Kingdom (parl.)
	United States (pres.)

Note: pres. indicates the state is a presidential system, parl. indicates that the state is a parliamentary system.

included.[4] Verdier (2002) argues that the degree of state centralization will affect the development of a national financial system, with federal political systems producing decentralized financial systems and centralized political systems producing centralized financial systems. This, therefore, produces another alternate thesis, that central states should have more clout and be less susceptible to political influence than federal states and therefore be more likely to resist the pressure from the financial sector for more generous terms. Thus, a federal central dummy is included. Additionally, Weaver and Rockman suggest that presidential systems should be more permeable to outside influences, including the financial sector, than parliamentary systems and thus less able to resist the influence of financial sector actors. Therefore, a presidential/parliamentary dummy is included as well (Weaver and Rockman, 1993).

The impact of these variables is evaluated on the likelihood of three policy outcomes in a cross-sectional time-series multinomial probit analysis, appropriate to the binary outcomes in the dependent variables. Three dependent variables are analyzed. Broadest is *capital support*, whether the state provides operating capital to banks, whether through ownership stakes, open grants, or bad bank provisions. States with capital market–based systems, and therefore more limited private governance, should provide capital support more often. Without private assistance organized by private governance networks, the narrow self-interest of healthy banks means that ailing banks will have fewer alternatives and will be more likely to turn to the state for assistance. More narrowly, *nationalization* captures whether the state fully nationalized any banks in its crisis response. In general, nationalizations, which socialize all future profits, should be harsher than other forms of bank support. As such, nationalizations should be more common in capital market–based systems, in which other banks will favor harsh terms for failing rivals, and there are no strong private governance associations to lobby against expanded state ownership or harsh terms for failing banks. Finally, *recapitalization recovery* measures whether the state was able to recapture any of the money it invested in its banks, regardless of the form of investment. This is an imperfect measure, as a state can adopt stringent policies, but the magnitude of the crisis may still make a recovery impossible. However, if the state provides capital on generous terms, the likelihood of a recovery of that money is low regardless of the terms of the crisis. As such, as with nationalization, recapitalization recovery should be more common in capital market–based systems than in bank-based systems, as, in the

[4] All party ideology and political structure variables are taken from Beck, Clarke, Groff, Keefer, and Walsh (2001) as updated by Keefer (2012).

latter, healthy banks and stronger private governance associations will lobby for more favorable terms to failing banks.

The results, as shown in Table 2.2, show a consistent pattern in line with theoretical expectations.[5] States with capital market–based systems, where atomized relationships between banks produce fewer and weaker private governance associations, are more likely to provide capital support, more likely to nationalize, and more likely to recover at least some of their money when they provide capital support. These predictions are all in line with the model outlined above, where weaker private governance creates a greater need for the state to intervene in the absence of private solutions and where weaker private governance associations and more competitive interbank relationships mean that the state will be more able to impose stricter terms on failing banks. Of the other controls, a greater exposure to trade makes nationalization more likely, a product of international exposure both increasing the need to resolve crises quickly and increasing the force of global norms of nondiscrimination, which would be more tolerant of punitive nationalization than generous subsidies of private banks. Interestingly, party control has no significant effect, suggesting that financial structure matters more than ideology. Political structure similarly seems to matter less than financial structure. Central and federal systems have no significant effect. Presidential systems are more likely to provide capital support and to nationalize, which is contrary to the predictions of the institutional literature. However, the presidential systems in this dataset are overwhelmingly found in Latin America, suggesting that this may be a proxy for some other regional variable. Finally, wealth as measured by GDP per capita is strongly associated with all three outcomes. That wealthier states can better afford to provide capital support, including nationalization, is obvious. The association of wealth and recapitalization recovery may be attributable to a wealthier state having greater leverage or having greater ability to hold on to an investment until it produces a profit, rather than selling it early at a loss in order to free up scarce capital resources.

Qualitative Case Selection

Quantitative analysis demonstrates clear patterns in state response to financial crises with capital market–based financial systems favoring more intensive forms of capital support and on terms more likely to recover state funds. However, it has limitations that are better addressed

[5] Statistical analyses across multiple specifications of the model, as well as tests of other forms of state aid, are available in the Appendix (see Tables A.1 and A.2) and in Mitchell (2016).

Table 2.2 *Regression Results*

	Cap Support	Nationalization	Recap Recovery
Financial system (0 = bank-based, 1 = market-based)	0.770* (0.467)	0.816* (0.429)	1.695* (0.879)
Trade as %age of GDP	6.77E–03 (5.69E–03)	0.011** (5.24E–03)	0.012 (0.011)
Central bank independence	2.034* (1.133)	–0.019 (0.976)	1.928 (3.223)
IMF program	–0.135 (0.472)	0.146 (0.424)	–0.011 (0.680)
Political system (0 = pres., 1 = mixed, 2 = parl.)	–1.076** (0.328)	–1.150** (0.324)	–1.177 (0.760)
Federal/central state (0 = federal, 1 = mixed, 2 = central)	–0.148 (0.316)	–0.071 (0.274)	–0.601 (0.530)
Executive party (0 = left, 1 = center, 2 = right)	9.09E–05 (9.08E–03)	0.109 (0.188)	1.18E–03 (0.011)
Legislative majority party (0 = left, 1 = center, 2 = right)	–1.77E–03 (6.93E–03)	–3.57E–03 (0.020)	0.212 (0.341)
GDP per capita (constant USD)	8.06E–05** (3.11E–05)	8.28E–05** (2.63E–05)	1.50E–04** (7.64E–05)
Constant	–0.543 (0.946)	–0.856 (0.767)	–2.000 (2.128)
Observations	66	66	29
Groups	43	43	27

Cross-section time-series analysis; $^{*}p < 0.1$, $^{**}p < 0.05$.

through qualitative case study analysis. Two of these issues are observational. While public support is generally subject to public disclosure requirements and therefore hard to conceal, private support has no such limitations. Indeed, because disclosure that a firm accepted outside support may make the firm's problems worse, there may be strong incentives to keep private support secret. As such, it is difficult to systematically evaluate the provision of state aid across a statistically significant number of cases. A second observational problem concerns the terms of state aid. Determining the price of state aid presents data collection difficulties similar to those of tallying private rescues. Additionally, whether aid is generous or punitive is highly context-dependent, as what matters is the price relative to current market prices for liquidity support or capital and not an absolute price paid. These two observational challenges are both best addressed via case study analysis, which allows for both greater detail and greater contextualization.

The other advantage of qualitative research is in tracing causality. While the quantitative analysis demonstrates a statistically significant correlation, the actual causal chain requires more careful attention. This is not just an issue for quantitative analysis, as the nature of business influence on policymaking has generally been taken for granted but undertheorized. Much of the capture literature merely demonstrates that capture is a viable story, without being able to clearly specify the channels by which industry actors are able to shape regulators' decisions. Carpenter and Moss provide a valuable template by identifying not only plausible forms of capture but also standards by which capture may be evaluated. For Carpenter and Moss, this entails first outlining a defensible model of the public interest, then demonstrating a clear policy shift away from the public interest and toward special interests. This shift, however, is insufficient to demonstrate capture unless it can also be shown that there was sufficient action and intent by the industry in pursuit of that shift. This can present a daunting barrier to demonstrating capture. Models of the public interest may be highly contentious, and that a scholar has a different definition of public interest than regulators is insufficient to prove that the regulator was not acting outside of the public interest. Additionally, action and intent of the industry may be difficult to prove, as both firms and captured regulators may be reluctant to illustrate such action.

This task is made somewhat easier when capture is evaluated in comparative perspective, instead of single-case studies. The issue of establishing a baseline, for instance, would be one of the most contentious problems in establishing evidence that regulators acted against the public interest. In comparative perspective, however, it may be sufficient to highlight that different states adopted different response plans. So long as the problems policymakers confront are essentially similar, as, for instance, confronting the failure of several large and systemically important financial institutions due to a collapse in asset prices, one need not identify any given policy option as superior or inferior. It is enough to identify that state policy responses diverge. The baseline becomes not some ideal-type policy response but simply how other states with similar resources respond to similar problems. The comparative method also helps focus attention on whether industry action and intent is likely. If the most prominent difference between two cases is that industry actors have both the incentive and the ability to shape outcomes, this is a more compelling story than merely noting that, in a single case, it is possible that industry influence shaped outcomes. In other words, given that, for instance, the United Kingdom and Germany were similarly dominated by neoliberal ideology, had similar democratic pressures, and shared other elements in common, but differed in the incentives and access of healthy banks, this is more strongly suggestive of bank influence than other standards.

Case study work explores the dynamics of state response to financial crises across Germany, the United Kingdom, and the United States in their responses to the 2007–2009 financial crisis. All three of these are crucial cases, both because of their international importance and also because they are the most commonly cited exemplars of organized capitalist and liberal systems in the literature. Figure 2.1 depicts the ratio of capital market turnover to private bank–supplied capital in these three cases, showing the relative importance of each sector. In Germany, bank capital dwarfs that supplied by capital markets, making banks the key source of capital for firms. In the United Kingdom, private banks provide a roughly equivalent amount of capital as a percentage of GDP, but a much larger capital market means that firms have much greater opportunity to rely on capital market sources. In the United States, meanwhile, the massive capital market turnover overwhelms private banks as a source of capital.

Additionally, all three of these cases are large advanced economies. Focusing on large advanced economies in a common crisis minimizes variation on a number of potentially significant dimensions, enabling a focus on the key independent variable under examination – the organization of the financial system. The focus on large advanced economies minimizes differences in vulnerability to capital flight and fiscal limits on financial rescue policies. Developing states are generally much more vulnerable to capital flight than their advanced counterparts. Smaller advanced states, too, have different dynamics in times of crisis. The smaller size of their overall economies means they are both more vulnerable to capital flight than larger, more diverse economies and will sooner run into budgetary constraints on rescue policies. State guarantees and other intervention policies are generally regarded as risk-free by markets, on the assumption that states are more capable of running long-term deficits than firms. This holds until the state's debt-to-GDP ratio rises enough to call that into question. The smaller economies of smaller states or developing states mean that they run into debt-related constrains more quickly than large advanced economies.

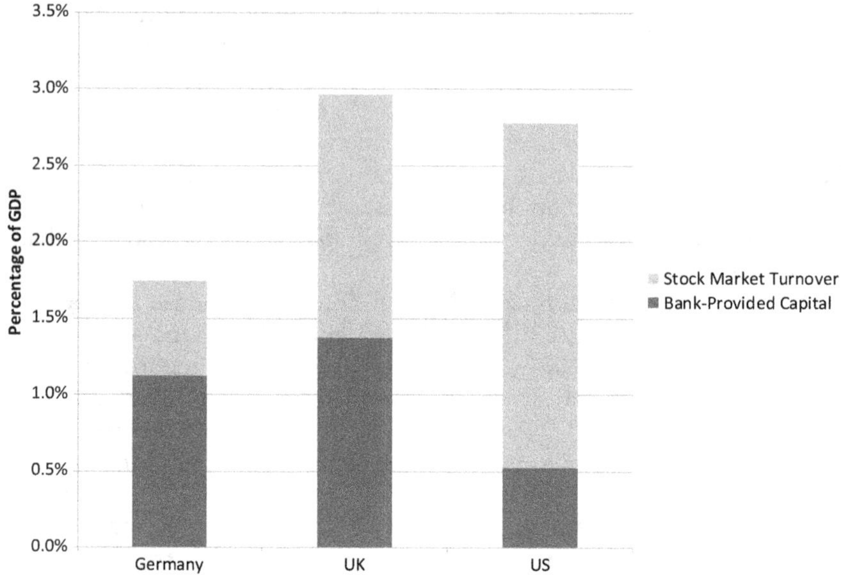

Figure 2.1 Sources of capital in Germany, the United Kingdom, and the United States.

The cases selected also control for cause of crisis. In all three cases, financial institutions ran into trouble based on essentially the same twin problems – the collapse of a global bubble in subprime mortgage securities and the attendant contraction of global credit markets. The housing bubble was largely centered on American subprime mortgages, although Spanish and Eastern European housing markets saw similar dynamics. In any event, since the derivative securities from those mortgages were traded globally, the point of origin mattered very little in the actual unfolding of the crisis. Moreover, even those banks that did not trade in subprime securities felt the effects from the credit crunch once banks exposed to those securities started to run into difficulties. Controlling for the cause of crisis, therefore, means that the essential problems were the same in all cases and obviates concerns that different types of crisis may produce different dynamics that could explain variation in responses.

Additionally, as indicated in Figure 2.2, these cases provide variance on two other potentially important causal variables: European Union membership and federalism. The European Union, far more than any other international organization, can play a significant role in shaping state economic policies. The European Commission has significant authority to restrict state responses seen as providing undue state aid. Comparing a

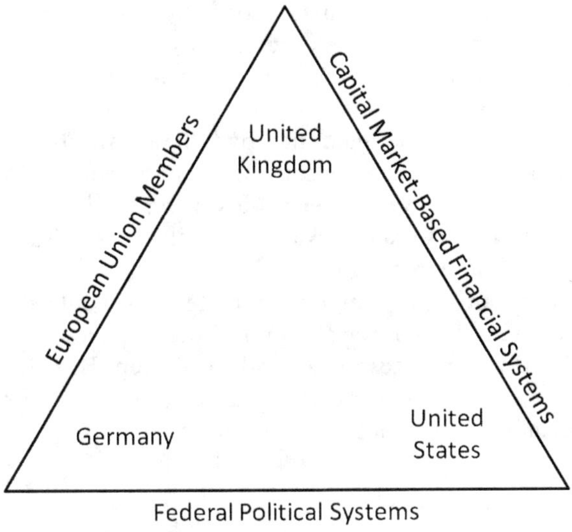

Figure 2.2 Case selection.

major economy outside of the European Union with two within it allows for a control on the influence of the European Union. If the British and German responses closely resemble each other, this suggests that the European Union played a crucial role. Alternately, if the American and British responses have more in common with each other, this indicates where the national financial system, and the influence of banks, played a determinative role in shaping policy. Additionally, whether a state is federal or unitary may affect the capacity of that state to respond, as power may be more decentralized in a federal system and banks may be able to turn to subnational units as alternate sources of assistance, weakening the bargaining power of the central state. Multiple scholars argue that the federal or unitary nature of the state will govern in part the long-term development of financial markets (Gourevitch and Shinn, 2005; Katzenstein, 1978; Verdier, 2002). It follows that the structure of the state may also play a role in how states respond in the short term to financial crises. A unitary state, without a delegation of powers to federal units, will be more powerful vis-à-vis the banks, having both a broader electoral base and greater economic resources than the central state of a federal system. Therefore, it may be in a better position to dictate terms to the banks. Conversely, in a federal system, not only is the central state weaker than a unitary state but that the federal units may also play a role in shaping responses. The federal units may have their own reasons to favor more generous terms to the banks, especially if a bank is a primary economic actor in that region. A bank may be large enough to dominate economic activity in a federal region but only be a relatively small part of the national economy, so its ability to influence policymakers, especially at the federal unit level, may be magnified by federalism. Therefore, federal systems may produce more generous terms of assistance for banks, both because the state will be weaker vis-à-vis the banks and because the central and federal units may work at cross-purposes, with the banks favoring whichever is more generous.

The United States and Germany are both federal, while the British state is unitary, allowing for an examination of the impact of state structure. Similar US and German responses and a divergent British response would, therefore, suggest that state structure may be more important than either financial system structure or EU membership.

3 Germany and the 2007–2009 Crisis

Germany, along with most of the major Western economies, experienced severe effects from the global collapse of mortgage-backed securities prices and subsequent financial crisis. German real estate itself escaped the boom-and-bust cycle felt elsewhere, but German banks held significant exposure to real estate busts in the United States, as well as in Ireland, Spain, and Eastern Europe. Consequently, confronted with bank failures of systemic importance, Germany, like the United States and the United Kingdom, responded with a massive state support program for its banks. However, while the US and UK plans resembled each other closely in terms of both intervention and attention to moral hazard concerns, the German plan differed greatly. The Germans, to a far greater extent than their Anglo-American counterparts, favored support on generous terms, with relatively inexpensive liquidity and consistently below-market capital injections. The Germans also proved far less willing to use nationalization as a policy tool, fully nationalizing only one institution and taking direct stakes in only two more. Moreover, the dynamics of bank–state relations were considerably different. German aid was voluntary in nature. While US and UK firms were largely presented with nonnegotiable terms for state aid, German banks could negotiate the terms of their assistance and in some cases seek alternate public sources of aid from the federal states, or Länder. Conversely, however, the Germans were able to extract a relatively large private contribution toward bank rescues, with banks contributing billions to their peers, while private rescues were virtually unknown in the United States and the United Kingdom.

The key difference between the German and US/UK experience lies in the different structure of their financial systems. German finance is highly organized and relatively interdependent. This gives banks an incentive and means to support their peers, but also a means by which to influence state aid policies. Private consortium rescues could be more easily organized in Germany, enabling the German state to lean on private associations to extract private contributions toward containing the financial crisis. At the same time, these stronger sectoral institutions gave the German financial sector greater political clout to shape the terms on which state aid was offered. Unlike in the US and UK plans, the German financial sector, including banks that would receive state aid, participated in drafting response plans, resulting in more generous state aid terms.

Structure of German Banking

The comparative capitalisms literature holds Germany up as an exemplar of private bank–based finance, in which private banks provide the key source of capital to businesses in the real economy. This can be overstated somewhat; like in capital market–based systems, companies' chief source of capital is their own retained earnings (Allen and Gale, 2000). However, in Germany, banks play a considerably more important role in financing companies than capital markets, which have been relatively small in Germany. The relationship between firms and banks, known as the *hausbank* system, involves the long-term provision of loans from banks to firms, as well as the bank taking an ownership stake in the firm. By law, this ownership is capped at 25 percent+1 of a firm, short of a controlling interest but large enough to hold a veto under German corporate law (Deeg, 1999).

This system offers a way to solve the information problem inherent in the provision of finance to firms. Lenders and investors want to do business with firms with a high likelihood of repayment, but that information is largely private and known most clearly to the firm seeking a loan. That firm may have an incentive to misrepresent itself as healthier, to gain access to more money at better rates. In a capital market system, this problem is addressed by firms seeking short-term capital from markets, selling shares and taking short-term loans. The price of a share provides a good sense of how the population of investors as a whole values the firm, circumventing the private information problem by relying on the collective judgment of the crowd. This method is, of course, imprecise, and as a consequence, provision of capital in market systems tends to be short term and more favorable to firms with established reputations. The hausbank system instead solves the private information problem through large ownership stakes. As part owner, the bank gains access to the firm's private information as well some control over the direction of the firm. The bank can, therefore, better safeguard its investment than investors in capital market systems who have minimal access and control. The firm in a hausbank system in turn gets a source of capital committed to the firm in the long term and is unlikely to rapidly withdraw its support.

The hausbank system shapes both the nature of the German economy and the politics of finance in Germany. The bank–firm relationship is inherently a more long-term one, as disentangling the two is a much more complicated and costly process than selling shares in a capital market. This makes it easier for smaller and newer firms to survive than in a capital market system, where the relative lack of information available to capital markets puts them at a disadvantage relative to large firms with well-established histories of share values. The hausbank system is generally seen to explain the success of the Mittelstand, Germany's small and medium-sized enterprises (Allen and Gale, 2000). Such firms have typically outperformed their liberal system equivalents, as they can more easily access financing. It also explains the success of Germany's diversified quality production approach, which is made possible because of an emphasis on long-term profits, rather than the next-quarter returns that preoccupy investors in capital market systems.

The system also diminishes the competition between banks somewhat. The hard-to-disentangle bank–firm relationship makes it relatively difficult for banks to poach clients from each other. This directs interbank competition more toward new business than to acquiring rivals' clients. The hausbank system is only one aspect of an extensive network of cross-holdings among firms, between firms and banks, and between banks and other financial institutions, such as insurance companies. Although two banks are rarely both investors in a single firm, their interests can overlap insofar as they will both be investors in firms that are interconnected through cross-holding.[1] Because banks are less directly competitive with each other, they have more space for collaborative action in their mutual interest. Less intense competition diminishes the incentives to pursue short-term gains by defecting from collective arrangements. Because of this, bank competition in Germany is far more between banking categories, or "pillars," than between individual firms.

German finance, like in the United States, has traditionally been divided between different types of firms. However, while US banking has been divided functionally, between investment and commercial banking, German banking is divided by ownership. German banking has, since the nineteenth century, consisted of three pillars: the privately owned commercial banks, the Land- and municipality-owned savings bank system, and the mutually owned cooperative banks (Deeg, 1999). Each of the three pillars has traditionally focused on different segments of the market. The cooperatives have focused on the needs of agriculture and

[1] For a detailed explanation of patterns of German cross-holdings, see Höpner and Krempel (2004).

small rural industry; the savings banks have focused on the Mittelstand; and the commercial banks have generally served the needs of larger industry. This division is by no means absolute, and the savings banks and commercial banks have competed intensely over the larger firms of the Mittelstand. The overlap between the markets of the commercial and savings banks has only grown in recent decades, increasing competition between the pillars.

The various pillars differ not only in their ownership but also in their organization. The private banks are independent and privately owned, although coordinated through a stronger sectoral organization than their liberal equivalents. The savings and cooperative banks, however, exist within their pillars in what can best be described as a federal organization (Deeg, 1999). Banking within the savings bank and cooperative pillars is hierarchically structured, with local banks under regional banks, all overseen by a national-level sectoral association. Individual banks, at all levels, retain significant autonomy to themselves. The individual banks are independent, but also noncompetitive, dividing markets along geographic lines and in some cases along functional lines as well. Within the savings banks pillar, the local or municipal banks, known as *Sparkassen*, are in this federal relationship with the Land-level *Landesbanken* and the national DekaBank. The Landesbanken serve as wholesale banks for the Sparkassen, while also engaging in their own banking operations, focused primarily on larger businesses and international investment. This relationship is marked by extensive cross-ownership, with the Sparkassen often significant owners of the Landesbanken and vice versa. The other chief owners of the Landesbanken are the Länder themselves. Traditionally, each Land had its own Landesbank, although, by the eve of the 2007–2009 crisis, consolidations had brought the total number of Landesbanken to nine. At that time, all the Landesbanken but one were entirely owned by a mix of Sparkassen and Länder.[2]

Each of these pillars, including the commercial banks, is overseen by its own peak association. For the savings banks and the cooperatives, the *Deutscher Sparkassen- und Giroverband* ("German Savings Banks Association," abbreviated DSGV) and *Bundesverband der Deutschen Volksbanken und Raiffeisenbanken* ("Federal Association of German Cooperative Banks," abbreviated BVR) are the peak associations of their respective federal systems. The commercial bank association – the *Bundesverband deutscher Banken* ("Federal Association of German Banks," abbreviated BdB) – serves a similar role for the commercial

[2] That one exception was HSH Nordbank, which in 2007 was 25 percent owned by American private equity firm JC Flowers & Co. (Bulkeley, 2008d).

banks, although the commercial banks lack the hierarchical federal structure of the other two pillars.

Each of the pillars of German finance is marked by a substantially greater degree of self-regulation than their liberal peers in the United States and the United Kingdom. For the cooperatives and the savings banks, this follows from their federal ownership structure. The commercial banks, while lacking this federal structure, nevertheless have diminished intrapillar competition and strong incentive to act collectively in response to the collective action of the other pillars. Each peak association runs a private deposit insurance scheme for its members, and all of them have some provision to provide emergency liquidity support to their members. This gives the associations a financial stake in maintaining the stability of their respective banks. Moreover, each association plays a semiformal role in monitoring their member banks and reporting problems as necessary to the Bundesbank or BaFin, the German central financial regulator (BdB representatives, interview by author, 2011). The associations are "almost equal" partners with state regulators in monitoring and regulating the banks (BdB representatives, interview by author, 2011). Each association is also the chief lobbying organization for the respective pillars.

Competition in German banking has generally not been between banks directly but between the pillars as a whole, in what is termed *Gruppenwettbewerb* ("group competition") (Deeg, 1999). The federal structure of the cooperatives and the savings banks eliminates direct competition within the pillar. The commercial banks, lacking this federal structure, do compete directly with each other. However, the hausbank system and reliance on coordination mechanisms through cross-ownership and the BdB mean that this competition is considerably less intense than the competition between American or British banks. Competition between savings bank and commercial bank pillars in particular can be intense. This competition gains an additional layer of complexity due to the legal protections enjoyed by the savings banks. The Landesbanken are not publically traded, and ownership is generally restricted to the Länder and the Sparkassen (Deeg, 1999). Therefore, the Landesbanken can engage in takeovers of commercial banks, but commercial banks cannot purchase Landesbanken and must compete purely in terms of market share. Additionally, until ruled to be illegal state aid by the European Commission, the Landesbanken enjoyed open-ended guarantees of support from their Länder, another advantage over the commercial banks (European Commission, 2001). The competition between the pillars is, therefore, often as much in the political realm as the economic. The commercial banks have historically focused a great deal of attention on rolling back the unique prerogatives of the Landesbanken. This conflict goes back as far as the Great Depression, when the commercial banks attempted to use the pressure for banking reform and rescues to remove traditional privileges of the Landesbanken (Deeg, 1999). More recently, the commercial banks pushed for the European Commission to act against Länder support of the Landesbanken.

The three-pillar *hausbank* system in Germany has endured in some form since the nineteenth century. Increasing access to international capital markets beginning in the 1970s, however, puts pressure on the system. Access to international capital was by no means uniform for all German firms. Large firms, with some international presence and reputation, found international capital markets to be a fruitful alternative to bank financing. These firms themselves played a role in pressing for further opening of capital markets (Beyer and Höpner, 2003; Deeg, 1999). Smaller firms found their access considerably more limited, such that the opening of international finance actually increased the importance of the hausbank system to the Mittelstand (Beyer and Höpner, 2003; Deeg, 1999).

This change in turn altered the balance between the commercial banks and the Landesbanken. As the large firms came to rely less upon the banks, the commercial banks turned more of their attention to the Mittelstand, increasing their competition with the Landesbanken. The commercial banks shifted their focus to what became known as the *Allfinanz* strategy, adopting a universal banking model in which they provided not only financing but also consulting, investment banking, and equity investing (Beyer and Höpner, 2003; Deeg, 1999). This strategy not only enabled the commercial banks to present themselves to the Mittelstand as a sort of financial one-stop supermarket for all of their financial needs but also allowed the banks to better assess their risk exposure. The Landesbanken responded in kind, also moving toward universal banking.

Increased international exposure increased international risk for German banking, to which the pillars responded by enhancing institutional structures for collective responses to firm distress. Historically, German finance had experienced relatively few firm failures. This is broadly typical of private bank–based financial systems, as banks both take on less risk and have greater access to private channels of support before a downturn becomes a crisis than in liberal systems. However, when banks fail in a private bank system, their integration with other banks makes the problems much more severe (Fecht, 2004).

The last major financial firm failure prior to 2007 in Germany was the failure of Herstatt in 1974. A medium-sized commercial bank, Herstatt experienced severe difficulties related to its exposure to the Secondary Banking Crisis in the United Kingdom and was subsequently wound down by the German state (Becker, 1976, p. 1290). The failure of a peer drove the other commercial banks to develop a cooperative response capability comparable to that of the savings banks and cooperatives. This resulted in the creation of the Liquidity Consortium Bank (the LIKO Bank), a standing institution managed by the BdB and funded by the commercial banks to provide emergency liquidity support to commercial banks (Beck, 2002). Although not used in the 2007–2009 crisis because it was too small and liquidity-focused to confront solvency problems, the LIKO Bank nevertheless demonstrates the much greater capacity of the German commercial banks to act collectively than in the United States or the United Kingdom.

The second major reform to come out of the Herstatt crisis was the creation of privately funded deposit insurance programs in all three pillars. These were largely intended to head off the creation of a public deposit insurance program, which would have expanded public oversight. Rather than submit to such oversight, the three pillars organized their own deposit insurance programs (Beck, 2002). These would be funded by the members and overseen by the respective peak associations. These reforms proved highly successful at providing private management of financial crises, and until 2007, few bank failures attracted the attention of the chancellor or other national political actors (Foreign Ministry representative, interview by author, 2011).[3]

The next major shift came in 2001, when the European Commission's Directorate General for Competition ruled that the Länder's longstanding guarantees of Landesbank obligations constituted illegal state aid, providing the Landesbanken with an unfair competitive advantage. This support consisted of a guarantee that the Länder would honor the Landesbank's obligations if it were to default (*Gewährträgerhaftung*) and a guarantee that the Länder would provide capital or liquidity support to enable the Landesbank to maintain its financial obligations (*Anstaltslast*) (Deeg, 1999). To ease the transition, the Commission gave the Länder until 2005 to remove these protections (European Commission, 2001). The Commission intended for the Landesbanken to use this time to consolidate in anticipation of higher borrowing costs. Instead, the Landesbanken took advantage of their remaining years of unlimited state guarantees to borrow and expand extensively. Supporters of the Landesbanken argued that this was done to put the banks in as strong a

[3] The largest of these was Schröder, Münchmeyer, Hengst, & Co. in 1983 (Beck, 2002, p. 16).

position as possible. Critics argued that the Landesbanken were stepping up their abuse of the guarantees now that their removal was a certainty (Foreign Ministry representative, interview by author, 2011; Handke and Zimmermann, 2012). In any event, by 2006, on the eve of the financial crisis, this approach left the Landesbanken considerably larger and more leveraged, with a rapidly acquired international portfolio of assets, including substantial mortgage-backed security holdings in the United States, Spain, and Eastern Europe.

Systemic Approaches

In the 2007–2009 crisis, the Landesbanken would be among the first German banks to run into difficulties and among the largest recipients of state aid. The crisis, however, would begin in a commercial bank – Industrialkreditbank, or IKB. Initially, as in the United States and the United Kingdom, the Germans attempted to address the failure of banks on an individual basis. Some of these rescues involved the Federal Republic contributing directly, in partnership with private sources, as in the rescues of commercial banks IKB and Hypo Real Estate. In others, the Federal Republic played no more than an advisory or coordinating role, and funding for rescues came either from the other banks or the Länder. This was the case in the initial Landesbanken failures. SachsenLB was rescued predominantly with money from the other Landesbanken and a small contribution from Saxony, while WestLB was initially rescued with funds from North Rhine–Westphalia and its Sparkassen shareholders.

As the number and scale of failures grew, however, Germany began to feel pressure to respond systemically, both domestically and from the Irish and French governments. The Irish, feeling the brunt of the collapse in housing prices, were straining to protect their own banks and urged the Germans to do more to shore up German banks with Irish subsidiaries. Angela Merkel, the German chancellor, rejected the Irish pressure, maintaining that German banks were not substantially at risk (Cody, 2008). Nikolas Sarkozy, the French president, attempted to orchestrate a European Union–wide bailout, in which member states would contribute to a common pool to rescue European banks. The Germans steadfastly rejected this plan over concerns that they would be the primary source of funds in a pool they would not have control over, effectively placing Germany in the position of funding bank bailouts in their neighbors (Smyth, 2008). More important was pressure from domestic sources. Representatives from Deutsche Bank, the Bundesbank, and the Economics Ministry all came "knocking on the Chancellor's door" the same day, demanding action on the growing crisis (Foreign Ministry representative, interview by author, 2011).

The German state resisted pressure for a systemic plan longer than the British or Americans, but on October 6, 2008, Merkel and Finance Minister Peer Steinbrück announced a complete guarantee of German bank deposits, a day after Merkel condemned the equivalent Irish deposit guarantee (*Belfast Telegraph*, 2008). Although both Merkel and Steinbrück subsequently walked back their guarantee as "symbolic" and "political," rather than legal, it nevertheless was a radical about-face (Corkery, 2008; Lichfield and Paterson, 2008). It also created significant moral hazard problems, by offering a free and unlimited guarantee to banks and depositors at taxpayers' expense. The subsequent walk-back, making the guarantee symbolic rather than legal, increased uncertainty around the guarantee and diminished its effectiveness, but did not resolve the moral hazard problem.

The Germans unveiled their guarantee not only as a way to prevent runs system-wide but as a part of negotiations between the state and the commercial banks over the public–private rescue of Hypo Real Estate (HRE). As will be discussed in more detail later, Merkel and her negotiating team managed to extract a significant private contribution to a public–private consortium rescue of HRE, a distressed and systemically important commercial property lender. Merkel managed to increase the commercial banks' contribution to the Hypo rescue by €5.5 billion in direct negotiations with Deutsche Bank CEO Josef Ackermann (Scally, 2009c). In those same meetings, Ackermann pressed Merkel to implement a system-wide approach (Evans-Pritchard, 2008b). Neither Ackermann nor Merkel confirmed that the open-ended guarantee was linked to the increase in private contributions to the Hypo rescue, but the two were announced within hours of each other. It appears highly likely that the guarantee was a concession by Merkel to extract a private contribution for the Hypo rescue.

The most significant system-wide response by the German state would be the creation of the *Sonderfonds Finanzmarktstabilisierung* ("Special Financial Market Stabilization Funds"), known as SoFFin. Equivalent in size to the US and UK systemic rescue plans, SoFFin established a €500 billion pool and conditions for the German state to provide liquidity and capital support to distressed German banks (*BBC Monitoring Europe*, 2008a). In the United States and the United Kingdom, the systemic rescue plans were constructed by regulators and politicians, with bank input limited to technical advice from not-at-risk banks. In Germany, banks that would likely need to call upon the plan were integral to the drafting process. This would be reflected in the form the plan ultimately took.

Primary negotiations were headed by Joerg Rasmussen, the state secretary of the Finance Ministry, in collaboration with Jens Weidmann from the Federal Chancellery's Department of Economics and Bundesbank chief Axel Weber. Weber, along with European Central Bank agents, pressed for the Federal Republic to take direct stakes in banks to address solvency issues. While industry representatives had no presence in the United States and the United Kingdom, both Deutsche Bank CEO Josef Ackermann and Commerzbank CEO Martin Blessing took an active role in the negotiations, representing not only their own banks but also the BdB and German banks more generally (*BBC Monitoring Europe*, 2008c). Blessing's presence is especially noteworthy, as Commerzbank's share prices were beginning to fall due to its similar profile to Hypo and other struggling banks (Dougherty, 2008a). Therefore, Commerzbank was widely expected to need state aid to survive, and Blessing was able to use his institutional access as a BdB representative to negotiate directly with the state over the general terms for aid.

SoFFin as originally constructed consisted primarily of money for liquidity support, in the form of loan guarantees. Smaller pools of money were set aside for capital injections and guarantees of state securities. €400 billion was marked for loan guarantees, in which repayment of loans made to at-risk banks would be guaranteed by the state. Such guarantees were to carry a minimum 2 percent per-annum cost for banks taking them, and no bank would be allowed to guarantee more than €5 billion (Braude, 2008; Walker, Munoz, and Gauthier-Villars, 2008). An additional €80 billion was set aside for capital injections to address solvency issues. Such assistance was to take the form of silent participation, providing capital to distressed banks but not diluting shareholder control of the institutions. As originally constructed, such silent participation was to generate a return of no less than 10 percent of the amount provided, and no firm would be allowed to take more than €10 billion in capital injections (Braude, 2008; European Commission, 2009c, p. 2; Walker, Munoz, and Gauthier-Villars, 2008). Finally, €20 billion was set aside under SoFFin to guarantee state securities. Additional conditions were set on banks accepting state aid, including restrictions on paying dividends to shareholders and a €500,000 cap on executive pay (*BBC Monitoring Europe*, 2008b).

In theory, the conditions placed on SoFFin aid were fairly stringent, although the emphasis on liquidity support over solvency support reflected a widespread belief among banking association representatives and bankers that German banks were essentially solvent and only distressed because of fallout over the collapse of Lehman Brothers.

This narrative, placing primary blame on US banks and policymakers, absolved the German banks of much of the blame for their fate and was promoted by, among others, Ackermann and the BdB (BdB representatives, interview by author, 2011; Landler and Bennhold, 2008). This narrative, in turn, could be used to justify liquidity provisions on nonpunitive terms. As such, capital support was more expensive than liquidity support. The overall stringent terms reflected the role played by the European Commission in setting out the terms necessary to ensure compliance with state aid directives. European Commission representatives gave ex ante approval of the plan even before its approval by the Bundestag (Foreign Ministry representative, interview by author, 2011). In practice, however, both liquidity support and capital support would be provided on far more generous terms than drafted in the original legislation, and limits on maximum aid to firms would be disregarded. Other restrictions on firm activities, such as the cap on executive compensation, would be similarly waived.

The core weakness of SoFFin in practice lay in its voluntary nature. In the United Kingdom, banks were given mandatory new capital requirements and would be required to accept public money if no private investors could be found (Darling, 2012). In the United States, Treasury officials made state capital injections essentially mandatory for the largest US firms (Paulson, 2010; Sorkin, 2009). In Germany, firms could choose whether to accept any aid at all. The state wanted banks to take assistance early, when a relatively small amount of state aid would cover losses. Firms, however, had incentive to "gamble for resurrection," attempting to find private solutions knowing they could tap state capital later on. This let firms potentially avoid taking public money, but forced the state to inject greater amounts later on if banks' problems worsened. Moreover, since taking state money was a public signal that the bank was in trouble, banks were extremely reluctant to do so. This created a scenario where the state wanted firms to accept aid and the firms wanted to refuse it.

The dangers of a voluntary plan were known in advance by German policymakers, and some elements, especially in the Bundesbank, lobbied for a mandatory plan (Bundesbank representative, interview by author, 2011). The banks strongly opposed a mandatory plan, and although the BdB never formally took a position on the issue, its representatives would press for a voluntary plan behind the scenes (BdB representatives, interview by author, 2011). Ultimately, a combination of bank pressure and legal issues in establishing new mandatory policies for banks that had met their microprudential requirements led to the adoption of a voluntary plan (Bundesbank and Foreign Ministry representatives, interviews by author, 2011).

The German state attempted to encourage banks to take money early and in large amounts, while the banks sought to resist, holding out for more generous terms. The organized nature of German finance increased the state's problem. The DGSV, the association of Landesbanken and Sparkassen, proposed a joint Landesbanken take-up state aid, which would both minimize the stigma associated with aid by providing it even to healthier banks and enable the association to negotiate the terms of aid for the banks as a whole (Braude, 2008). Such a joint take-up would have given the DSGV greater clout to negotiate favorable terms. Although this joint take-up never occurred, it nevertheless illustrated the organizational advantages enjoyed by the Landesbanken in their negotiations with SoFFin and shaped the negotiating context for those Landesbanken that did seek state aid.

The commercial banks had no such joint take-up proposal and highlighted instead the "stigma" problem of taking state aid. In leaked comments, Deutsche Bank CEO Josef Ackermann said he would be "ashamed" to take state money, reinforcing the stigma (Braude, 2008). Ackermann's comments were intended to be heard only by internal Deutsche Bank staff, and BdB representatives would lament that they were made public, increasing pressure on other commercial banks (BdB representatives, interview by author, 2011). Regardless, the comments had a chilling effect, increasing the reluctance of commercial banks to take state aid. The state meanwhile grew increasingly nervous at the possibility of having to provide greater aid later for institutions as large as HRE or Dresdner Bank, Germany's third largest financial institution at the time. The German state attempted to incentivize participation in SoFFin by lowering the costs associated with the assistance in one-on-one negotiations with the relevant banks (Dempsey, 2008; Dougherty, 2008b). Those banks that took state aid, therefore, received it on far more generous terms than specified in the plan as written, as will be discussed in more detail below.

Even after lowering the cost of assistance, German banks continued to struggle and increasingly called for a bad bank to remove their toxic assets. Here again, German banks demonstrated their influence on the policymaking process. The proposal for a bad bank originated with the BdB and would be adopted by the state with only slight modifications.[4] Under the final plan, banks would buy state bonds in exchange for toxic

[4] The chief difference between the BdB's proposal and the bad bank plan actually enacted was in the number of bad banks created. The BdB favored a single bad bank pooling all participants' bad assets, while the ultimate plan set up individual bad banks for each participating firm (BdB representatives, interview by author; Scally, 2009b).

assets valued at 90 percent of their book value, a value either much higher than their current market value or a reasonable estimate of their postcrisis value. The banks would then be obligated to buy back their assets at that value in twenty years (Scally, 2009a). If the bank failed in that intervening time, the state would be left holding a potentially worthless asset. This plan, therefore, gave banks a way to unload illiquid assets at above-market value and left the state exposed if the bank failed in the following two decades. If the bank did not fail, however, it would be required to repurchase the asset and so came to be seen by markets as an accounting sleight-of-hand, albeit one that increased the state's risk exposure (*Euromoney*, 2009).

German banks would continue to struggle into 2012, especially as the European sovereign debt crisis unfolded. German banks were among the largest holders of sovereign debt in the so-called "PIIGS" (Portugal, Italy, Ireland, Greece, and Spain). Therefore, as with mortgage-backed securities in 2007–2009, the banks were forced to choose between holding assets of questionable value and taking significant write-downs. In early 2012, Germany renewed the SoFFin fund to confront continued weaknesses in the German banking system (Ford, 2011).

Like its counterparts in the United States and the United Kingdom, SoFFin ultimately proved effective at containing the larger financial crisis in Germany, but differed sharply from the US and UK plans in both development and implementation. In both its initial creation and subsequent bad bank expansion, industry representatives, including likely recipients of the state aid, had a greater role in shaping the systemic rescue plan than in the United States or the United Kingdom. They used this access to secure a voluntary plan, which forced the German state to negotiate with failing banks to a far greater degree than in the other cases, where the state could compel banks to accept terms of aid. This in turn made the ultimate terms of assistance more generous and the likelihood of repayment of assistance lower than with a compulsory plan.

Commercial Bank Rescues

Industrialkreditbank

The first German bank to run into trouble and the first to receive assistance from the state was the commercial bank IKB. The case of IKB demonstrates the way in which a corporatist financial system enables rapid private responses to financial crises. In its later developments, however, IKB illustrates how those private institutions may push the state to intervene in increasingly industry-favorable ways, as well as the extreme reluctance of the German state to take ownership of a financial institution. Initial aid to IKB came through a public–private consortium, demonstrating how bank interdependence can lead to private contributions to rescues. However, the state's stake in IKB would ultimately be sold at a loss, rather than held until profitability as comparable stakes in US and UK institutions would be. This loss-making sale, under pressure from the German banks and a German public reluctant to extend state ownership, illustrates the limited capacity of the German state to use nationalization as a policy tool, especially at minimal cost to the state.

As would be the case for many later bank failures, IKB's problems began in a subsidiary's heavy losses on subprime mortgage assets. In IKB's case, its Rhinebridge subsidiary faced heavy losses from US mortgage assets, with losses approaching €24 billion, about 20 percent of IKB's total value (European Commission, 2009a, p. 32; Scherer, 2007). IKB was not generally regarded as large enough to be systemically important, but its distress threatened to impose losses directly upon the German government. At the start of the crises, IKB was 38 percent owned by Kreditanstalt für Wiederaufbau (KfW), the state-owned development bank (European Commission, 2008, p, 32). Although IKB's failure did not threaten the German economy generally, it did threaten to impose high, potentially disastrous, losses on KfW. Accordingly, KfW acted to preserve its own interest by rescuing IKB and initiated negotiations for a public–private rescue. At the same time, initial aid to IKB included a significant private component, through a rapidly organized shield provided jointly by KfW and the peak associations of the three pillars of German banking (European Commission, 2008, p, 32).

This first wave of aid to IKB was organized with remarkable speed. On July 27, 2007, a German bank informed BaFin, the German financial regulator, that it would be suspending credit lines to IKB (European Commission, 2008, p, 32). BaFin in turn convened a meeting of the Finance Ministry, KfW, the Economics Ministry(KfW's owner), and representatives of the three banking associations – the BdB, DGSV, and BVR (Economics Ministry representatives, interview by author, 2011; European Commission, 2008, p. 35). In just four days, the group produced a risk shield for IKB, covering €8.1 billion of losses from the Rhinebridge subsidiary and an additional €1 billion of related losses at IKB proper. Of this, the private associations agreed to cover 30 percent of losses up to €1 billion, split 50 percent to the BdB, 33.3 percent to the DGSV, and 16.7 percent to the BVR. KfW would cover 70 percent of expected losses until the banking associations reached €1 billion in coverage and then 100 percent of losses above that. Losses, split between the four consortium partners, were expected to be €3.5 billion (Buergin, 2007; European Commission, 2009, p. 35). This was soon followed by a second round of aid, extending an additional €350 million, in which KfW and BdB each provided an additional €150 million, while BVR and DSGV together contributed another €50 million (European Commission, 2009a, p. 36).

Both waves of assistance were assembled with great speed and spread the burden of the rescue broadly across both public and private actors. KfW and BdB shouldered the greater share of the burden, but both also faced direct exposure in the event of an IKB collapse, KfW as a significant shareholder and BdB through claims on the private deposit insurance scheme (Economics Ministry representatives, interview by author, 2011; European Commission, 2008, p. 36). The other two organizations had no such direct exposure and faced only the indirect costs from the collapse of a large – but not systemically crucial – German bank. Nevertheless, the German state was able to prevail upon them to contribute to IKB's rescue by appealing to the banking associations to contain a systemic crisis, and not "start the [global] financial crisis on German soil" (BdB representatives, interview by author, 2011). In addition to spreading costs across the industry broadly, the rescue was assembled quickly, over a single weekend. Requiring only three representatives of the banking sector made the process of constructing such a rescue considerably simpler than it would have been in the United States, where heads of all the relevant major banks would need to be both present and in agreement. Minimizing the number of actors both reduced the risk of defection and made negotiation and implementation relatively simple.

This first rescue is somewhat difficult to evaluate from a moral hazard standpoint. Undeniably, the German government, through KfW, provided the majority of the support IKB received through 2007. However, as IKB was 38 percent state-owned, the Economics Ministry argued that KfW was simply acting as a self-interested shareholder (Economics Ministry representatives, interview by author, 2011). Moreover, given the size of KfW's stake in IKB, it could credibly argue that it needed to prevent IKB's failure to minimize costs to the state. Additionally, securing aid from the banking associations reinforced the precedent of public–private cost-sharing. If banking associations believed that they would need to contribute to future bank rescues, they would have an incentive to adopt prudential practices, rather than simply relying on state assistance.

Future rescues of IKB, however, would prove more problematic. While the banking associations were willing to contribute through 2007, they balked once additional problems became apparent in February 2008. To cover these additional losses, Finance Minister Peer Steinbrück sought an additional €1.5 billion for IKB, this time in the form of capital injections rather than loans. Steinbrück envisioned this aid as being one-third private and two-third public (Evans-Pritchard, 2008a). The banking associations, however, resisted providing additional support for IKB. IKB was not a systemic risk, but was a risk to KfW. KfW's losses on IKB had already reached €5 billion, and IKB's failure risked bringing down KfW as well (Evans-Pritchard, 2008a). KfW therefore needed IKB to survive much more than the banking associations did. As such, the three associations combined offered only a relatively paltry €300 million, while the vast majority of this capital injection (€2.3 billion) came from KfW. €1.25 billion took the form of direct shares, bringing KfW's ownership stake to 90.8 percent. The remaining €1.05 billion was loans, with repayment subject to a better fortune clause that waived repayment until the bank recovered (European Commission, 2008, p. 36).

Even this assistance failed to secure IKB, and as losses continued to mount, KfW faced a choice. It could continue to hold IKB as an all-but-fully nationalized firm, until such time as it returned to profitability, and the state could recover its stake. Alternately, it could sell the bank immediately, which would guarantee immediate and substantial losses for KfW but avoid further losses in the future. While American and British policymakers generally chose to hold banks until profitability, in Germany, political pressure against state ownership pushed strongly for the second option (Economics Ministry representatives, interview by author, 2011). Economics Minister Michael Glos urged as early as August 2007 that KfW sell its stake as soon as IKB recovered (Gould, 2007). The Landesbanken similarly pressured the German state to abandon its ownership in IKB, both through the DGSV and by applying pressure through the Länder. Early in IKB's struggles, the Landesbanken even proposed a Länder purchase of the bank, until its troubles became more apparent (*Irish Times*, 2007). Economics Ministry officials, therefore, never seriously considered holding the bank to profitability, arguing that the political will almost uniformly favored a sale at a loss (Economics Ministry representatives, interview by author, 2011). In August 2008, KfW did just that, selling its 91 percent stake to American private equity firm Lone Star Funds for €100 million. This was well below the €800 million KfW hoped for and required KfW to retain €1 billion of IKB's bad assets and waive repayment of the €1.05 billion loan made in February (European Commission, 2008, pp. 37–38). All told, the sale resulted in a €14.8 billion loss for KfW (*Sunday Times (London)*, 2008). Even after the sale, however, IKB would seek state aid, tapping the SoFFin fund for €7 billion in loan guarantees spread across four separate requests in 2009 (Sonderfonds Finanzmarktstabilisierung, 2011).

Hypo Real Estate

The failure of IKB demonstrated the willingness of the German state to take a significant loss rather than maintain ownership of a bank. This reluctance was seen throughout the financial crisis. In only one case did the German state take full ownership of a financial institution. The nationalization of HRE would be the first nationalization of a German bank since Darmstädter & National in 1931 and would be done in a voluntary and above-market way that illustrated the extreme reluctance of the German state to nationalize a financial institution (*Irish Times*, 2009; Scally, 2009f). Rather than take a hard line with shareholders, which would have both limited state losses and contained moral hazard problems, this approach insulated shareholders from losses to soften the blow of nationalization, at a cost to the state. It therefore illustrates how the German financial sector retains significant power to assure above-market state aid even for a firm with virtually no value or chance for survival without the state. The Hypo case, however, also illustrates how rival firms in corporatist financial systems may come together to assist their peers and how the state may lean on healthy firms' exposure and ability to organize to extract greater private aid than would be available in liberal systems. Before it was nationalized at above-market rates, Hypo enjoyed a consortium rescue on a greater scale and with greater reach than the rescue of IKB and on terms more favorable to the state.

Prior to running into difficulties in 2007, Hypo was one of the largest of Germany's commercial banks, specializing in commercial property lending. It also held about 10 percent of the German covered bond, or Pfandbrief, market. A covered bond is a bond with recourse to a pool of assets. In other words, the issuer guarantees to repay the bond, but if the issue fails, the bondholder can seek repayment directly from that pool of assets. Because of this added assurance of repayment, covered bonds are thought to be safer than conventional corporate bonds[5] (Aldrick, 2009; European Commission, 2010a; Scally, 2009e). As would be the

[5] A covered bond is a bond with recourse to a pool of assets. In other words, the issuer guarantees to repay the bond, but if the issue fails, the bondholder can seek repayment directly from that pool of assets. Because of this added assurance of repayment, covered bonds are thought to be safer than conventional corporate bonds.

case for several Landesbanken that ran into trouble, Hypo's problems originated in its exposure to foreign real estate markets. In Hypo's case, the troubles originated in its Irish-based Depfa subsidiary, which experienced major losses when the Irish housing bubble collapsed in late 2007 and early 2008 (European Commission, 2010a, p.3). Depfa's failure has been attributed in part to regulatory gaps, between the various German regulators and between the German and Irish regulators. BaFin, the German financial regulator, later claimed to have seen problems as early as spring 2008, but had no authority over a bank-holding company operating in Ireland (Crawford and Walker, 2009). The Bundesbank and Irish regulators, meanwhile, argued that Depfa was the other's responsibility (Tinning, 2008). Slipping through the regulatory gap, Depfa was able to accumulate substantial exposure to Irish real estate markets, and its sharp decline threatened to bring down the parent company as well.

Unlike IKB or SachsenLB, the first German financial institutions to run into trouble, Hypo was indisputably of systemic importance. A failure of Hypo was widely regarded by both private and state actors as potentially more devastating than the collapse of Lehman Brothers (Scally, 2009g). Not only was Hypo large, but it held approximately 10 percent of the Pfandbrief market (*BBC Monitoring Europe*, 2009d). The German Pfandbriefen had not experienced a default in 100 years and consequently enjoyed extremely good credit ratings (Aldrick, 2009; Scally, 2009e). A Hypo failure would be disastrous to the broader Pfandbriefen market. In addition, the *Verband deutscher Pfandbriefbanken* (VdP), the association of German Pfandbrief banks, was generally considered one of the most powerful financial lobbies, with substantial links to both industry and political actors. The VdP had both a strong interest in seeing Hypo rescued and the organizational means to press for such a rescue (Wookey, 2008).

As with IKB, the German government initially sought to organize a public–private consortium rescue for Hypo. BaFin and the Bundesbank organized a meeting with the heads of major German commercial banks and the BdB, with the private negotiators chiefly represented by Josef Ackermann, CEO of Deutsche Bank, member of the BdB board, and chair of the Institute of International Finance (Boyes, 2008; Bundesbank representative, interview by author, 2011; Scally, 2009g). As with IKB, the preexisting organizational structures and interdependent nature of corporatist finance enabled the rapid assembly of a consortium rescue. The other commercial banks faced even greater losses and less potential gain in market share from the collapse of Hypo than the American banks faced after Lehman. They therefore were much more willing to contribute to a rescue than the American banks were in the aborted Lehman consortium rescue. They were also able to coordinate more easily, by having a single representative of the industry as a whole in Ackermann.

The outcome of the consortium rescue also demonstrates how these organizational structures can work in the state's favor. The German state was able to lean on the private organizations to extract private aid more easily than in a liberal system. When the banks initially met, they hoped to contribute only €3 billion to the rescue effort, with the rest to be provided by the Federal Republic (Boyes, 2008). The state refused these terms. BaFin and the Bundesbank declined to even send a representative to the first day of formal negotiations. Representatives later described this move as strategic on their part, to demonstrate the state's willingness to risk the collapse of a systemically important institution to ensure a private contribution (Boyes, 2008; Bundesbank representative, interview by author, 2011). Although the negotiations failed to produce the 55 percent privately funded rescue the German state wanted, the move convinced Ackermann to increase the banks' contribution to €7 billion, and subsequent direct negotiations with Chancellor Merkel raised that to €8.5 billion (Boyes, 2008; Scally, 2009g, p. 18). The plan revealed on September 28, 2008, consisted of €35 billion in guarantees to Hypo in two tranches, the first of €14 billion and the second of €21 billion. The first tranche would be 60 percent privately funded, while the second would be entirely public. Therefore, if Hypo's losses came in under €17 billion, the rescue would be majority privately funded (Bulkeley, 2008c). When Hypo's losses proved substantially greater than expected, Merkel convinced Ackermann in direct negotiations to not only retain a private element in the rescue but to actually increase the private contribution by €15 billion. The ultimate €50 billion rescue was, therefore, split into €23.5 billion private and €26.5 billion public, a 47 percent privately funded rescue (Board, 2008a; Tyler, 2008).

As with IKB, the organization of the German banking sector helped policymakers, allowing them to win a nearly 50 percent private rescue in only a short period of time. It also enabled the state to credibly threaten to walk away from negotiations, knowing that the private sector could, in extremis, develop its own private rescue. The banks could bluff the state, but the state could bluff the banking associations as well.

Subsequent rescue efforts for Hypo, however, illustrate how the organizational strength of the German financial sector limits the ability of the state to take a hard line with failing banks. After the initial €23.5 billion, no more private aid for Hypo would be forthcoming. Once €50 billion in loss guarantees proved insufficient to save Hypo, the chances of restoring the bank to health dimmed considerably. Instead, aid focused increasingly on "soft-landing" Hypo, winding down its operations in an orderly fashion to minimize the disruption to the broader economy. At this point, the private banks had less incentive to be involved and could instead rely on the state to handle Hypo's rescue. Moreover, as of October 17, 2008, the SoFFin fund had been established, and Hypo could simply tap state aid directly, without the need for an emergency ad hoc rescue. Unlike in the United Kingdom and the United States, therefore, the creation of a system-wide aid mechanism worsened the state's ability to provide aid to banks on state-favorable terms.

Once Hypo began relying exclusively on state aid, the terms of that aid would be consistently at moral hazard–generating levels, with guarantees provided at below-market rates and share purchases at above-market rates. On October 29, Hypo became the first commercial bank to tap the SoFFin fund, for €15 billion in loan guarantees (*BBC Monitoring Europe*, 2008d). The rates it paid for those guarantees, 0.1 percent for unused guarantees and 0.5 percent for called-upon guarantees, were both well below market rates for such guarantees and below the legal requirements set out in the Financial Market Stabilization Act (FMSA), the SoFFin-creating legislation. Under the FMSA, guarantees were to carry a fee of at least 2 percent per year, and the European Commission required guarantees to be above-market rates (Governing Council of the European Central Bank, 2008; Walker, Munoz, and Gauthier-Villars, 2008). Guarantees were also to be capped at €5 billion per institution. Nevertheless, by January 2009, when nationalization began to be discussed in earnest, Hypo would call upon a total of €102 billion in SoFFin guarantees, all at below-market rates and well in excess of the €5 billion cap (*BBC Monitoring Europe*, 2009d).

Hypo was able to extract such generous terms because the voluntary nature of the SoFFin plan created incentives to gamble for resurrection. Hypo, as the most distressed commercial bank, both needed aid first but also presented the clearest costs to Germany if it refused aid for much longer. In order to induce Hypo to take aid, SoFFin removed or lessened many of the conditions of that aid, including restrictions on firm activities and costs for loan guarantees. Guarantees, however, proved to be insufficient to rescue Hypo. Increased losses on Depfa made it clear that Hypo's problem was fundamentally about solvency, and not liquidity. Moreover, Hypo needed so much capital that if the state provided it, it would almost inevitably become the majority owner of the bank. Therefore, by January 2009, discussions began about the need to nationalize Hypo, the first nationalization of a German bank since 1931 (Bulkeley, 2009g; Walker, 2009).

Nationalization produced significant resistance both for cultural reasons and because of the resistance of the financial sector to state ownership. Culturally, nationalization was strongly associated in national memory with the Nazi expropriation of Jewish property, and the last nationalization of a German bank had happened under Nazi rule (Mason, 2009). At the same time, the prospect of an uncontained financial crisis prompted others among the German elites and public to recall the Nazi period in other ways. Interior Minister Wolfgang Schäuble, in discussing the need to rescue Hypo, warned that a financial crisis had caused the Great Depression and that "the consequences of that Depression were Adolf Hitler and indirectly World War II and Auschwitz" (Boyes, 2008). Therefore, debates over nationalization and state aid to banks became highly contentious, as they rapidly became connected to rival narratives of the rise of the Nazis, the Holocaust, and Second World War.

More prosaically, Hypo shareholders wanted to ensure state aid on generous terms. In this, they had allies in the rest of the commercial banking sector, as other banks seeking aid wanted a precedent of generous state aid. *Deutsche Schutzvereinigung für Wertpapierbesitz* (DSW), the German association for private investors, pressured the German state to take only a 75 percent stake in Hypo, preserving private owners whose shares could increase in value with the injection of state capital (Bulkeley, 2009d). Especially prominent among Hypo shareholders was American investor JC Flowers. Between a €1.1 billion stake in Hypo and a €1.85 billion stake in HSH Nordbank, Flowers' private equity firm faced almost €3 billion in losses from the German financial crisis (Bulkeley, 2008d, 2009g). As a major shareholder, Flowers was able to negotiate directly with Merkel over the nationalization of Hypo and attempted to build a political coalition for a shareholder-favoring nationalization (*BBC Monitoring Europe*, 2009a). Flowers sought to limit the state's ownership to 90 percent and to win a share price of ideally €5 per share but no less than €3 per share (Aldrick, 2009; Bulkeley, 2009j; Whitfield, 2009).

On February 18, 2009, the German cabinet drafted legislation giving it authority to nationalize Hypo by fiat (*BBC Monitoring Europe*, 2009b). It passed the Bundestag on March 31, and on April 3 the Bundesrat approved the measure (*BBC Monitoring Europe*, 2009c; Bulkeley, 2009h). The state could take ownership without the consent of shareholders and pay compensation as determined after the fact. Unlike the broader authority to nationalize held generally by the American FDIC and obtained in the crisis by the UK government, the new German nationalization authority was severely restricted, with an expiration date designed to ensure that it could only be used for Hypo (Aldrick, 2009). Even within these limitations, the German state showed extreme reluctance to use its new power, preferring to use the threat of expropriation to negotiate a voluntary sale by shareholders. Policymakers sought to purchase a majority of existing shares and then issue new shares to be purchased by the state. Once the state reached 90 percent ownership in this fashion, German corporate law would allow it to compel the remaining shareholders to sell their stakes (Bulkeley, 2009k). This strategy promised to be more expensive and time-consuming than an expropriation, but memories of 1930s' expropriations and the lobbying strength of the financial sector combined to make the new nationalization law too politically costly to use.

The state consistently paid above-market prices to induce shareholders to sell rather than use expropriation. In its first purchase of shares, on March 30, 2009, SoFFin purchased 20 million shares for €60 million, giving it an 8.7 percent stake in Hypo. The €3 per share price was significantly above the €1.52 per share current trading value, an overpayment of €29.6 million (Bulkeley, 2009h). On April 4, the state offered to pay a 16 percent premium on the Hypo share price, €1.62 per share for shares trading at €1.39 per share. The state purchased a majority for €290 million, a €40 million premium over market value, in order to obtain a voluntary sale, despite possessing the legal authority to expropriate (Bulkeley, 2009f). Hypo management urged shareholders to sell to the state rather than risk expropriation (Dougherty, 2009). It was described by market observers as "a gift to shareholders" whose bank had "no value anymore" and as "a good deal for Hypo, but a bad one for taxpayers" (Dougherty, 2009; Duncan and Lewis, 2009).

Having obtained a majority, the state issued €5.6 billion in new shares at the still-above-market rate of €1.50 per share and purchased them immediately (Scally, 2009d). Doing so brought the state to a 90 percent share and enabled it to compel the sale of the remaining shareholders. These included JC Flowers, who continued to demand €5 per share and preservation of a minority private stake (Whitfield, 2009). Even though it was widely reported that German politicians "despised" Flowers, the state continued to pay an above-market rate (Dougherty, 2009). The remaining shareholders, squeezed out on October 5, 2009, were paid 1.30 for shares technically valued at €0 (Dougherty, 2009). Flowers' tactics failed to produce a profit on his stake, but despite delaying the nationalization by eight months and increasing the cost to the German state, he still ultimately received an above-market rate for his shares.

Once in public ownership, Hypo, now rebranded Deutsche Pfandbriefbank, would still require significant amounts of state aid. A further €3 billion of capital would be injected by the state, and new guarantees of €52 billion would be extended (Bulkeley, 2009a). Despite this aid, and total guarantees as of May 2010 of €103.5 billion, the bank would continue to struggle (*Irish Times*, 2010). Exposure to sovereign debt in southern Europe would cause the bank to fail European stress tests in 2011, and the bank would continue to struggle into 2012 (Bulkeley, 2010).

Commerzbank

Commerzbank, the second largest bank in Germany after Deutsche Bank, was the largest bank to face severe distress in the 2007–2009 crisis and in some ways the most important. It was far more important than IKB, a relatively small bank of no systemic importance but for KfW's exposure to it. It also differed from HRE, both because it was considerably larger and more central to German finance and because its problems were less severe, meaning that Commerzbank could survive outside of majority public ownership more readily than Hypo. The case of Commerzbank, therefore, shows how a struggling but not collapsing firm can use its position to extract favorable aid from Germany.

Commerzbank has traditionally been one of the Big Three commercial banks of Germany, together with Deutsche Bank and Dresdner Bank. At the beginning of the financial crisis, Commerzbank trailed Deutsche Bank in size and was negotiating the purchase of Dresdner from insurance company Allianz (Jolly, 2008). Both Commerzbank and Dresdner, however, soon ran into troubles. Despite a net productive year for the bank as a whole, Commerzbank's Eurohypo subsidiary recorded €1.4 billion in losses in 2008, largely from real estate securities (European Commission, 2009e, p. 3). Dresdner ran into far greater problems. In February 2008, Dresdner was forced to inject €18.8 billion into its own real estate special investment vehicle to keep it solvent (*Gazette (Montreal)*, 2008).[6] Dresdner would struggle through 2008, and by September, Allianz would stake its hopes of addressing those problems on selling Dresdner to Commerzbank. Commerzbank faced its own problems, chiefly from Eurohypo, but those problems were generally not regarded as insurmountable (Clark, 2009). A Commerzbank–Dresdner merger was, therefore, analogous to the merger of Lloyds and HBOS in the United Kingdom. A struggling but essentially healthy bank would

[6] A Special Investment Vehicle (SIV) is an investment portfolio kept separate from the main accounts so that its profits and losses are not reflected on main balance sheets, but nevertheless remains under the control of the main institution.

take on a failing one, propping it up in the short term and hopefully making the united banking group stronger in the long run.

Shortly after the merger was announced, however, Commerzbank's troubles increased. Commerzbank, with its heavy reliance on overnight financing, was seen as Hypo-like by investors, and its shares began to fall along with Hypo's (Dougherty, 2008a). Through October 2008 speculation grew that Commerzbank would turn to the German state for assistance. However, it feared doing so would signal its distress to other market actors. This problem was compounded by Deutsche Bank CEO Josef Ackermann's statement that he would be "ashamed" if Deutsche took state aid. Commerzbank CEO Martin Blessing sought to avoid this problem by lobbying Peer Steinbrück to raise capital requirements for all German banks. This would make capital injections effectively mandatory, as the British had just done in their own state recapitalization plan, and provide cover for Commerzbank by compelling Deutsche and other banks to also seek new capital (*BBC Monitoring Europe*, 2008e). Steinbrück, however, refused Blessing's request, and SoFFin aid remained purely voluntary.

Blessing did, however, win generous terms from SoFFin, when, on November 3, 2008, he did ultimately seek capital assistance from the state. This first wave of capital assistance was €8.2 billion of silent participation from SoFFin. The first €4.1 billion tranche of this aid carried an 8.5 percent dividend, and the second paid a 5.5 percent dividend (Levitin, 2008). Both of these dividends were well below both the market rate for silent participation and the 10 percent minimum remuneration required by the European Commission (2009c, p. 2). As silent participation, the Commerzbank aid did not dilute shareholder control and gave the Federal Republic no direct influence on Commerzbank's operations. In addition to this below-market capital injection, Commerzbank received €15 billion in guarantees. Again, Commerzbank paid both below-market rates and below the legally prescribed minimum of 2 percent annually. Commerzbank would pay 0.5 percent on guarantees that lasted three to twelve months, and 0.948 percent for guarantees over twelve months, up to a maximum of thirty-six months (European Commission, 2009e, p. 5).

Commerzbank was able to secure such favorable terms for several reasons. The voluntary nature of SoFFin meant that the state wanted banks to take aid earlier than the banks themselves wanted it. Since the state could not compel the banks, it was forced to incentivize them offering aid on generous terms. Commerzbank enjoyed additional advantages as well. Blessing, as a member of the BdB board, enjoyed significant access to the policymaking process. Together with Deutsche's Ackermann, Blessing played a role in advising and drafting not only the original legislation that created SoFFin but also later revisions to the plan (*BBC Monitoring Europe*, 2008c, 2008d). Blessing could therefore shape legislation in the interest of Commerzbank. Additionally, the state needed Commerzbank to help save Dresdner Bank. If Commerzbank both refused state aid and rejected the Dresdner merger, the state would need to take far more drastic and expensive steps to save Dresdner.

The leverage from Dresdner Bank would help Commerzbank again in January 2009, when it sought additional state aid. In advance of the completion of the sale from Allianz to Commerzbank, Dresdner sought to tap the SoFFin fund itself (Bulkeley, 2009e). This would enable Commerzbank and Dresdner to circumvent legal limits on maximum aid to individual banks by counting them as separate banks and taking aid before the merger would be completed. Commerzbank and Dresdner were unable to secure a separate injection, but by threatening to scuttle the merger, Commerzbank was able to extract an additional €10 billion in capital from SoFFin. €8.2 billion of this aid came in the form of additional silent participation, on similar terms as the money injected the previous November. The final €1.8 billion would be ordinary shares, the first time SoFFin would take a direct stake in a financial institution, and only the second time in the crisis that the Federal Republic took ownership stakes. €1.8 billion gave SoFFin a 25 percent stake, which under German corporate law gives the holder a veto over decisions at the company (Bulkeley, 2009c). SoFFin also received three seats on the Commerzbank board, although both Blessing and state officials denied that the state would use its position to exert any influence over decisions made by the bank (Scally, 2009a, p. 19). Despite owning over a quarter of Commerzbank shares and €16.4 billion in silent participation, the state vowed not to dilute ownership control by private shareholders. Repayment was to be made at below-market rates, private control remained in place, and share values remained high, making this an overall gain for Commerzbank shareholders.

The German state worried less about avoiding moral hazard than avoiding the full nationalization of Dresdner Bank. Commerzbank itself could have survived the crisis without state aid, albeit with difficulties. However, as with HRE, an independent Dresdner would have required a full nationalization (Clark, 2009, p. 48). This gave Commerzbank leverage to negotiate more favorable terms with Germany. Commerzbank's leverage was enhanced because, unlike in the United Kingdom, Germany could not mandate a capital raise or credibly threaten to withhold aid. In the United Kingdom, the state could persuade an ailing but not failing Lloyds with HBOS to avoid needing to nationalize the latter because the ability of the state to require or withhold aid meant that it could compel private banks in a way the Germans could not. Instead, Germany needed to offer sweeteners to ensure the merger's completion. Commerzbank also enjoyed greater support from the rest of the industry than Lloyds did. In the United Kingdom, other large banks opposed the merger, fearing the new Lloyds/HBOS would be a far stronger rival. In Germany, however, Deutsche Bank welcomed the merger. The conditions attached to the merger meant that the new Commerzbank would withdraw from big corporate business to focus on the Mittelstand, leaving Deutsche Bank the sole German purveyor of services to Germany's largest companies (Scally, 2009a, p. 19).

The Commerzbank–Dresdner merger was completed on March 12, 2009. Commerzbank paid €4.5 billion to Allianz, which retained a 19 percent share in the merged bank (Bulkeley, 2009b). Commerzbank's troubles were far from over, however, as its exposure to sovereign debt would drag it down in subsequent years. This again demonstrates the weakness of SoFFin's voluntary nature. Commerzbank took only what it needed to survive, and not the capital it needed to address future problems. This avoided paying the state more in the short term, but necessitated greater state support later on. In late 2011, Germany revived the SoFFin legislation to make additional injections into a weak Commerzbank that never recovered completely from the financial crisis. Additionally, the state support of Commerzbank remained controversial. The European Commission ruled it to be state aid and demanded strict conditions to avoid distorting the market. Therefore, although Commerzbank was able to obtain Dresdner Bank, the European Commission forced it to sell its own Eurohypo wing, representing 45 percent of Commerzbank's total assets (Bulkeley, 2009k).

Conclusions on Commercial Banks

The commercial banking sector is the pillar of German banking that most closely resembles liberal banking systems. Although the emphasis on long-term investment and the hausbank system changes the relationship both between the banks and other industries and between the banks themselves, the commercial banks lack the federal organization of the savings banks or the cooperatives. Nevertheless, they showed a far greater capacity for cooperative action in the crises than their liberal counterparts. Initially, this worked in the state's interest: by relying on the preexisting institutional structures of commercial banking, German policymakers could construct consortium rescues for IKB and Hypo with a significant private contribution on relatively short notice. IKB's initial rescue was a public–private mix, but a mix in which the state provided the majority of support, in part because of KfW's direct exposure. In the case of Hypo, the state even managed to secure a more even public–private split initially. The common interest and organization of the German banks worked for the state initially. Because the commercial banks likely had both the means and incentive to organize a private rescue, the state could credibly threaten to walk away. This enabled Merkel to extract an additional €15 billion from the banks without matching state aid after the initial €35 billion proved insufficient.

However, once it became clear that the commercial banks required even more significant support, the organization and influence of the banks became a liability for the state. The savings bank association, the DSGV, had no desire to compete against a state-subsidized IKB and so pressured the state to sell its stake at a loss rather than run the bank as a state-owned enterprise. This produced a €14.8 billion loss for the taxpayer on IKB. In the cases of both Hypo and Commerzbank, that the influence of the banking associations produced a voluntary plan would cost the state much more than comparable cases in the United States or the United Kingdom. The state was forced to offer generous terms to induce Hypo to take aid, even as its need increased steadily. Once nationalization became discussed, the German private investors' association DSW would play a role in lobbying for a voluntary above-market nationalization. Similarly, the state could not compel Commerzbank into a merger with Dresdner Bank and so was forced to offer generous terms or else engage in a more costly full nationalization of Dresdner.

Landesbank Rescues

The Landesbanken, with their stronger institutional coordination, enjoyed several advantages over their commercial bank peers in seeking aid in the financial crisis, both organizationally and in their relationship to various elements of the German state. As a sector, the Landesbanken were even more capable of collective action than the commercial banks. The commercial banks, as discussed above, generally compete less intensely with each other than their peers in other states, but the Landesbanken, with their federal organization, do not compete with each other at all. Rather, the Landesbanken coordinated their activities through their peak association, the DSGV. As such, some observers have argued that the Landesbanken are more properly considered a single decentralized national bank than a group of firms (Hackethal and Schmidt, 2005). The DSGV took a lead role in both coordinating assistance from Landesbanken to ailing peers and in negotiation with the state. Because of a lack of direct competition and a preexisting coordinating organization, consortium rescues among the Landesbanken were even easier than among the commercial banks.

The Landesbanken also enjoyed advantages in negotiating terms of state aid because they were better able to tap multiple sources of state aid. The DSGV enabled coordinated action in dealing with the German state and in negotiating the terms of state aid to the Landesbanken. A proposed coordinated take-up of SoFFin aid among the Landesbanken enabled the sector both to negotiate standard terms for the Landesbanken and to diminish the stigma associated with taking aid by individual Landesbanken (Braude, 2008). The Landesbanken also had multiple sources of state aid. Unlike the commercial banks, which had to rely on either Berlin or private investors, the Landesbanken could negotiate aid from the Länder. Although the European Commission had barred the traditional guarantees from the Länder, they remained free to provide emergency assistance so long as the Commission ruled it did not rise to the level of unfair state aid. Moreover, the Länder, as shareholders in the Landesbanken, had a direct fiscal stake in preserving the value of the banks. This, coupled with the voluntary nature of the central state's SoFFin aid, put the Landesbanken in an advantageous position in negotiation for state aid. While the commercial banks had only one source of state aid, the Landesbanken had two and could turn to the Länder if the terms SoFFin offered were too onerous. This enabled the Landesbanken to both get more aid than they otherwise would have and to get that aid on more generous terms.

SachsenLB

The first of the Landesbanken to run into trouble, SachsenLB, provides a clear example of how the Landesbanken will work together to support an ailing fellow Landesbank. Much like commercial banks IKB and Hypo RE, Sachsen's problems stemmed from subprime losses from an off-balance sheet subsidiary, which in Sachsen's case was Ormond Quay (European Commission, 2009b, p. 34). Like IKB and Hypo, Sachsen received aid from a consortium of banks. Unlike those commercial banks, however, Sachsen's assistance was organized by and largely funded by the banks themselves, with no role for the Federal Republic and a relatively small role for Saxony, Sachsen's 50 percent owner (European Commission, 2009b, p. 35).

Immediately after Ormond Quay's inability to refinance itself threatened Sachsen, the Landesbanken and the DGSV convened to address the situation. Although regulators kept an eye on Sachsen, this meeting and subsequent action would be organized by the DSGV, and not by BaFin or other state agents. Initially, the Landesbanken and DGSV met Sachsen's needs with a €17.1 billion purchase of commercial paper on August 19, 2007, a loan for which Sachsen paid market rates (European Commission, 2009b, p. 36). The consortium and Sachsen immediately began negotiating the sale of Sachsen to another Landesbank. After BayernLB and HSH Nordbank declined to bid, Landesbank Baden-Württemberg (LBBW) agreed to purchase Sachsen on August 26 (Bulkeley, 2007b).

Before the sale could be completed, however, additional unexpected losses from Sachsen's Ormond Quay subsidiary caused LBBW to balk, fearing that Sachsen's losses would drag down the merged institution (Bulkeley, 2007a). Once again, the Landesbanken met to negotiate a rescue package and preserve the merger. This time the Landesbanken agreed to purchase €17.5 billion in bad assets from Sachsen prior to its sale to LBBW, to be moved into a bad bank. LBBW would also contribute to the bad bank, but take a junior tranche, receiving repayment last, and take no more than 50 percent ownership, to keep the Super SIV off LBBW's own books. Saxony, Sachsen's 50 percent owner, agreed additionally to guarantee the first €2.75 billion of losses from the bad bank (Bulkeley, 2007a). With the bad bank and its Land-provided guarantee in place, the sale of SachsenLB to LBBW went ahead as planned, ending the crisis at Sachsen.

WestLB

The next Landesbank to run into trouble, North Rhine–Westphalia's WestLB, was considerably larger than SachsenLB. With €286.5 billion in assets, WestLB was large enough to be considered a systemic risk. Like Sachsen, WestLB's essential problem was overexposure to subprime assets, chiefly in the United States (European Commission, 2009d, p. 3). But while the resolution of Sachsen was relatively straightforward and organized and funded by the Landesbanken and the relevant Land, the resolution of WestLB would reveal deep divisions between its Land 49 percent owner, North Rhine–Westphalia, its Sparkassen 51 percent owners, and the Federal Republic, represented by BaFin and the Bundesbank. The bank would be able to take advantage of these divisions and the voluntary nature and multiple sources of German state aid to play the Land and Federal Republic off each other to its own advantage.

WestLB first ran into trouble when it realized losses of up to €2.5 billion on its subprime portfolio (European Commission, 2009d, p. 4). BaFin and the Bundesbank, which had long advocated consolidation of the Landesbanken, pushed for WestLB to be sold to another Landesbank (Bulkeley, 2008b). At that time, LBBW was the most likely purchaser. WestLB's owners resisted this pressure to merge. The Sparkassen feared redundancies, while North Rhine–Westphalia's Prime Minister Jürgen Rüttgers was loathe to reduce his influence in the merged bank (Bulkeley, 2008b). Together, WestLB's owners provided the bank with a €2 billion capital injection, proportional to their ownership stakes (European Commission, 2009d, p. 4). Since the aid came from the owners and not the Federal Republic, WestLB was able to resist merger pressures initially.

As problems worsened, North Rhine–Westphalia's government began to advocate for a merger with Helaba, the Landesbank for Hesse and Thuringia (Bulkeley, 2008b). As Helaba was considerably smaller than LBBW, North Rhine–Westphalia could hope to have a greater continued influence in a merged WestLB–Helaba than a merged WestLB–LBBW. To incentivize the merger and to limit further damage at WestLB, North Rhine–Westphalia proposed offering an additional risk shield on losses from subprime assets. The Sparkassen, however, continued to oppose merging WestLB with any other bank, fearing that as many as 2,000 of WestLB's 6,000 employees would be let go (Bulkeley, 2008b). With the Sparkassen refusing to shoulder any additional burden, North Rhine–Westphalia would provide an additional €3 billion in aid to WestLB alone, in the form of loss guarantees (Bulkeley, 2008b). This aid came on extremely generous terms. WestLB paid 0.1–0.2 percent per annum for the guarantees, a price well below market rates, and North Rhine–Westphalia did not immediately increase its control of WestLB (European Commission, 2009d, p. 5). Rather, should the guarantees be called upon, WestLB would be required to repay them either with cash or shares valued at €200 per share. €200 per share was well above market price, making this advantageous for the bank and bad for the Land. If the share price was under €200 per share, WestLB could lower its burden of repayment by paying in shares rather than cash. If shares should climb above €200 per share, the bank could pay the lower cash value instead. WestLB's repayment maximum was capped, but its minimum was determined by how low share prices might fall. Without increasing its ownership stake, North Rhine–Westphalia could not compel the sale of WestLB to Helaba, and the Sparkassen continued to balk at any move to threaten WestLB's independence. European Commission reports argued that this continued paralyzing division between owners itself indicated the need for WestLB to be taken into new ownership (European Commission, 2009d, p. 13).

WestLB would remain independent, although by no means healthy. Its next infusion of state aid came in November 2009, when it decided to move €85.1 billion of assets into a bad bank and sought a €6 billion injection from the federal government's SoFFin fund to facilitate that action (*Total Securitization*, 2009). SoFFin's price proved too expensive for the Sparkassen, however, which instead lobbied North Rhine–Westphalia for cheaper aid, following the precedent of HSH Nordbank earlier that year. Because the Federal Republic and the Land had different visions for how to reform the Landesbank, both wanted to be the one to aid and restructure it. This created space for WestLB to bargain with both federal and Land authorities for favorable terms.

Ultimately, WestLB received a €3 billion capital injection via silent partnership from SoFFin into its new bad bank. The silent partnership left the ownership structure unchanged but paid a theoretical 10 percent dividend, the minimum allowed by the European Commission. However, payment was deferred until the bad bank was profitable (European Commission, 2010b, p. 19). The deferred payment clause meant that it was highly unlikely that SoFFin would recoup anything close to the full value of that fee (European Commission, 2010b, p. 23). In exchange for providing aid on such generous terms, SoFFin did obtain some assistance from WestLB's owners, in the form of an additional €1 billion in guarantees, split proportionally between North Rhine–Westphalia and the Sparkassen. In return, however, the bad bank plan ensured a cap on Sparkassen losses of €4.5 billion (European Commission, 2010b, p. 23).

Throughout the crisis, WestLB's shareholders were able to use their multiple sources of assistance both to obtain favorable state assistance and to resist pressures from the European Commission. This aid was generous to WestLB's shareholders, in that ownership was undiluted and repayment terms were generous but was insufficient to restore WestLB to health. Attempts to find buyers through 2010 and 2011 failed, as would-be partners either produced insufficient offers or declined to take on WestLB's obligations (Braude, 2010; Risk, 2010; Scally, 2010). North Rhine–Westphalia, the Sparkassen owners, and the Federal Republic remained divided over how best to resolve the bank, such that when required by the European Commission to submit a restructuring plan, the lack of consensus at the European Commission deadline required them to submit three separate plans (Bulkeley, 2011a). Ultimately, the bank was split into a Sparkassen-owned clearing bank and a land-owned financial services and management firm (Bulkeley, 2011b).

HSH Nordbank

HSH Nordbank, the Landesbank for Hamburg and Schleswig-Holstein, did not face the same degree of existential threat from the crisis as

SachsenLB and WestLB. Nevertheless, it did require state aid and, like WestLB, illustrates how the Landesbanken can use their ability to draw on aid from both the Federal Republic and the Länder to extract favorable terms. Nordbank first ran into trouble after the SoFFin fund had already been established. Therefore, it did not need to establish an emergency mechanism to draw on support. Rather, the bank tapped SoFFin for €30 billion in guarantees, which it received on January 20, 2009. As a term of this aid, Nordbank was required to keep a core capital ratio of 7 percent (European Commission, 2009f, p. 3). Therefore, when it needed additional capital to maintain that level in February 2009, the bank again turned to SoFFin. This time, however, SoFFin's proffered aid came at too high a cost for the bank (Bulkeley, 2009i). Nordbank balked at the terms and sought instead to raise capital from the Länder. Its Land owners, Hamburg and Schleswig-Holstein, proved willing to offer aid on more generous terms. The two Länder provided €1.5 billion each in new core capital, as well as €10 billion in new guarantees. In exchange for this new capital, the Länder received an enlarged ownership stake, at an above-market rate of €19 per share. This increased their stake from 59.51 percent split between the two Länder to approximately 80–87 percent.[7] The remaining owners, the Sparkassen of Hamburg and Schleswig-Holstein and the private equity firm JC Flowers & Co., saw their ownership stakes reduced accordingly, to 4–6 percent and 8–10 percent, respectively (European Commission, 2009f, p. 4). They were not, however, required to contribute to the capital injection, enjoying the benefit of an above-market injection without needing to contribute to it. Both the Federal Republic and the European Commission, therefore, considered this capital injection to be state aid above market terms. The second component of assistance to Nordbank, the €10 billion risk shield, came at a fee of 3.5 percent per annum, significantly above the 2–2.75 percent coupon on equivalent guarantees from SoFFin (European Commission, 2009f, p. 4). Like the capital injections, only the Länder provided the aid, and the Sparkassen and private equity shareholders did not contribute.

BayernLB

BayernLB, the Landesbank for Bavaria, may have been the most distressed of all of the Landesbanken (Ewing, 2010). In seeking assistance, it followed much the same pattern as HSH Nordbank, using its ties to Bavaria and systemic importance to play the Federal Republic and Land off each other and secure more favorable terms of aid. BayernLB,

[7] The uncertainty is due to a lack of precise figures in European Commission reports.

however, accomplished this to greater success than Nordbank. Therefore, it offers additional evidence that the Landesbanken received favorable treatment from the German state.

As with HSH Nordbank, BayernLB first required assistance after the SoFFin fund was already in place. Its initial needs were much greater, however, and it obtained €5.4 billion in SoFFin guarantees, plus €700 million from Bavaria and €300 million from its Sparkassen owners (Bulkeley, 2008a). These guarantees proved insufficient, and by November 2008, Bayern sought a €3 billion capital injection from SoFFin. Like the other Landesbanken, Bayern found SoFFin's conditions too expensive, and with too many strings attached (*Globe and Mail (Canada)*, 2008). Instead, Bayern lobbied Bavaria for aid. Bavaria obliged and provided a €10 billion capital injection and €20 billion in additional guarantees (*Globe and Mail (Canada)*, 2008). As with Nordbank, Bavaria's Sparkassen shareholders were diluted, but otherwise not required to participate in an injection to save their Landesbank.

BayernLB once again illustrates how the Landesbanken can play their status and links to the Länder to their advantage. Both the Federal Republic and Bavaria provided guarantees and capital on generous terms. The only government to treat BayernLB harshly was Austria. On December 14, 2009, Austria nationalized Hypo Group Alpe Adria, an Austrian banking group that was 50 percent plus one share owned by BayernLB. BayernLB, which has invested €6.25 billion in the bank, received a single euro for its share (Ewing, 2010). Austria, therefore, performed an archetypal nationalization of a valueless firm, comparable to the United Kingdom's nationalization of Northern Rock and Bradford & Bingley, valuing the firm as worthless without state support and compensating shareholders accordingly.

Conclusions on the Landesbanken

The Landesbanken enjoyed all of the advantages of the German commercial banks and more. Like the commercial banks, the Landesbanken boasted a strong industry association that provided access to policymaking and enabled the banks to win key concessions both in the construction of the systemic rescue package and in the individual bank rescues. Like the BdB, the DGSV's quasi-public function, collectively self-regulating its member banks, gave it superior access to policymakers than their liberal equivalents, and like the BdB, the lack of competition among the DGSV's member institutions meant that the peak association had greater ability to organize and act in the interest of the sector as a whole. Therefore, ailing Landesbanken enjoyed the support of their fellow banks, while in liberal systems, healthy banks stood to gain from the distress of peers and had no incentive to help them.

As with the commercial banks, the organization of the Landesbanken produced a bank component to rescue efforts, at least in early rescues. Because the Landesbanken and Sparkassen stood to lose directly if one of their members fell, they had an incentive to support their members. This is especially true because the DGSV ran the savings bank deposit insurance scheme and so would need to pay out in the event of a Landesbank failure. That payment indirectly would come from the DGSV member institutions. Because of their tight federal structure, the savings banks, even more than the commercial banks, could be leaned upon to provide bank funding for rescue efforts.

The Landesbanken differed from the commercial banks most clearly, however, in their ability to rely on the Länder for aid, both because the Länder were exposed to losses as part owners and because they had an interest in continued influence over their Landesbanken. The other owners could compel the Land to put up most or all of the rescue funds, and on generous terms, by simply refusing to participate. Additionally, because only other savings banks could purchase Landesbanken, the DGSV represented the interests of both potential buyers and the Sparkassen co-owners. This was a highly advantageous position which enabled the DGSV to control negotiations and extract Land assistance. Moreover, the Länder and the Federal Republic had conflicting visions for the future of the Landesbanken, which meant that each wanted to be the one to supply aid and use conditions on the aid to shape the Landesbanken in their chosen direction. For the Federal Republic, this meant pushing the Landesbanken toward consolidation, while the Länder generally wanted to retain a controlling position over their respective Landesbank, the better to keep it as a tool to advance other policy aims. The Landesbanken were able to take advantage of these two competing sources of state aid by soliciting rival bids. SachsenLB and WestLB took federal support, while Nordbank and BayernLB received support from their Länder, but in all cases it was more generous than would have been offered had there been only source of state aid. While failing banks in the liberal states had to accept state terms as the only aid available, the Landesbanken enjoyed not only access to private support but also multiple sources of state aid. Aid for the Landesbanken was a buyer's market, and the Landesbanken took advantage to their benefit.

Conclusions

The German response to the financial crisis illustrates how a corporatist financial system creates different dynamics in response to crises than a liberal system. The greater organization and interdependence of the financial sector creates two paradoxical dynamics, the first creating the incentive and means for greater private rescues and the second creating greater pressure from the industry for state aid on terms favorable to the banks. In effect, this creates a "tipping point" model of financial crisis response in Germany: while the crisis is relatively small, the state can lean on the peak associations to develop fully or partially industry-funded solutions, as seen at SachsenLB and the initial consortium rescues for IKB and Hypo RE. In these cases, the state was able to pressure the relevant peak associations to provide billions in support for failing banks, both by appealing to the self-interest of interconnected banks and by taking advantage of the greater ease of organizing consortium rescues provided by a more institutionalized financial sector. In smaller bank failures, the peak associations even provide privately funded automatic rescue plans, such as each association's deposit insurance scheme and the LIKO Bank liquidity support program. In liberal systems, private rescues are generally limited to fire-sale purchases of failing banks by healthier ones. Liberal consortium rescues are rare, fragile, and almost always organized by the state. Private standing support facilities such as the deposit insurance schemes and the LIKO Bank are unheard of in the United Kingdom and the United States.

Private rescues are more extensive in Germany because of the differing interbank relationships. There is no interbank competition among the Landesbanken and Sparkassen, the members of the savings bank pillar, nor in the cooperative banks pillar. Rather, these institutions are organized on federal lines, with coordination of activity and cross-shareholding among members, and the focus of competition is instead on the other pillars. Therefore, member banks have an incentive to aid their peers, to better support the pillar as a whole in interpillar competition. The commercial banks lack this federal relationship, but still have substantially greater interbank interdependence than in liberal systems. This reflects the longer-term relationships in a private bank system, which diminishes the intensity of interbank competition, increasing the relative advantage of stronger private governance. Private governance benefits all of the German banks, minimizing state regulation and allowing the banks to negotiate with the state on more advantageous terms, negotiating as a pillar or even as a banking industry as a whole, rather than on a bank-by-bank basis. It also makes banks more willing to provide their own funds to assist failing peers, both because they are directly at risk from greater interdependence and to prevent the state from increasing its influence over the sector through invasive rescue policies.

The greater organization of corporatist finance also ensures that when the state does commit its resources to a financial rescue, it is on more favorable terms for the banks. The regulatory and support role of the peak associations reveals itself as a double-edged sword. The private associations self-monitor and even offer some privately funded rescues, but that close relationship with public regulators also means that the peak associations play a role in shaping the state's responses. In the United States and the United Kingdom, when consultation with financial sector experts was used, it was always from institutions judged not to be future recipients of state aid. In contrast, in Germany, the CEO of Commerzbank, as a board member of the BdB, played a direct role in shaping the state's response plan despite Commerzbank already showing clear signs that it would ultimately require state assistance. This access let industry associations shape a voluntary response plan, which in turn empowered the banks to negotiate favorable terms for actual aid, whatever the letter of the law initially. Moreover, in those negotiations, industry links ensured that even failing banks retained sufficient political influence to negotiate favorable terms. Whereas representatives of failing institutions such as Lehman Brothers in the United States and Northern Rock shareholders in the United Kingdom found few allies and little access as their fate was debated between state representatives and potential buyers, JC Flowers found significant institutional support from the DSW and VdP, which enabled him to lobby successfully for a higher sale price in the Hypo nationalization than its equivalents in the United States and the United Kingdom.

Party politics were almost entirely absent from the German debates on responses to the crisis, to a much greater degree than in either the United Kingdom or the United States. In part this derives from the Grand Coalition governing Germany to 2009; with both the center-right CDU/CSU and center-left SPD in government, neither was likely to be sharply critical of state responses. The two chief political actors in Germany, Chancellor Angela Merkel and Finance Minister Peer Steinbrück, came from the CDU and SPD, respectively. Although they would be the two chief rivals for the chancellorship in 2013, in the crisis they presented a united front and any disagreements between them were kept hidden. The smaller parties of the left and right, outside of the governing coalition, also offered far less criticism of state responses than the opposition parties in the United Kingdom and elements on both the left and right in the United States. Party politics would intrude on German crisis response debates only after the Grand Coalition was replaced by a CDU/CSU–FDP coalition in 2009. Even then, however, debate centered primarily on state aid to auto manufacturer Opel, while proposals to extend SoFFin aid to banks passed relatively uncontroversially.

A more important source of tension was between the German state and the European Commission. Although the European Commission was an observer in the original debates over construction of the SoFFin plan and approved it as written, the European Commission would take a more critical line on subsequent implementation of the plan. Its influence was somewhat limited, however, restricted to criticizing the implementation after the fact rather than blocking action. German policymakers preferred to implement their favored policies and deal with the consequences later, rather than seek European Commission's approval in advance (Foreign Ministry representative, interview by author, 2011). Therefore, while the European Commission was able to insist on modifications to existing aid packages, most notably in insisting on the break-up of WestLB, it did not shape the response terms of the German state. Its most significant influence may have been its 2001 decision barring traditional aid from the Länder to the Landesbanken, a move that was designed to limit state aid but which instead, in the eyes of many critics, led to the Landesbanken overleveraging themselves and deepening the extent of the crisis and need for state assistance.

German policymakers had both more opportunities for private contributions to bank rescues and more constraint in developing state rescues. This meant that, when the funding needs of banks were smaller, the state could rely on other banks to play a role in both organizing and funding a rescue and decreasing the demands on the state. However, the corollary of this greater engagement by the healthy banks and bank associations was that they also brought pressure on the state to provide more generous terms in shaping the state component of assistance. This happened in the policy-drafting stage, when representatives of the banking associations and several of the major banks were part of the body that drafted the SoFFin plan and its later revisions. It also happened in the implementation phase, when the Landesbanken used their ability to act jointly and to tap the Länder for aid to secure more favorable terms of aid. This left German policymakers far more constrained than the US or UK equivalents, who were free to choose a policy that minimized moral hazard and maximized the chance of the state seeing a positive return on its assistance.

4 The United Kingdom and the 2007–2009 Crisis

Turning from corporatist Germany to more liberal systems reveals a strikingly different pattern in response to the financial crisis. Germany and the United Kingdom are comparable in population and GDP. Both are also European Union members, meaning that not only are their economies closely integrated but that, in the 2007–2009 crisis, their national response patterns were constrained by the same European Commission directives on the terms of state aid. Nevertheless, clear differences between the patterns of response emerge. The German state took a "soft touch" approach, favoring voluntary and generous aid to its failing banks. In the United Kingdom, state assistance consistently came at an extremely high cost to bank shareholders, who were given little to no choice on accepting state aid, and lost significant value, in some cases being all but wiped out entirely. Moreover, while the German state showed extreme reluctance to use nationalization and state control, in the United Kingdom, state ownership and control were both advocated and used early on in the crisis. Germany would wholly nationalize only one firm, Hypo RE, and would be quick to sell its shares in the firm it held the largest partial stake in, IKB, choosing to take a loss rather than continuing to hold an ownership stake. The United Kingdom would turn to compulsory nationalization and part-nationalization early in the crisis and would show a willingness to hold full or significant stakes in banks for an indefinite period until they could be sold at a profit to the state.

The key variable explaining these different patterns is the structure of the two countries' respective banking systems. While the German banks are tightly integrated, the UK banks hold each other at an arm's length, lending to each other only on good collateral and zealously avoiding any actions that would aid a competitor at their own expense. As such, UK banks lacked both the strong institutions for collective action of their German equivalents and the will to act in the interest of failing peers. Whereas the German banks both organized private and public–private rescues and lobbied the state for favorable state rescue terms, in the United Kingdom the healthy banks refused to participate in private consortium rescues, save one small rescue under heavy state pressure, and would take on failing firms if the terms were generous to the purchasing bank. Equally importantly, the healthy banks played no advocacy role on behalf of the failing banks over the terms of state intervention. Instead, they protested if they saw state aid as overly generous. The lack of private governance institutions meant that bank representatives had no formal role in the regulatory process and thus no seat at the table in policy discussions. This left British policymakers free to develop state responses independent from industry influence, and they chose policy tools that minimized moral hazard and maximized the chance of a positive return on taxpayer assistance.

The United Kingdom is on the surface where an observer would most and least expect to see nationalization used as a policy tool. On the one hand, nationalization in the United Kingdom is less politically charged than in Germany, where it is closely tied up with the expropriation of Jewish property in the 1930s, or in the United States, which has a far weaker tradition of state-owned enterprises than elsewhere in the advanced capitalist world. In the United Kingdom, state ownership of banks had long been part of the political discourse. Historically, the Labour Party had called for state ownership of banks, though the "New Labour" Party of Tony Blair and Gordon Brown rejected state ownership as a goal in itself. This history of public calls for state ownership of banks meant that nationalization produced less normative resistance than it would in the United States or Germany, cases where bank nationalization never had much popular appeal. Both major parties in the United Kingdom had, in times of distress, relied on nationalization of failing industries in the past. The most recent bank nationalization in the United Kingdom prior to the 2007–2009 crisis took place in 1984, when Conservative Prime Minister Margaret Thatcher oversaw the state takeover of Johnson Matthey Bank. On the other hand, the financial sector in the United Kingdom plays a more central role in the national economy than elsewhere. Finance accounts for a larger share of GDP than in either Germany or the United States, and successive Conservative and Labour governments have emphasized the importance of maintaining the City of London as a major global financial hub in driving economic growth in the United Kingdom (Beck, Demirgüç-Kunt and Levine, 2009). Once out of office, Gordon Brown testified to the clout of financial actors in spurring a disastrous program of deregulation:

> In the 1990s, the banks all came to us and said: Look, we don t want to be regulated, we want to be free of regulation. Everybody in the City was saying look, you re regulating them too much. And actually the truth is that, globally and nationally, we should have been regulating them more. (McArdle, 2011)

This clout, however, was chiefly felt in good economic times, when the banks were healthy. Ultimately, the United Kingdom proved to be among the states willing to take the hardest line in rescuing its banks. The Bank of England resisted pressure to supply markets with emergency liquidity longer than the US Federal Reserve or the European Central Bank (ECB), and when it did provide liquidity, it did so at penalty rates. Once it became necessary to address solvency issues, the United Kingdom also proved willing to use compulsory nationalization at minimal compensation as a policy tool. The United Kingdom fully nationalized two smaller banks against the wishes of shareholders and for *de minimis* compensation. It also attempted to part-nationalize two larger firms at below-market rates, though it would be frustrated by those firms' rapid collapse in value. Moreover, virtually all policy decisions made by the United Kingdom were made without input from the financial sector. Because UK banks rapidly lost influence once they started to fail, the failing banks were unable to persuade UK authorities to adopt more generous policies, and the healthy banks were unwilling to do so. Absent pressure from the banks, policymakers could adopt options that stabilized the financial system while minimizing costs to taxpayers and imposing costs on failing banks.

The Structure of Banking and Regulation in the United Kingdom

The key to the success of the British state in limiting moral hazard in its bank rescues lies in the structure of British banking, in which there are relatively few interbank linkages and thus both fewer incentives and weaker mechanisms for interbank coordination in financial crises. The structure of UK banking is considerably simpler than in either the United States or Germany. UK banking is divided by neither function nor by ownership. While some smaller deposit-focused mutual banks remain, most major banks are universal banks, engaging in both investment and retail banking. The chief division in UK banking is simply on size, with a significant gap between the largest banks – in 2007 Barclays, HBOS, HSBC, Lloyds/TSB, RBS, and Standard Chartered – and the smaller, generally more regionally focused banks. Several of those smaller banks, including the important cases of Northern Rock and Bradford & Bingley, were formerly mutual banks that converted to conventional banks in the aftermath of the "Big Bang" of UK banking deregulation under Margaret Thatcher in the 1980s. Relationships between UK banks tend to be at arm's length, especially following the Big Bang. Interbank lending plays an important role in the system but on the basis of good collateral and risk-based interest rates, meaning that banks lend on terms that minimize their vulnerability to borrower failure. Cross-holding, both among banks and between banks and industry, is extremely limited, with banks generally providing loans or advising rather than equity for clients. As such, banks have little direct exposure when other banks run into distress and little incentive to help their failing rivals. This is different in Germany, where banks are often directly and substantially exposed to each other's decline. Therefore, there have been no major private or consortium rescues since the Secondary Banking Crisis of 1974–1975, when the smaller number of banks and greater level of interconnectedness of pre–Big Bang UK banking made banks more inclined to act collectively (Reid, 1982).

This combination of competition and limited direct exposure produces little incentive for collective action. There are industry associations representing UK banking, chiefly the British Banking Association, but unlike in Germany they have little clout relative to the banks themselves. This can be attributed to their differing functional roles. The German associations wield significant influence over their members by serving as not just a lobbying group but also a clearing bank, deposit insurance provider, and even a regulator in some limited capacities. This gives them the ability not only to speak on behalf of their member banks but also to sanction or otherwise compel their members toward joint action. The British associations are limited to lobbying. Even in this capacity, they are less powerful than their German equivalents. While they can represent the consensus views of the banks, they have no power to negotiate for the banks or to compel individual banks to fall in line with industry-wide policies. This lack of control over their members limits their usefulness as a partner in negotiations with the state.

In the crisis, this meant that other banks provided only limited assistance, and only where they saw a direct economic interest. The healthier UK banks proved largely unwilling to act in other banks' interest, with no significant consortium rescues or lobbying on behalf of distressed banks. Instead, healthy banks poached clients from their weakened rivals, deepening their distress (Stewart and Connon, 2007). UK authorities exploited this division to their advantage, persuading the healthy banks to side with the state in pressuring the weaker ones to accept compulsory part-nationalization.

The regulatory structure of the United Kingdom, following Labour reforms in the late 1990s, took the form of the "Tripartite Authorities" of the newly independent Bank of England, the Financial Services Authority (FSA), and the Treasury. Under the system implemented in 1997, the Bank of England would take charge of maintaining the overall stability of the system, including liquidity provision, while the FSA would monitor individual banks, and the Treasury would oversee the overall regulatory structure, reporting to Parliament and providing any necessary capital injections (HM Treasury, 2006). Prior to the 2007–2009 crisis, this system appeared to work reasonably well, although it would prove considerably more unwieldy once the crisis began. Dividing responsibilities and tools among the different agencies, especially between the FSA and the Bank of England, proved to be extremely destabilizing. Success depended on a good working relationship between the leadership of the Bank, the FSA, and the Treasury (Darling, 2012, p. 20). Both the Bank of England and the FSA were formally independent entities, meaning the Treasury could only persuade and not compel them to act. The Treasury and the Brown government could not compel the Bank of England to release liquidity. Because much of the individual bank regulatory authority remained with the FSA, the Bank lacked many of the tools that the Federal Reserve had to compel banks to restrict their capacity to increase systemic risk (Darling, 2012, pp. 21–22). In the 2007–2009 crisis, the prime minister's office also played a key role in negotiating the terms of state response. Brown's involvement was driven both by his experience as the previous Chancellor of the Exchequer and a personal and political divide between Brown and his current Chancellor, Alistair Darling, a supporter of Brown's predecessor and rival, Tony Blair (Darling, 2012).

This division within the regulatory authorities did not, however, provide an opening for banks to exploit in pursuit of more favorable terms. To the contrary, a remarkable consensus on the importance of imposing costs on the banks and on the viability of nationalization as a policy tool reigned over not just the Labour government but the opposition parties as well. The Liberal Democrats and their Shadow Chancellor, Vince Cable, would be among the strongest advocates for nationalization, often pushing for nationalization before the incumbent Labour government considered the option publically. The Conservatives generally favored placing the banks in administration and letting them fail but, like Labour and the Liberal Democrats, favored punitive terms for failing bank shareholders. Critics of the Conservatives asserted that their rejection of nationalization was driven primarily by a desire to cast the Labour government in a bad light, as past Conservative governments had relied on nationalization when confronting the failure of systemically important firms. This consensus followed patterns of response to financial crises by both Labour and Tory governments. Banks typically have been either allowed to fail – as with BCCI in 1992, Barings Bank in 1995, and numerous small banks in the 1970s – or nationalized with minimal shareholder compensation, as was the case for Johnson Matthey Bank, nationalized by the Thatcher government for £1 in 1984 (Brummer, 2008; Darling, 2012). Liquidity support generally has followed the prescriptions laid down by Bagehot in his discussion of the proper role of the Bank of England in 1873: liquidity should be made freely available, but at a penalty rate of interest and only backed by good collateral, to ensure that only banks with a capacity to repay can access central bank liquidity and that a penalty rate of interest will discourage them from doing so, save as a last resort.

The 2007–2009 Crisis in the United Kingdom

The financial crisis in the United Kingdom began in summer 2007 with the tightening of European interbank credit markets following the distress of the French bank BNP Paribas. As in other parts of the advanced capitalist world, UK banks had extremely high capital ratios, enabling them to maximize returns in good times, but leaving them extremely vulnerable in a downturn. Moreover, these highly leveraged banks were highly dependent on overnight financing to fund operations, meaning that even a slight fluctuation in credit markets could cause disastrous results. As in Germany, the problem began in relatively small banks of relatively little systemic importance, which the United Kingdom attempted to address in an ad hoc manner. However, after a period of relative calm in early to mid-2008, the crisis reached a fever pitch in September of that year. That fall, as in the United States and Germany, several major banks of systemic importance ran into trouble, compelling the state to abandon ad hoc rescue plans in favor of a systemic approach. That approach in the United Kingdom took the form of mandatory partial nationalization among distressed banks, intended to be at below-market rates to maximize the return to the state and minimize moral hazard concerns. Continued distress by major institutions would thereafter require additional assistance, again focusing on attempting to ensure the full repayment of state aid and ultimately pushing the cost of the rescue onto the financial sector itself.

The Fully Nationalized Former Mutuals

Northern Rock

The first bank to run into trouble in the United Kingdom was Northern Rock, a midsized former mutual bank based in Newcastle. Like many smaller UK banks, Northern Rock was a mutual bank that converted into a regular commercial bank (Comptroller and Auditor General

National Audit Office (UK), 2009b, p. 13). Typical of many of the banks that ran into trouble in the crisis, Northern Rock was highly leveraged and strongly dependent on overnight financing to fund its daily operations. On the eve of its distress, Northern Rock's loan-to-deposit ratio was at 323.1 percent, the third highest of any European bank (Heath, Dunne and Burroughes, 2007). This made Northern Rock highly vulnerable to any disruption of its access to overnight funding. On August 9, 2007, overnight markets experienced such a disruption, stemming from the decision by BNP Paribas to suspend investment funds (Doward et al., 2007). Given its well-known vulnerability, skittish investors began abandoning Northern Rock. Its fellow UK banks, looking to profit from Northern Rock's distress rather than seeking to assist it, attempted to poach Northern Rock clients (European Commission, 2009b, p. 34; Stewart and Connon, 2007). While the German Landesbanken would organize a consortium rescue of SachsenLB early in the crisis, UK banks had less exposure and less incentive to help. Rather than acting to contain the crisis, the UK banks exacerbated it.

Unable to secure private funding, Northern Rock instead turned to the Bank of England for assistance. From the beginning, however, British officials, especially Bank of England Governor Mervyn King, showed extreme reluctance to extend state aid to banks and a willingness to only do so on punitive terms. King initially resisted providing any extraordinary assistance to Northern Rock, until pressured by Darling (2012, pp. 22–24). Even at that point, King only offered aid to Northern Rock on punitive terms, offering loans at a penalty rate of 1 percent over the London interbank base rate (Comptroller and Auditor General National Audit Office (UK), 2009b; Smith, 2007). In doing so, King hoped to keep Northern Rock running, but in a market-conforming way. Northern Rock, unable to find an alternative source of aid or persuade King to be more lenient, had no alternative but to accept the Bank's terms of aid.

This aid proved insufficient to stem a panic, however, and may have worsened the situation for Northern Rock by publicizing its distress more widely. On September 13, depositors started lining up *en masse* to withdraw their funds before the bank ran out of cash on hand. This was a classic bank run not seen in the United Kingdom on such a scale since the nineteenth century (*Economist*, 2007a, 2007b). Several factors contributed to this run. Seeking Bank of England assistance broadly publicized the bank's distress. King later lamented that, prior to new disclosure rules, the Bank of England could have secretly funded Northern Rock and that might have diminished the likelihood of a run (Wilson,

2007). A second factor was that the British deposit insurance scheme only covered 90 percent of an individual's deposits (Comptroller and Auditor General National Audit Office (UK), 2009b, p. 53; FDIC representatives, interview by author, 2011). In theory, leaving some risk with the depositor compelled individuals to evaluate the soundness of banks, but in practice it left an incentive to still participate in a run that US FDIC's 100 percent guarantee up to a fixed amount did not (FDIC representatives, interview by author, 2011). Finally, Northern Rock's account closure procedures were time-consuming and nonautomated. It therefore did not take long for a queue to run out the door, attracting television cameras and escalating the pressures for depositors to participate in the run (Darling, 2012, pp. 24–25).

Faced with the first major UK bank run in over a century, the Tripartite Authorities hurriedly responded with a 100 percent guarantee of Northern Rock deposits (Livesey and Menon, 2007). The disruption from the Northern Rock panic was severe enough to cause a 0.5 percent overnight fall in the British pound against the dollar following the announcement of emergency liquidity assistance (*Investors Chronicle*, 2007). The guarantee introduced moral hazard problems, but was judged to be necessary to contain the panic. The other UK banks critiqued the guarantee for giving a rival an unfair advantage (Kaletsky, 2007). From early in the crisis, UK banks placed their narrow self-interest and an opposition to overly favorable aid to rivals above systemic concerns.

With the guarantee in place, the government began looking for a buyer for Northern Rock. Pressure for a rapid sale met pushback from shareholders, especially large investment firms SRM and RAB Capital, which feared losses from a fire sale on Northern Rock (Duke, 2007). Initial attempts at finding a buyer proved unsuccessful. The bank's management sounded out over a dozen buyers, including all of the "Big Five" of UK banking and several foreign banks, including Santander, Crédit Agricole, and Citigroup (*Birmingham Post*, 2007). Only Lloyds/TSB showed interest and only if the Bank of England would provide a £30 billion bridge loan for two years (Darling, 2012, p. 22; Watkins, Buckingham and Atkinson, 2007). This would have kept Northern Rock both private and operational, but only by providing a subsidy to a private firm, in a manner comparable to the state-subsidized purchase of Bear Stearns by JP Morgan-Chase in the United States. UK policymakers again demonstrated their unwillingness to subsidize private losses and rejected Lloyds' proposal. FSA head Hector Sants advocated accepting the Lloyds offer, but was overruled by King in the Bank of England and

Darling in the Treasury[1] (Bentley, 2012). King advocated a rapid and early nationalization of Northern Rock to secure the taxpayers' interest and minimize uncertainty and disruption. Lack of existing legal authority and reluctance by Brown and Darling to be seen as returning to "Old Labour" practices meant, however, that the search for an alternative to state ownership would continue for several months (Wighton, 2012).

The Treasury also attempted to orchestrate a consortium rescue, in which the major banks would provide a facility to assist small distressed banks (Darling, 2012, p. 54). With little direct exposure to Northern Rock, the banks balked at such a move. HSBC chairman Stephen Greene told Darling that it simply was not in the banks' commercial interest (Darling, 2012, p. 54). A healthy Northern Rock would be a rival, and moreover if any other bank declined to participate in the consortium, that bank could free-ride on the others' participation.

Without a potential buyer by the end of September, British officials began to consider nationalization of Northern Rock (Comptroller and Auditor General National Audit Office (UK), 2009b, p. 7). Increasingly, politicians within both the Labour Party and the opposition Liberal Democratic Party criticized the unlimited guarantee of Northern Rock deposits as a nationalization of the bank's liabilities that left its assets in private hands (Hutton, 2007). On October 9, the guarantee was extended from deposits prior to September 19 to include new deposits as well (Comptroller and Auditor General National Audit Office (UK), 2009b, p. 16). As more of Northern Rock's liabilities were effectively nationalized, increasing the risks to taxpayers, calls increased for its assets to be nationalized as well (Hutton, 2007; McRae, 2007).

Representatives of the Tripartite Authorities and Brown met in a closed debate to consider potential ways to resolve the bank, without input from Northern Rock or other banks. Ultimately, they considered three options to deal with the ailing Northern Rock: administration, nationalization, and a private sale (Comptroller and Auditor General National Audit Office (UK), 2009b, p. 20). In an administration, the bank would be run down, with its assets sold off to pay for its liabilities. Doing so would cost the government £10 billion, according to National Audit Office estimates, given the fire sale prices Northern Rock's assets would command (Comptroller and Auditor General National Audit Office (UK), 2009b, p. 21). Moreover, once put into administration, the bank could no longer borrow on the interbank market, requiring the Bank of England to

[1] It is worth noting that Sants only made this position public upon his resignation in June 2012, well after the consequences of failing to take Lloyds' offer became clear. Public statements at the time indicated a unified position by the Tripartite Authorities.

increase its loan to £100 billion (Hutton, 2007, p. 31). Therefore, despite being the course of action advocated by the opposition Conservative Party, administration received only cursory consideration by British officials (Comptroller and Auditor General National Audit Office (UK), 2009b, p. 21).

Nationalization would rescue the bank and contain the threat to the rest of the UK financial system and the pound. By granting *de minimis* compensation to the shareholders, moral hazard would be minimized while still enabling the state to contain external costs from such a failure. Nationalization also meant that a restored Northern Rock might replay state aid through profits and eventually reprivatization. This course of action was supported strongly by Vince Cable, the Liberal Democrat shadow chancellor, and only weakly opposed by the Conservatives, who favored administration, and elements of Labour, who feared criticism of a return to "Old Labour" practices (Hutton, 2007, p. 31). Given the *de minimis* compensation to be expected, nationalization understandably attracted the opposition of Northern Rock shareholders and their allies in the UK Shareholder Association (UKSA) (Brogan, 2008). The other UK banks, however, offered no resistance to the nationalization of Northern Rock.

The first choice of government officials, however, remained the sale of Northern Rock to another private bank (Comptroller and Auditor General National Audit Office (UK), 2009b, pp. 21–22; McDonough, 2008). The search for a buyer was handicapped by the need to address the conflicting interests of Northern Rock shareholders and the British government. While the Northern Rock shareholders sought to maximize share value, the British government above all wanted to ensure the repayment of the sizeable aid provided to Northern Rock. By January 1, 2008, this had reached £57 billion (McDonough, 2008). The government maintained the right to veto any potential sale, in order to safeguard its repayment, but was reluctant to take a lead role in negotiating the sale. The Treasury feared that if the government took such a lead role, it might be vulnerable to legal action by Northern Rock shareholders arguing that their rights had been overrun by the state (Comptroller and Auditor General National Audit Office (UK), 2009b, p. 22). Therefore, Northern Rock management was in charge of the bidding process and seeking to maximize the initial sale price, but the Treasury retained a veto and favored whatever plan that would maximize the longer-term likelihood and speed of repayment of state aid.

Those bidders that emerged did not provide compelling offers. All offers were below Northern Rock's market value and required continued government support for several years. The British government initially favored Virgin Money's offer, which valued Northern Rock at 25 p per share, and would have immediately repaid £10 billion to the Bank of England and injected £1.3 billion into the bank (Comptroller and Auditor General National Audit Office (UK), 2009b, p. 24; Thompson, 2007). However, major shareholders SRM and RAB Capital strongly opposed Virgin's bid, arguing it undervalued the bank (McDonough, 2007). They initially supported an offer from British investment group Olivant, Ltd., which proposed injecting £800 million of equity from a consortium of investors, in conjunction with a £450–£650 million sale of new shares (Lyons, 2007). After Olivant ultimately declined to put forward a formal bid, they favored a proposal from Northern Rock management to raise £400 million from existing shareholders, but this was dismissed by the government as unrealistic (Griffiths and Aldrick, 2008; McDonough, 2008; Slater and Marques, 2008). The government too became increasingly dissatisfied with the Virgin Money bid, as the terms offered meant that Northern Rock would need to grow to £2.75 billion from a current market value of £380 million before taxpayers would see repayment (Griffiths and Aldrick, 2008). The Virgin offer, therefore, failed to meet the hopes of either shareholders or the state.

By December 19, government guarantees on Northern Rock had been extended to wholesale liabilities, meaning that the state now guaranteed all of Northern Rock's liabilities, but controlled none of its assets (Neligan, 2007). Northern Rock by this point owed the British government £55 billion in loans and guarantees (Brogan and Chapman, 2007). Although the search for a private buyer continued until early February 2008, policymakers increasingly saw nationalization as the "least bad" option (Aldrick, 2008). In addition to a growing political consensus, Treasury advisor Goldman Sachs, after evaluating the bid offers, recommended nationalization as the best way to protect taxpayer interests (Comptroller and Auditor General National Audit Office (UK), 2009b, pp. 27–29). Therefore, on February 18, 2008, Darling stopped negotiation with the remaining bidders, and Labour passed legislation authorizing the nationalization of Northern Rock. This legislation, the Banking (Special Provisions) Act 2008, became law on February 21, and Northern Rock was nationalized under this new authority the following day (Comptroller and Auditor General National Audit Office (UK), 2009b, p. 29). This was in sharp contrast to Germany, where the state acquiring the authority to nationalize triggered additional months of negotiation in an attempt to cajole a private sale. Nationalization was involuntary, with shareholders receiving compensation to be calculated at a later date. The Treasury warned that such compensation would be low at best, based on a valuation of what shares would have been worth had Northern Rock not received any state aid (Seib and Andrews, 2008).

Predictably, Northern Rock shareholders strongly opposed the move and demanded compensation between £4.25 a share, the price when the bank was nationalized, and £9.60 a share, the precollapse share price (Russell, Griffiths and Aldrick, 2008). Outside of Northern Rock shareholders and the UKSA, which promised to launch a legal challenge for greater compensation, the nationalization received a positive reaction and only muted criticism. Brown and Darling defended their actions as best serving the interests of taxpayers, and Liberal Democrat Cable agreed that "belatedly, the government has made the right decision" (Morris, 2008). Richard Branson of Virgin Money expressed disappointment that his offer was not accepted (Morris, 2008). The rest of the banking industry, however, showed very little reaction to the decision, apart from a few slightly positive statements. The CEO of the West Bromwich Building Society argued that nationalization was better than other options while hoping that it would not set a precedent. Similarly, a spokesman for the Confederation of British Industry conceded that nationalization was the "least bad" option for Northern Rock (Tift and Cranage, 2008).

Among the most vocal critics was Conservative Shadow Chancellor George Osborne, who reiterated his argument that a Bank of England–led administration, which avoided state ownership, would have been superior to nationalization (Chapman, 2008). Even Osborne, however, opposed subsidizing a privately owned Northern Rock and in fact argued that administration was superior precisely because it offered even less danger of moral hazard by guaranteeing virtually no compensation to shareholders.

Bradford & Bingley

When Bradford & Bingley, another former mutual bank-turned-commercial bank, ran into trouble in summer 2008, the state's pattern of response would closely follow the Northern Rock precedent. The state initially attempted to rely on private market solutions but, when those proved insufficient, turned to an involuntary nationalization with *de minimis* shareholder compensation. As with Northern Rock, Bradford & Bingley failed to attract support from other industry actors, who were willing to neither support their peer economically nor lobby politically for more advantageous terms.

Bradford & Bingley first ran into trouble when its spring 2008 losses proved higher than expected, losing £8 million in the first four months of 2008, versus a profit of £108 million the previous year (Waples, 2008).

The bank initially responded to this downturn by seeking capital injections from both its own shareholders and outside sources. A planned sale of a £179 million stake to American equity company Texas Pacific Group collapsed after existing shareholders objected to the new investors being offered shares on more favorable terms in comparison to their existing shareholders (Duncan, 2008; Essen, 2008; Waples, 2008). After Texas Pacific Group backed out, the FSA attempted to convince either Lloyds or HSBC to purchase Bradford & Bingley outright, but to no avail (Farndon, 2008). HBOS, which itself was struggling and desperate for the cash reserves Bradford & Bingley held, made an offer, but was rejected by state officials. Alistair Darling judged that HBOS' bid was one of desperation and that it was too weak to save itself or Bradford & Bingley through a merger (Darling, 2012, p. 65).

Without either an external injection of capital or a buyer, Bradford & Bingley was forced to rely solely on a £258 million capital raise from its own shareholders. As this raise was underwritten by a consortium of major banks, it is the lone example of a consortium rescue in the UK crisis (Hosking and Seib, 2008). It occurred under the direct pressure of the FSA and involved only £20 million each from the five major UK banks (Hosking and Seib, 2008). Even then, they only served as underwriters, agreeing to purchase that portion of the capital raise not purchased by existing shareholders. Ultimately, as Bradford & Bingley share price collapsed below the offer price for the capital raise, very few shareholders took up the offer, and the underwriters were forced to contribute the bulk of the £258 million injection (Hosking and Costello, 2008).

The disappointing capital raise meant that Bradford & Bingley's value continued to fall and the Tripartite Authorities soon began to consider nationalization of the troubled bank. As with Northern Rock, public support to keep the private bank running was never considered, and the choice was between administration, nationalization, and a private sale (Darling, 2012, pp. 133–134). Administration, as with Northern Rock, was a deeply problematic option, as it would take months and risk another UK bank run while the bank's assets and liabilities were processed (Darling, 2012, p. 133). As with Northern Rock, the Tripartite Authorities favored a private sale, but found no takers. Even after they offered Bradford & Bingley for nothing and backed by a consortium of other UK banks, no buyer stepped forward (Darling, 2012, p. 65).

The FSA ruled that the bank could no longer continue to function as a deposit-taker (Lynch, 2008). Without a buyer and facing closure, the bank was nationalized under the state authority gained in the Northern Rock nationalization legislation. Bradford & Bingley's shares were cancelled, with shareholders to receive state-determined compensation after the fact (Lynch, 2008). This was expected to be quite low, as the price at nationalization was 25 p per share (Barrow, 2008). Once nationalized, the state immediately split Bradford & Bingley into a "good bank" of its quality assets and a "bad bank" of the more troubled assets. The good bank, including the deposit book and branches, was immediately sold to Abbey National, a UK subsidiary of the Spanish bank Santander, for £612 million, realizing an immediate return on the still saleable assets of the newly nationalized bank (Comptroller and Auditor General National Audit Office (UK), 2009b, p. 54). The remaining "bad bank," consisting chiefly of Bradford & Bingley's mortgage book, would be merged with the nationalized Northern Rock and run down in state ownership, hopefully returning an eventual profit to the taxpayer (Comptroller and Auditor General National Audit Office (UK), 2009b, p. 54).

Government officials justified their actions, as with Northern Rock, as the best available option. As with Northern Rock, actors both inside and outside the government hailed nationalization as the "least bad" option for protecting taxpayers' interests and the overall stability of the British banking system (*Bristol Evening Post*, 2008). The Conservatives again argued that administration would have been a preferable option, though the Liberal Democrats endorsed nationalization. The other UK banks made no criticism of the move, and the chief voices of opposition came from Bradford & Bingley shareholders, who were slated to receive only minimal compensation (*Bristol Evening Post*, 2008). The shareholders, however, lacked the clout to win more favorable terms.

Evaluating Initial Responses to the Crisis

The two small former mutuals demonstrate a pattern of response by both the state and the other banks consistent with expectations from a liberal system. The other banks showed no willingness to contribute to a rescue of their smaller rivals except in the case of the consortium underwriting Bradford & Bingley's share raise. Even in this instance, the direct pressure of the FSA and the clear and present threat of Bradford's collapse destabilizing UK banking only extracted approximately £20 million in underwriting from each of the banks, a meager provision given the size of their operations. The other banks also showed no inclination to oppose the state's ultimate decision to force nationalization at *de minimis* compensation, a move that ensured the stability of the system but did not require the other banks to contribute to that effort. From the state's perspective, nationalization was an optimal strategy, as it both guaranteed systemic stability and minimized moral hazard. Because shareholders in the two banks received virtually no compensation, they paid a steep price for their banks' failures. Letting the banks fail would have accomplished a similar shareholder-punishing function, but the extremely panicking condition of financial markets at the time meant that such a move might have sparked an even larger crisis, despite the banks' relatively small size. Nationalization punished the shareholders while avoiding such a panic. In this, the Labour government had the consistent support of the Liberal Democrats. The Conservatives similarly opposed a state subsidy of shareholders, though they favored administration, which minimized state ownership but also minimized chances of the state recovering the aid money already invested. Although as of 2015 the state continues to be in the red on both banks, both the relevant policymakers and the National Audit Office remain optimistic that the nationalized mortgage operations of the two banks will ultimately net a profit for the British taxpayer (Comptroller and Auditor General National Audit Office (UK), 2010b, 2015).

Moving Toward a Systemic Approach: The Special Liquidity Scheme and Mandatory Capital Injections

Both Northern Rock and Bradford & Bingley were relatively small institutions, and Northern Rock ran into distress well before other institutions in the United Kingdom or elsewhere. By spring 2008, however, it had become clear that the banking crisis would be broader than one small northern institution, and the United Kingdom began looking at systemic solutions. Although the ultimate UK plan would be praised as one of the boldest state responses to financial crisis, the British were initially extremely reluctant to move toward a general solution. The Bank of England, in particular, resisted pressure to provide emergency liquidity assistance much longer than either the US Federal Reserve or the European Central Bank. This reflected Bank of England chair Mervyn King's deep aversion to any intervention that might increase moral hazard, fearing that any such intervention would, in his own words, "sow the seeds of a future crisis" (McConnell, 2007). King only offered liquidity support to Northern Rock after being pressured by Darling, and even then at a punitive rate. In offering liquidity more generally, the Bank of England's terms remained expensive, a point above the London Interbank Offer Rate (LIBOR) (Brummer, 2007; Fincher, 2007). King's moral hazard stance was undermined, however, by the ability of British banks to access ECB liquidity. By providing an alternate lender of last resort, the ECB undercut the Bank of England's bargaining power and complicated King's attempts to use conditional access to liquidity to entice UK banks to increase their capital reserves. Additionally, the ECB made liquidity available at a lower rate, in October 2007 at 4.63 percent versus 6.75 percent from the Bank of England, although much of that savings was wiped out in currency exchanges (Seib, 2007). The chief advantage of ECB funding, however, was anonymity. Banks could tap ECB liquidity without fear of signaling their distress to market observers, which could exacerbate their distress (Seib, 2007). By contrast, Bank of England aid was not only more expensive but would publically signal a need for liquidity despite the costs. This desire to avoid signaling distress by the banks continued to bedevil King's efforts to cajole banks into reinforcing their liquidity and capital positions. Following a March 2008 public statement by King urging banks to recapitalize themselves, several responded instead by further depleting their reserves by paying dividends (Warner, 2008a). In doing so, they hoped to send a strong signal to markets that they were in a good position, even if doing so in fact weakened an already precarious capital position. Unlike in Germany, there was no discussion of a joint bank take-up of liquidity to alleviate these signaling concerns.

The Special Liquidity Scheme

In late April 2008, the heads of Barclays, RBS, HBOS, Lloyds, HSBC, and thirty other UK financial institutions met with Gordon Brown (Dey and Smith, 2008). They urged the British government to act to provide greater liquidity to the banks on less punitive terms, but continued to insist that their problems were rooted in liquidity – and therefore external and not in a capital shortfall – and of their own making. After meeting with the banking heads, UK policymakers began debating a new liquidity program. Although spurred to action in part by the lobbying of the banks, the actual debate over shaping the policy was restricted to the cabinet, the Treasury, and the Bank of England (Darling, 2012, p. 94). Mervyn King continued to zealously defend against moral hazard, insisting that any central bank intervention must be driven by two principles: that the risk of loss remains with shareholders, and that any longer-term solution must focus on the overhang of existing assets, and not simply serve as a means of subsidizing new asset purchases (Dey and Smith, 2008). Without the presence of banking industry representatives, the ultimate plan presented would conform to King's principles.

The plan agreed to was the Special Liquidity Scheme (SLS), under which banks would provide collateral in exchange for access to Bank of England bonds. Although dubbed a "giant pawn-broking operation" by media sources, it was designed as a way to provide banks liquidity with a minimum of moral hazard effects (Seager, Elliott, and Treanor, 2008).

Under the terms of the SLS, banks would pledge AAA-rated assets to the Bank of England in exchange for Treasury bills, discounted 10–30 percent, insulating the Bank of England against losses so long as the highly rated assets kept their value. Banks would pay a penalty rate of interest of 1 percent over the base rate (Fleming, 2008a). Therefore, the terms of the SLS were as strict as earlier Bank of England programs and considerably harsher than comparable Federal Reserve or ECB programs. The SLS nevertheless carried two advantages for the banks. The first was the scale of the program. Earlier Bank of England liquidity auctions were relatively small, on the order of £10 billion. The SLS's initially announced scale was £50 billion, but did not have a fixed upper limit and was widely anticipated at the time of announcement to reach as high as £100 billion (Pratley, 2008). Policymakers hoped to ensure that no bank with acceptable AAA-rated collateral would fail from lack of liquidity, however punitive the terms of access. The second key advantage over earlier programs was the agreement of all UK banks to participate in the SLS, removing the stigma of accepting state liquidity (Comptroller and Auditor General National Audit Office (UK), 2009b, p. 2). This provided banks the cover for accepting state aid, but also helped insulate taxpayers from losses. The participation of healthy banks increased the amount of funds issued, but healthy banks were also more likely to repay in full, minimizing the risk of net losses. The SLS proved widely popular with UK banks, and in October the Bank of England would widen the scope of acceptable collateral to include AAA corporate and consumer loans and extend the window for participation as part of the broader systemic rescue (West, 2008). These extensions, however, did not change the costs of SLS participation, which still aimed to only provide liquidity for good assets on punitive rates, in the classic Bagehot formula.

In addition to the SLS, the Bank of England provided secret funding to both RBS and HBOS. Under the terms of this program, the two banks, the most distressed of the Big Five of UK banking, pledged collateral to the Bank of England in exchange for liquidity support. RBS's usage peaked at £36.6 billion on October 17, while HBOS peaked at £25.4 billion on December 13. The terms for both were more stringent than other Bank of England loans, paying 1.7 percentage points above the base rate and requiring over £100 billion in collateral from the two banks (Hopkins and Treanor, 2009). Both would pay back these loans in their entirety by January 16, 2009, though no disclosure was made to the public until November 2009 (Hopkins and Treanor, 2009; MacNamara and Lynch, 2009). The program was only disclosed because the banks' subsequent part-nationalization gave the public access to their books. Bank of England representatives refused to confirm or deny the participation of other financial institutions (Peev, 2009). This program, extending support while minimizing publicity, demonstrates the attention UK officials paid to fears of stigmatizing participants in state aid. In Germany, this fear drove state officials to provide aid to distressed banks on terms generous enough to overcome the costs of this stigmatization. In the United Kingdom, however, where banks had less direct influence on policymakers, it would culminate in the state providing compulsory, rather than voluntary, state aid.

Mandatory Capital Injections

By October 2008, it had become clear to UK officials that the problem facing the banks was fundamentally about capital and could not be addressed by liquidity support alone. The failure to find a buyer for Northern Rock or Bradford & Bingley illustrated that a privately funded solution was unlikely. Additionally, both cases illustrated the limits of a private consortium rescue. UK banks refused to assemble a consortium for Northern Rock and could only be prevailed upon to provide a small consortium for Bradford & Bingley, insufficient to prevent that bank's failure. Some elements within the Treasury favored simply letting the banks fall, citing the precedent of Barings in 1995, BCCI in 1991, and a series of smaller bank failures in the 1970s (Darling, 2012, p. 141). This was also the course of action publically advocated by the opposition Conservatives. The heads of the Tripartite Authorities and Gordon Brown, however, felt that the cost of allowing UK banks to fail was too high and the likelihood of a private solution appearing was too low, meaning that no acceptable "do nothing" option existed (Comptroller and Auditor General National Audit Office (UK), 2009a, p. 20). Mervyn King, with the backing of FSA chairman Adair Turner, argued that the optimal solution was compulsory injections of capital by the state. The banks had already demonstrated their reluctance both to raise more capital and to accept state liquidity assistance for fear of signaling their weakness to markets; so King argued that a compulsory program could best both provide the necessary capital and avoid severe moral hazard issues (Darling, 2012, p. 140). Brown advocated a similar position while Darling agreed in principle, with some reservations about its practical viability (Darling, 2012, pp. 140, 142).

Therefore, UK policymakers came to an agreement that some form of state recapitalization would be necessary. Temporary full nationalization, as used in Northern Rock and Bradford & Bingley, was seen as a last resort, for both political and practical reasons. Politically, Gordon Brown's "New Labour" government was determined to avoid being seen as returning to the "Old Labour" advocacy of state-owned banking (Darling, 2012, p. 54). The British public was sensitive to moral hazard concerns, but also opposed to a general nationalization of the financial sector. Perhaps more important, however, were practical concerns: banks such as RBS, HBOS, and Barclays were much larger than the relatively small Northern Rock and Bradford & Bingley. Taking on the liabilities of these large banks might inflict serious damage on state finances if they continued to falter (Darling, 2012, p. 128). Therefore, policymakers favored some way to inject capital without taking full ownership.

This meant two basic options: a toxic asset purchase into a "bad bank" or state ownership stakes in the banks themselves (Comptroller and Auditor General National Audit Office (UK), 2009b, p. 5; Darling, 2012). The former faced the general problem of bad banks: a successfully implemented toxic asset purchase scheme requires a valuation of assets that is low enough to contain moral hazard problems and losses to the state but high enough to prevent the bank's failure. State officials simply lacked the time necessary to produce an accurate valuation, though they did not dismiss the possibility of such a program later on, when greater due diligence might be possible (Comptroller and Auditor General National Audit Office (UK), 2009b, p. 5).

State officials therefore instead favored direct capital injections into banks. Not only would this be simpler to implement than a bad bank, but it would minimize both moral hazard and losses to taxpayers by giving the state a share of future profits (Comptroller and Auditor General National Audit Office (UK), 2009a, p. 15; Darling, 2012). Under the initial recapitalization program, capital injections were to primarily take the form of preferred stock paying a punitively high dividend of 12 percent, well above comparable German or American programs (Comptroller and Auditor General National Audit Office (UK), 2009b; United States Congress House Committee on Financial Services, 2011). Moreover, preferred stock was senior to other claims, meaning that any losses would be felt by ordinary shareholders before the state.

British officials paired their capital injection with loan guarantees to stimulate interbank lending, calculating that such a move would lower the total amount of required capital injected and thus lower the potential risk for taxpayers (Darling, 2012, p. 157). Such loan guarantees would be provided at market rates, unlike the under-market German loan guarantees (Comptroller and Auditor General National Audit Office (UK), 2009b, p. 11). The final form of the program consisted of £50 billion in recapitalization, £250 billion in loan guarantees, £100 billion in short-term loans, and an extension of the existing £100 billion SLS (Darling, 2012, p. 156). The capital injections would come from the state underwriting a private capital raise, in which shares would first be offered to existing shareholders but the state purchasing any shares the shareholders declined to take up. This method would allow shareholders to take on a portion of the costs of the rescue directly, reducing the costs to the state and the dilution of their own stake in the bank.

The plan was not negotiated with the banks but presented as a *fait accompli* to representatives in a special meeting on October 7, 2008. It came to be dubbed the "Balti Bailout," after the Indian food served as the meeting ran late into the night (Armitstead, Aldrick, and Griffiths, 2008). Banks were presented with specific capital raising requirements, with the worst-off banks – RBS and HBOS – presented with the highest capital requirements, and the healthiest banks allowed to avoid mandatory recapitalization (Comptroller and Auditor General National Audit Office (UK), 2009b, pp. 6–7). Such levels were to be set by the FSA, based on stress tests of the banks' existing capital positions (Comptroller and Auditor General National Audit Office (UK), 2009b, pp. 6–7). Those levels would be nonnegotiable, though banks would be free to substitute private capital for state capital, if such a source could be found. Without a private alternative, however, banks would be compelled to accept part-nationalization on the state's terms. Those banks requiring recapitalization contested, at times bitterly, but without success. Sir Fred Goodwin, the CEO of RBS, steadfastly maintained that his problems were purely liquidity-based, and not capital-related, and would later compare the meeting to a drive-by shooting (*Observer (England)*, 2010). Representatives of Lloyds and HBOS were similarly upset, but also could not prevail on policymakers to change the terms of recapitalization (Darling, 2012, pp. 171, 173). The only bank to make use of the private alternative was Barclays. Barclays' chief executive John Varley was "almost on his knees" pleading that he could raise the required capital without participation in the government scheme (Darling, 2012, p. 173; Rayner, 2008). With the understanding that Barclays would still be compelled to raise the capital from some source, the bank escaped compulsory state recapitalization. This would spare the British taxpayers but ultimately cost Barclays shareholders more than the state recapitalization would have.

While the German failing banks had the support of the healthy ones in negotiating terms of state aid, British officials were able to take advantage of the divided nature of British banking to their advantage, making temporary allies of the healthier banks against the weaker banks. The liquidity provision, which all banks wanted, was available only if the package as a whole was accepted by all the major banks. This gave the healthy banks, especially Standard Chartered and HSBC, incentive to pressure the weaker banks, especially RBS and HBOS, to accept the terms as offered (Darling, 2012, p. 162). Standard Chartered and HSBC were judged by the FSA to not need significant recapitalization, but did want to avail themselves of the loan guarantees and liquidity provisions of the state assistance package. The tension between the banks culminated the night of the Balti Bailout with another banker angrily declaring to Goodwin that the crisis was "all [his] fault" (Griffiths, 2009). The atomized nature of their banking system had pushed the banks to turn against each other and allowed the state to press for more punitive terms.

As with the nationalization of Northern Rock and Bradford & Bingley, reaction to the plan outside of the affected banks was generally that the partial nationalization was not ideal but was the best available option. Even the other banks and the Conservatives gave the plan grudging support. HSBC CEO Michael Geoghan stated, "I don't think it is right that the British taxpayer should need to bail out banks ... it sets a bad precedent, but the Government had no alternative" (Blackhurst, 2008). Conservative Shadow Chancellor George Osborne also accepted part-nationalization as a necessary step, although he argued that it was only necessary because of earlier errors by the Labour government (Settle, 2008a). Others responded more positively. Liberal Democrat leader Nick Clegg praised nationalization but called for broader stimulus measures, especially a tax cut (Clegg, 2009). Other critics similarly called on the state to go further, either taking ordinary shares or outrightly nationalizing the banks (*Sunday Telegraph (London)*, 2008). Apart from people arguing that the banks should be allowed to fail, there was no serious critique of nationalization. Internationally, the plan attracted significant praise, both in the op-ed pages of major newspapers and among policymakers (Krugman, 2008). Henry Paulson, the US Treasury Secretary, would credit the UK approach as a factor guiding him toward a similar mandatory state recapitalization in the United States, and other international leaders would also move toward part-nationalizations after the British action (Darling, 2012, p. 168).

State Aid to Individual Institutions under the Systemic Response Programs

Barclays

Alone among the major UK banks singled out for recapitalization, Barclays was able to avoid part-nationalization. This was not due to a stronger position, however. Barclays early on had been one of the banks seen as most vulnerable. As of February 2008, most of the United

Kingdom's £5 billion in subprime losses were concentrated in Barclays and RBS (Goodway, 2008c). In October 2007, both Barclays and RBS tapped the US Federal Reserve for a combined $30 billion in liquidity (Dey, 2007). Barclays was also widely rumored to be the unidentified other bank that had tapped the emergency fund the Bank of England set up for Northern Rock in November 2007 (Inman, 2007). By April of 2008, JP Morgan estimated Barclays had a capital shortfall of £8 billion (Hosking, Seib and Kennedy, 2008). In September 2008, the UK Treasury and FSA refused to grant a waiver allowing a rapid purchase of Lehman Brothers by Barclays, fearing that Barclays was too weak to save the US investment bank and that the purchase would simply bring both banks down (Darling, 2012, pp. 123–124).

Therefore, it was not surprising that Barclays was identified as requiring recapitalization by the FSA when the compulsory recapitalizations were announced (Darling, 2012, p. 173). However, as noted above, Barclays' CEO John Varley was able to convince UK officials that his bank could raise the required funds from private sources and should therefore not be required to accept state capital. A private injection was preferable for Barclays for two reasons. The first was avoiding the stigmatization of requiring public assistance, allowing Barclays to claim it was not as distressed as RBS or HBOS. The second advantage was avoiding the additional restrictions that came with state capital. In addition to diluting the existing shareholders and the 12 percent fixed dividend required for government-preferred stock, banks accepting aid were subject to lending target requirements and a ban on payment of dividends or bonuses until the state was repaid (Comptroller and Auditor General National Audit Office (UK), 2009b, p. 41). Through these provisions, the state hoped to encourage rapid payback of state aid. In the case of Barclays, it convinced the bank to accept private aid on even more costly terms to avoid these restrictions on dividends and bonuses.

Barclays avoided state aid through a £7.3 billion capital injection from a mix of its own shareholders and a consortium of investors from Qatar and Abu Dhabi (Goodway, 2008a). Three billion pounds of the Middle Eastern consortium's investment would come in the form of Reserve Capital Instruments, a kind of preferred share paying 14 percent interest. About £2.8 billion of the Middle Eastern investors' money and £1.5 billion from Barclays' existing shareholders would be Mandatory Convertible Notes, preferred shares paying 9.75 percent interest until June 2009, when they would convert to ordinary shares at a share price of 153 p. This aid came at a higher cost than £3 billion of government-preferred shares, which charged only a 12 percent dividend, and diluted existing shareholders to a greater extent than the terms of state assistance would have.

From a government perspective, this was ideal. Barclays was recapitalized above the FSA's requirements and at no cost or risk to the taxpayer. The UKSA welcomed it as well, for avoiding another expansion of state ownership (Group, 2008). Barclays' management benefited by avoiding the ban on bonuses. Existing Barclays' shareholders, however, had less to celebrate. Not only were their shareholdings diluted, but their rights of preemption were violated. By offering the Middle Eastern consortium a deal that was not offered to existing shareholders, the deal violated City of London rules that shareholders be offered rights on equal terms (Boles, 2008). Several legal firms and shareholder advisors urged Barclays' shareholders to vote down the deal, but Barclays' management refused to renegotiate the terms (McCusker, 2008; Moir, 2008; Northedge, 2008). As a concession to contain a shareholder revolt, Barclays offered existing shareholders an opportunity to purchase £500 million in Reserve Capital Instruments at the same 14 percent dividend (*Global Banking News*, 2008). With that concession, the deal went ahead as planned.

The terms of that deal, while good for the government and Barclays' management in the short term, contained a provision largely overlooked at the time, which would substantially complicate later efforts at capital raising. Under the terms of the arrangement, should Barclays raise additional capital at a lower price than 153 p per share conversion price for Mandatory Convertible Notes before conversion to ordinary shares in June 2009, the Convertible Notes holders could convert at that lower share price. This effectively blocked Barclays from participating in the second system-wide support plan the United Kingdom would introduce – the Asset Protection Scheme (APS) – discussed in more depth below. Because Barclays in January 2009 was trading at only 66 p per share, any government capital support at market value would enable the Middle Eastern shareholders to convert their stake at that price. Converting at such a low price would have given the consortium a 55 percent controlling interest in the bank, an unacceptable outcome from the perspective of existing shareholders and management. This provision therefore effectively blocked any additional support for Barclays (Blackhurst, 2009).

The state's ability to take a hard line in negotiations with the bank was crucial in driving Barclays to find a private source of investment. The terms of the private investment were harsher from a shareholder's perspective than even the UK state terms, which were already harsher than other states' aid terms in the 2007–2009 crisis. It is highly unlikely that Barclays would have accepted those terms if the state's terms had been more generous or less compulsory. If the state had been more generous, the costs of stigmatization as an aid-taker could have been balanced against generous capital access, leading to the bank accepting state aid. This was the case in Germany, where state aid was cheaper than private alternatives. If the capital raising had not been compulsory, Barclays could have gambled for resurrection, continuing to place risky bets in the hope that they would pay off and get the bank out of trouble, but reasonably confident that the state would still rescue the bank if they failed. However, with neither renegotiation nor gambling for resurrection as options, Barclays was forced to choose between costly, stigmatizing state aid and even more costly but less stigmatizing private capital. That the bank chose a private capital route was nearly ideal from a government perspective, as the bank received a capital infusion without exposing the taxpayer to additional risk. It worked out well for the Middle Eastern private investors as well, who realized a £1.4 billion profit when their Mandatory Convertible Notes converted in June 2009 (Treanor, 2009a). It did not work out so well for Barclays' existing shareholders, who saw their holdings diluted and were limited in their ability to participate in later state aid schemes. In that sense, therefore, the Barclays case was moral hazard–limiting, as existing shareholders were forced to bear the costs of rescuing their bank. The case of Barclays, therefore, illustrates an instance of the state using its ability to threaten nationalization to push a bank into a private market solution. Although the state did not compel private investors to save Barclays, it was able to push Barclays into a willingness to pay a great deal for private capital. The state was able to do this because of its ability to dictate terms to banks, even to the point of compelling them to accept state aid on nonnegotiable terms. Without allies among either politicians or fellow banks, Barclays' only room for negotiation with the state was to offer to find a more expensive source of private capital, and not to bargain for cheaper state assistance.

The Royal Bank of Scotland

While Barclays managed to avoid state aid, the other major institutions to run into distress – RBS, Lloyds, and HBOS – would end up receiving substantial state aid, though on harsh terms. The Royal Bank of Scotland (RBS), like Barclays, was widely identified as a potential problem bank as early as 2007. It and Barclays held the majority of the United Kingdom's subprime losses (Goodway, 2008c). Like Barclays, RBS tapped the US Federal Reserve for liquidity in October 2007 and was widely rumored to be the unidentified other bank that tapped the Bank of England's Northern Rock liquidity fund in November 2007 (Dey, 2007). Its losses were considerably higher, however, and in April

2008, JP Morgan estimated a capital shortfall of £13 billion (Hosking, Seib, and Kennedy, 2008).

That month RBS embarked on the largest capital raise to that point in UK history, attempting to solicit €12.6 billion from its shareholders (*Daily Mail (London)*, 2008). This was speculated to be a quid pro quo negotiated in exchange for access to the Bank of England's SLS (Stewart, 2008). A fund manager referred to the arrangement as a "Faustian bargain," in which the state would provide liquidity, but not nationalizations, in exchange for which the bank would cut its dividends and raise additional private capital (Fraser, 2008). Such a bargain served the interests of the state, much like the later Barclays private capital raise, by increasing RBS' capitalization without exposing the taxpayer to risk the way state ownership would. The capital raising was generally successful in reaching its target, with 95 percent of the new rights issue taken up by shareholders. This was by virtue of a discounted rights purchase price of 200 p, below the trading value of 226 p per share on June 3 (Financial Services Authority (UK), 2011, p. 317; Young, 2008). Even after the rights issue, however, RBS would be in a weaker capital position than most of its UK peers (Financial Services Authority (UK), 2011, p. 196). It would not be enough to save RBS, given its further losses and subsequent loss of faith by investors, especially after the failure of European partners.

In 2007, RBS had partnered with the Dutch–Belgian bank Fortis to purchase the Dutch ABN AMRO, a massive expansion for both purchasers. ABN AMRO, however, held significant exposure to subprime assets, and as their value plummeted, losses from ABN AMRO dragged down both Fortis and RBS (Financial Services Authority (UK), 2011, pp. 170–171). On September 30, 2008, the Dutch and Belgian governments nationalized the failing Fortis (McIntosh, 2008b). The failure of RBS' partner in ABN AMRO, largely driven by losses from ABN AMRO, caused a corresponding drop in RBS' share price. The potential for the imminent collapse of one of the United Kingdom's largest banks became one of the chief factors spurring the British state to launch its own state recapitalization plan.

The FSA-determined capital injection for RBS would be £20 billion, more than the bank was worth at the time. This required new capital level was presented to the bank without space for negotiation. FSA chief Hector Sants' stated goal in setting such a high recapitalization was to make RBS "bulletproof," removing all doubt as to the viability of the bank going forward (Askeland, 2008). The aid was to consist of £5 billion of preferred shares, paying an "eye-watering" 12 percent dividend and £15 billion of ordinary shares, to be raised via an underwriting of a shareholder capital raise (Comptroller and Auditor General National Audit Office (UK), 2009a, p. 7; Forsyth, 2008). Without shareholder participation, this would give the state a 58 percent stake in RBS, but at the time it was hoped that a significant portion of that £15 billion would come from RBS shareholders (Goodway, 2008b). The offer price for the underwritten capital raise was 65.5 p per share, while the trading price was 90 p per share the day the plan was announced (Fleming, 2008b). This offered a substantial discount for shareholders looking to increase their stake in the bank. In addition to the high dividend on the preferred shares, the purchase of ordinary shares would be considerably below market value, and far below the trading price of 546 p per share a year earlier (Behrmann, 2008). Such a below-market nationalization served several purposes. It diminished the moral hazard effects of a part-nationalization. The bank would be saved by an infusion of state aid, but by paying below-market terms, the shareholders would be diluted and see the value of their own shares and any potential future dividends diminish. This dilution was compounded by the terms of the preferred shares, where no ordinary share dividend could be paid until the preferred shares were repaid (Comptroller and Auditor General National Audit Office (UK), 2009b, p. 41). Additionally, a below-market offer price encouraged shareholders to join in the capital raise themselves, potentially shifting some of the burden for the rescue off of the taxpayers.

As with Barclays, the terms of recapitalization to RBS were harsh. Unlike with Barclays, however, no private alternative could be found, and RBS had no choice but to submit to the recapitalization plan. However, the announcement of state aid failed to prevent a further collapse of the RBS share price. The third quarter report from RBS revealed £206 million in losses, driving the share price down (Goodway, 2008b). The sale price, 65.5 p per share, was well below the trading price of 90 p per share when it was announced, but RBS' share price plummeted to only 55.3 p per share on November 24, the day the offer expired (McConnell, 2008). With an offer price above the market price, there was little incentive for RBS shareholders to participate in the capital raise, and only 0.24 percent was taken up. The remainder, almost the full £15 billion, was taken up by the state, producing an immediate £2.5 billion paper loss on the now above-market nationalization and leaving the state the 57.9 percent majority owner of RBS (McConnell, 2008).

The picture continued to worsen at RBS into the new year, with the bank on track for £24 billion in losses, most (£20 billion) from toxic assets (Treanor, 2009b). This would be the biggest one-year loss in UK corporate history. At this point, with similar problems appearing at

HBOS, the Tripartite Authorities began to consider a second round of state aid to the banks. As with the initial capital injections, policy discussions were a closed process, without a role for industry representatives in shaping policy. RBS would be presented with the new terms from the state, drafted without RBS input. Because it was now majority state-owned, RBS was in no position to reject them. Three options were considered: a further injection of capital, a temporary full nationalization, and a scheme to underpin the value of assets on the distressed banks' balance sheets. Further recapitalization, on similar terms as the previous fall, would be the simplest to implement logistically. However, given that the £20 billion to make RBS "bulletproof" in the first round quickly proved inadequate, it would be difficult to determine how much further capital would be needed should the economy continue to deteriorate. Moreover, with the state already a 57.8 percent shareholder in RBS, further capitalization risked becoming effectively a full nationalization anyway (Comptroller and Auditor General National Audit Office (UK), 2010b, p. 3; Darling, 2012, p. 202).

A temporary full nationalization was also discussed at that time (Comptroller and Auditor General National Audit Office (UK), 2010b, pp. 3–4). Temporary nationalization offered the advantage of giving the state greater control over the bank's actions than even its majority shareholding did. Moreover, temporary nationalization offered a way to spread the costs to the subordinated debtholders of RBS, who had previously managed to avoid shouldering the costs of RBS' losses and state aid (Comptroller and Auditor General National Audit Office (UK), 2010b, p. 4). However, the Tripartite Authorities ultimately decided that nationalization raised too many problems. A full nationalization of a bank of the scale of RBS risked destabilizing markets even further, which might drive investors from the United Kingdom and force further nationalizations of UK banks, a step the state wanted to avoid. Even if there were no panic, nationalizing RBS might erode the depositor base of the other banks, as depositors made a "flight to safety" to the state banks. This had already occurred on a smaller scale at Northern Rock, forcing the state to cap the number of new accounts the nationalized bank could open. Even as depositors might flock to RBS, however, the best managers and clients might leave, making it harder to return to profitability and repay the taxpayer stake. Finally, leaving RBS partially privately owned left some of its shares publically listed, making it easier to calculate the market value of the bank and eventually unload the state's stake. Therefore, the Tripartite Authorities concluded that temporary full nationalization was not desirable at the current time (Comptroller and Auditor

General National Audit Office (UK), 2010b, pp. 3–4, 6). Significantly, the objection to nationalization was practical and not a rejection of state ownership in principle. Nor did it reflect opposition to nationalization from RBS' remaining shareholders. The Tripartite Authorities in fact drew up contingency plans for nationalization should the bank continue to deteriorate (Comptroller and Auditor General National Audit Office (UK), 2010b, p. 4).

If full nationalization was to be avoided, the state needed to act to shore up the eroding value of RBS' assets. Previous crises suggested two ways to confront such a problem. The first was a conventional bad bank or toxic asset purchase, and the second was a scheme in which the state would insure specific assets, which would remain with the bank, against losses above a certain level (Comptroller and Auditor General National Audit Office (UK), 2010b, p. 5). The former option presented the same difficulties as when it had been considered as a response to the previous fall. It would be too difficult to properly price the assets to avoid substantial moral hazard problems. It would also require an immediate outlay of additional state funds (Comptroller and Auditor General National Audit Office (UK), 2010b, p. 5). An asset protection scheme, by contrast, could theoretically avoid the direct use of state funds, as the guarantee itself might be enough to staunch the erosion of asset value.

Designing such a scheme, however, presented several challenges. Control of the assets and profits from it would remain with the bank, although losses would be shared with the taxpayer. There would, therefore, be fees to offset this imbalance in risk-sharing and incentives for the bank to maximize returns even once the loss guarantee scheme was activated. Additionally, the scheme should be structured in such a way that the bank has an incentive to exit the scheme and eliminate taxpayer exposure as soon as possible (Comptroller and Auditor General National Audit Office (UK), 2010b, p. 7).

In order to address these concerns, the APS as drafted for RBS involved several mechanisms designed to align the bank's incentives with the taxpayers'. As the scheme was originally devised, £325 billion of RBS assets would be protected, with RBS taking the first £42 billion of losses on that pool of assets, which the Treasury estimated as the most likely level of losses to be experienced (Comptroller and Auditor General National Audit Office (UK), 2010a, p. 6). An upturn in RBS' share price gave the bank a bit of space to negotiate, and the terms would be revised to cover £282 billion in assets, with a first-loss level of £60 billion, reflecting the fact that the assets in the smaller pool were of poorer quality and more likely to lose value (Comptroller and Auditor General National Audit Office (UK), 2010a, p. 4). Losses above that point would be split between the state and the bank on a 9:1 ratio. This ratio followed the precedent set by the United States in its similar arrangement with Citigroup (Comptroller and Auditor General National Audit Office (UK), 2010a, pp. 20–21). Payments from the Treasury on losses would be made two years after the loss, to provide opportunity for the asset to regain value while also providing further incentive for the bank to avoid losses. The bank would pay an annual fee for participation in the scheme of £700 million a year for the first three years and £500 million a year thereafter. In order for the bank to exit the scheme and avoid these annual fees, it would need to pay no less than £2.5 billion, including annual fees paid to date, plus pay back any losses covered by the Treasury plus interest (Comptroller and Auditor General National Audit Office (UK), 2010a, p. 23). Finally, the bank would grant the state £6.5 billion in shares as payment for participation, and the state would inject a further £19 billion of additional recapitalization. These new shares would be "B shares," preferred shares that would be convertible to ordinary shares if the share price climbed above 65.5 p per share (Behrmann, 2009; Lynch, 2009). Through such convertible shares, the state guaranteed itself a dividend if the bank remained unprofitable, but gained a mechanism to increase its share of profits if the bank returned to health. This additional recapitalization brought the state's share of RBS to 83 percent (Comptroller and Auditor General National Audit Office (UK), 2010a, pp. 4, 15). Finally, as part of the European Commission's approval of the APS, RBS was forced to sell off significant operations, including much of its branch network, its insurance divisions, and parts of its investment banking operations (European Commission, 2009g; Fleming, 2009). The construction of the APS was, therefore, quite complex, but designed to both impose costs on RBS for its participation and encourage RBS to exit the program as rapidly as it feasibly could.

The state ultimately invested a total of £45 billion directly in RBS, with more in loans and guarantees (European Commission, 2009g, p. 12). The bank, therefore, consumed a substantial portion of state resources, and as of 2015 still represented a net loss to the British taxpayer (Comptroller and Auditor General National Audit Office (UK), 2015). Nevertheless, the state's actions toward RBS consistently demonstrated concerns for minimizing taxpayer losses and moral hazards. The initial fall 2008 recapitalization was designed to be below market value, giving the state a share of the bank disproportional to its investment and diluting shareholders. That it failed to do so was because of an underwriting approach designed to encourage burden-sharing by private investors, and not a deliberate subsidization of losses. The punitive 12 percent dividend on preferred shares was substantially greater than in either Germany or the United States. The APS again sought to prevent the bank from falling while limiting moral hazard concerns, designed to be expensive enough both to produce a taxpayer profit in the long run and to incentivize the bank to rapidly repay the state and exit the scheme.

Throughout the crisis, RBS representatives were shut out of the policymaking process. The fall from grace of Sir Fred Goodwin, the CEO of RBS at the beginning of the crisis, represents in miniature how UK banks rapidly lost their influence as their market position fell. In 2004, near the peak of his clout as the head of a dominant UK bank, Goodwin received a knighthood for "services to banking" (*Telegraph*, 2012). In December 2007, Goodwin had enough clout to call on Alistair Darling at his home in Edinburgh, to urge the Treasury Secretary to pressure the Bank of England to provide additional liquidity to RBS (Darling, 2012, p. 61). Although unsuccessful in that effort, that he was able to arrange such a meeting indicates a substantial level of access to high-level policymakers. By October 2008, however, Goodwin's dismissal became one of the conditions of state aid to RBS (Darling, 2012, p. 171; Porter et al., 2008). After that, Goodwin became targeted by British politicians as emblematic of the problem with British banking. Politicians, bankers, and the general public came to see him as one of the chief villains of the 2007–2009 crisis (Aldrick, 2009; Hattenstone, 2009; Walker, 2009). Ultimately, although he would avoid criminal charges, Goodwin would be stripped of his knighthood in a move that attracted broad support across parties in Parliament (*Telegraph*, 2012).

More broadly, although RBS enjoyed significant access and influence while it was strong, it soon lost influence and control over its fate once it ran into trouble. The negotiation of both the recapitalization and the APS were closed processes, open to the Tripartite Authorities but not to the affected parties. The recapitalization plan was presented to RBS as a fait accompli. Negotiation on the APS, possible only because of a rise in RBS' share price, lowered the amount of assets RBS put in the scheme, but raised the amount of losses it would experience on those assets. Throughout the crisis, RBS had virtually no allies. The other bankers readily turned on Goodwin, unwilling to jeopardize their own access to liquidity to help pressure the Treasury for more favorable terms. This gave policymakers the space to shape whatever policy they thought best, and they consistently foregrounded concern with protecting the taxpayer from losses and limiting moral hazard problems.

Lloyds/TSB and HBOS

The other two major banks to receive state aid in the crisis were Lloyds/TSB and HBOS.[2] Although they would remain in majority private control, both would be provided state assistance on terms comparable to those of RBS, and with a similar lack of autonomy in dealing with the state. Prior to the peak of the 2007–2009 crisis, both Lloyds and HBOS encountered some difficulties, although Lloyds' issues were minor compared to HBOS'. In April 2008, Lloyds had an estimated capital shortfall of £4 billion, while HBOS' was £11 billion (Hosking, Seib, and Kennedy, 2008). The Scottish bank was widely seen as one of the most vulnerable in the United Kingdom. That spring, rumors of HBOS approaching the Bank of England for support prompted a massive collapse in share value and drove the Bank of England to take the highly unusual step of publically refuting the rumors (Tift, 2008). In order to address these issues, HBOS made several attempts to increase its cash reserves. The bank attempted to reinforce its capital position with a £4 billion raise from its shareholders (Pagano, 2008). However, much as happened with the state recapitalization of RBS later that year, the collapse in share price meant that the offer price fell below the market price of HBOS stock before the sale was completed. The offer price, 275 p per share, was a substantial discount to the 500 p per share market price at the time of unveiling (Young, 2008). However, in the ensuing three months, from May 4 to July 20, the market price of HBOS shares dipped to 265 p per share, causing only 8.3 percent of the rights issue to be taken up (*Guardian*, 2008).

This failed capital raising further weakened HBOS, and the government began to be concerned about the bank's precarious position. In September 2008, members of the Tripartite Authorities met to consider potential actions on HBOS (Darling, 2012, pp. 126–129). Temporary full nationalization was considered at that time but, given the size of the bank and the potential for less radical solutions, was reserved as a last resort. The option soon viewed as most desirable was a managed sale to another bank (Comptroller and Auditor General National Audit Office (UK), 2009a, p. 18; Darling, 2012, p. 128). If possible, this would avoid a collapse at HBOS without involving taxpayer money. It could potentially raise competitiveness issues, however. The size of HBOS meant that any UK bank large enough to acquire it would inevitably take a commanding share of the UK banking market. Purchase by a foreign bank

[2] HBOS formally is not an abbreviation, but the bank was formed from the merger of Halifax plc and the Bank of Scotland in 2001, so is widely presumed to stand for Halifax Bank of Scotland.

could avoid these issues, but no such foreign buyer expressed interest (Comptroller and Auditor General National Audit Office (UK), 2009a, p. 18; Market News International, 2008). However, letting HBOS fail would reduce competition in UK banking anyway, and a private sale was seen as preferable to state aid (Darling, 2012, p. 129). Therefore, policymakers began seeking a buyer for HBOS in earnest, with Gordon Brown controversially taking a central role. As in earlier cases, representatives of the bank at issue, HBOS, played little role in these discussions.

Few banks expressed much interest in HBOS. Barclays indicated that it would only make such a purchase if strong-armed into it by the UK government (Warner, 2008b). HSBC offered to take HBOS essentially for free, with no compensation to HBOS shareholders (Winnett, 2008). Only one viable merger partner emerged, Lloyds/TSB, which had expressed interest in acquiring HBOS as early as July, but had been dissuaded at that time due to concerns over the market share of a merged Lloyds/HBOS (Treanor and Elliott, 2008). By September, however, the potential benefits of such a merger outweighed the negatives in the eyes of policymakers. Should HBOS fail, competition in UK banking would be reduced anyway, and a merger could not only save HBOS but also prop up Lloyds. Lloyds was not as distressed as HBOS, RBS, or Barclays, but nevertheless was suffering in the financial crisis. A merger could not only avoid the nationalization of HBOS but also reduce the need to provide additional taxpayer support to Lloyds. It was precisely because of Lloyds' vulnerable but not dire position that the bank agreed to participate in the merger, seeing a greater chance for advancing its own interests than the healthier HSBC did. These factors not only overrided competition concerns but also drove policymakers to actively press HBOS to accept the merger. Brown personally contacted the chairmen of both banks to convince them to begin work on a merger (Prynn, 2008). Lloyds initially offered HBOS shareholders 0.83 Lloyds share per HBOS share. This was equivalent to £15.8 billion at current market value, 58 percent above HBOS' traded value but only one-fifth of its peak value in February 2007 (Board, 2008b).

Once announced, the merger attracted considerable controversy. Press accounts claimed that the merger was negotiated directly between Lloyds chairman Sir Victor Blank and Gordon Brown, and that Blank used his political influence to persuade Brown to push a merger (Darling, 2012, p. 129; Dey and O'Connell, 2009; Rees, 2009). State officials vehemently denied these claims, arguing that a merger served taxpayer interests better than any available alternatives (Darling, 2012, p. 129). Scottish National Party politicians were especially critical, accusing Brown of acting in the interests of Lloyds rather than the British taxpayers. Scottish First

Minister Alex Salmond even argued that pumping billions of pounds of taxpayer funds into HBOS was preferable to the loss of independence of one of Scotland's most prominent banks (Macdonell, 2008). HBOS shareholders resisted being pressured into a merger and sought to find other banks to make rival bids (Farrell, 2008; Macdonell and MacMahon, 2008; McIntosh, 2008a). Lloyds' shareholders complained as well, as a collapsing HBOS share price made the terms offered considerably less attractive. By October 1, thirteen days after the initial offer, Lloyds' offer has become shares worth £9.8 billion for a bank only worth £6.4 billion at current market value (Treanor, 2008). Since any merger required the state to waive competition requirements, Lloyds could not alter the terms of the deal without the consent of the Treasury, which above all wanted the merger to go through to save both banks. Therefore, Lloyds' CEO Eric Daniels vowed to push ahead with the original terms (Treanor, 2008).

Soon thereafter, both Lloyds and HBOS were compelled to accept capital injections from the United Kingdom. Lloyds was required to accept £4.5 billion in ordinary shares and £1 billion in preference shares, while HBOS was required to take £8.5 billion in ordinary shares and £3 billion in preference shares (Aldrick and Griffiths, 2008). As with RBS, the preference shares carried a 12 percent coupon. The ordinary shares would be injected via an underwritten below-market share raise, hopefully encouraging existing shareholders to participate (Settle, 2008b).

Salmond continued to contest the merger, and UKSA representatives argued that, after the share collapse, only the government now seemed to gain from the merger, and not shareholders at either bank (Bain, 2008; Barnes, 2008; Jamieson and McIntosh, 2008). Nevertheless, government officials publically insisted that recapitalizations for both Lloyds and HBOS were contingent on the merger going forward (Treanor et al., 2008). Privately, Darling and Brown felt that, while a weakened Lloyds might survive without the merger, the only way to save HBOS absent a merger would be a total nationalization (Darling, 2012, pp. 128, 202). Nationalizing HBOS would potentially expose the UK taxpayer to billions of pounds in losses and could not guarantee the survival of the bank. Therefore, they would use the threat of withholding state aid to pressure the banks into going forward with the merger.

An unmerged Lloyds would be damaged but likely survive, so could credibly threaten to withdraw from the merger. Therefore, Lloyds retained some space to renegotiate the terms of the merger. In recognition of the new context, Lloyds renegotiated the terms of the merger downward, offering only .605 share of Lloyds stock for one share of HBOS (Gallagher, 2008). The worsening terms for HBOS sparked an insurgent movement led by former HBOS board members Sir Peter Burt and Sir George Mathewson to scrap the merger and devise a plan by which HBOS could survive as an independent institution. Burt and Mathewson argued that the £12 billion in new capital the FSA required was only £500 million above the government recapitalization and therefore could be raised from existing shareholders (Lynch and Christie, 2008; Maddox, 2008). This plan attracted the support of First Minister Salmond, as well as numerous Scottish public figures, including actor Sean Connery (Cameron, 2008; Duncanson, 2008). The state, however, remained extremely wary of any plan other than the Lloyds merger. Darling argued that the merger offered greater security going forward, as wholesale funders would likely stay away from an independent HBOS and the bank had only survived to this point thanks to £11 billion in funding Lloyds had provided in recent weeks in anticipation of the merger (Hay, 2008). Moreover, an unmerged Lloyds and HBOS would together require greater taxpayer support than a single merged bank would and would have a lower chance of repaying the rescue money in a timely fashion. Ultimately, Darling defeated the Burt-Mathewson proposal by undercutting its central premise: that HBOS could access state capital on the same terms with or without a merger (Lydall and Jamieson, 2008). Once Darling made it clear that an independent HBOS would face more stringent conditions on any state aid, the Burt-Mathewson plan was no longer viable, and they declined to submit a formal proposal (Darling, 2012, p. 200). The state's power to grant or withhold aid on terms of its choosing gave the HBOS shareholders only a choice between accepting state terms or failing and becoming nationalized at minimal compensation. By acting in this fashion, Darling used the power of the state to compel a private bank to act in a way that served the interest of the UK taxpayer, and not the interests of HBOS shareholders. With the Burt-Mathewson proposal eliminated, both Lloyds and HBOS shareholders had little alternative but to vote forward the merger and the recapitalization.

Unfortunately for the state, as with the RBS recapitalization, the market value of shares for both Lloyds and HBOS fell below the offer price before the offer closed. What was intended to be a below-market nationalization, therefore, ended up being above-market. With an offer price above market price, very few private shareholders took part in the offering. Only 0.24 percent of new HBOS shares and 0.5 percent of new Lloyds shares were taken up. The state paid £13 billion for a 43 percent stake in the newly merged Lloyds/HBOS, realizing an immediate £3.5 billion paper loss. The state also took £4 billion in preferred shares, at the same 12 percent dividend as the RBS preferred stake (*Belfast Telegraph*, 2009). This left the state a 43.5 percent shareholder in the new bank.

The merged Lloyds/HBOS continued to struggle and was originally slated to participate in the APS along with RBS (Comptroller and Auditor General National Audit Office (UK), 2010a, p. 14; Cusick and Watt, 2009; Farrell, 2009). However, a surge in value in summer 2009 allowed the bank to escape participation by instead launching £13.5 billion rights issue (Sharp, 2009). This enabled the bank to pay back the state a net £2.3 billion of its preferred shares, though the state participated in the share raise to preserve its ownership stake (Jagger and Webster, 2009). The terms of participation in the APS were onerous enough to convince the bank to offer a below-market capital raise, relying on its own shareholders to bail out the bank rather than turning to additional state assistance.

HBOS, much like the other distressed banks, rapidly lost control over its own destiny once it became dependent upon state aid, losing virtually all leverage to negotiate with policymakers over terms. Lloyds was in a slightly better position, as it plausibly could have survived without state assistance. Lloyds maintained the ability to refuse a merger, while HBOS was given no alternative. Lloyds, however, still had no leverage to negotiate more favorable terms of state aid. Neither HBOS nor Lloyds had any allies among the other banks, which were more concerned about the potential threat from a merged Lloyds/HBOS.

Unlike the other failed banks, however, HBOS did have political support, from the Scottish National Party. Labour, the Liberal Democrats, and the Conservatives differed over specific policies, but all favored harsh terms for HBOS. The SNP and Scottish First Minister Salmond, however, argued for a subsidy to keep HBOS independent and at least partially private. The SNP supported HBOS not because it had been captured by banking interests but rather because an independent HBOS was a part of the party's case for Scottish independence. HBOS had been presented for years as evidence that Edinburgh could function as an international banking center and that Scotland need not be beholden to London banks (Linklater, 2008; Massie, 2008). This argument hinged on HBOS being a *Scottish* bank. RBS, with its significant operations in England and mainland Europe, was, name notwithstanding, less clearly Scottish and therefore did not attract the support of the SNP the way HBOS did (European Commission, 2009g, pp. 2–3). Moreover, even after nationalization, RBS remained independent and headquartered in Edinburgh, while a merged Lloyds/HBOS would be headquartered in London (*Scotsman*, 2008). HBOS alone among the UK banks had political allies, because of the politics of Scottish independence and not the political clout of HBOS.

Conclusion

The UK responses to the financial crisis of 2007–2009 followed the expected pattern for states with liberal financial systems. The atomized nature of the UK financial system gave healthy banks very little incentive to lobby on behalf of their ailing peers. The banking industry organizations, such as the British Bankers' Association, had very little ability to organize their own members toward a collective response or to influence the political process. Healthy banks deepened the distress of Northern Rock by poaching clients and depositors as it failed and opposed guarantees of its deposits as state aid to a rival. They pressured RBS and HBOS to accept partial nationalization, rather than helping them lobby for better terms. Although individual banks were tremendously influential prior to the crisis, with great access to high-level policymakers, they rapidly lost their influence once they failed and were forced to approach the state as supplicants. Unlike in corporatist systems, where healthy banks use their own resources and political influence to both aid distressed banks directly and lobby for more favorable terms, in the United Kingdom, healthy banks were either indifferent or hostile to failing ones.

This reflects their economic interests. While vulnerable to general systemic risk, the healthier banks faced few direct costs from the failure of their rivals, with whom they had an arm's-length relationship. There was very little cross-holding to impose direct losses, and any loans between banks were generally well collateralized. In some ways, they benefited from their rivals' distress, as customers fled to safety. The failing banks, meanwhile, without allies, lost the tremendous influence they had precrisis and were at the mercy of the state. Therefore, when setting bank rescue policies, policymakers were largely free from the influence of the banking sector. This allowed policymakers to focus on more general goals: containing systemic risk and minimizing losses to taxpayers.

Below a certain level of systemic risk, maximizing these goals meant letting banks fail. This was the case for BCCI and Barings in the early 1990s, as neither failure precipitated systemic collapse. In the early stages of 2007–2008, the Bank of England only went so far as to provide liquidity in the classic Bagehot formula: on the basis of good collateral to minimize potential losses and on punitive terms to avoid moral hazard from state aid. Once bank failures threatened the system as a whole, however, state aid became essential. Because the healthy banks had little exposure to their failing peers, private rescues were extremely limited. The small Bradford & Bingley underwriting consortium only developed because of intense pressure from the FSA. Private purchases were similarly offered if a bank saw a clear opportunity for profit. In the 2007–2009 crisis, this frequently meant that potential buyers insisted on a state subsidy, such as both Lloyds and Virgin Money demanded for Northern Rock. The one apparent example of banks in the United Kingdom collaborating in their response to the financial crisis was the illegal conspiracy to rig the LIBOR, in which at least three banks – but probably more – conspired to change the published interbank lending rate in a way that was advantageous for them. However, this both predated the financial crisis and, because the interests of the involved banks were in line, did not involve the kind of generosity to a peer bank found in the healthy banks in Germany, sacrificing some of their own capital to preserve an interdependent partner.[3]

[3] Officials at several banks involved in setting the LIBOR engaged in an activity to distort the value to their banks' advantage. The LIBOR, which is supposed to reflect the cost of interbank lending for twenty top London banks, is used by banks and firms around the world to determine the rates of lending and other financial transfers. As such, an artificially high or low LIBOR, with a gap between the LIBOR and the actual cost of interbank lending, can offer substantial advantages to the banks engaged in setting the LIBOR. The LIBOR is calculated by asking the twenty banks to report the cost of their interbank lending, then averaging the middle twelve values. For some unknown period of time, but at least since 2005, several banks, including Barclays, Swiss bank UBS, and possibly RBS, systematically misreported their cost of interbank lending. In good times, short-term manipulation of the LIBOR enabled these institutions to avoid losses or increase gains from trading positions. In the crisis, in addition to these advantages, underreporting of a bank's interbank lending sent a false signal of confidence to nervous investors, as a lower reported interbank lending rate indicates that other financial actors think the bank is a low risk. Because of this, the Bank of England sought to lower the LIBOR, both by increasing liquidity available to banks from the Bank of England and by pressuring the banks to lower their interbank lending rates through moral suasion. This may have risen to the level of suggesting that banks err on the side of lowering their estimation of their reported interbank lending rate.

The extent of the LIBOR scandal is unknown. Because the lowest and highest four reported rates are ignored in calculating the LIBOR, effectively manipulating the LIBOR to any significant degree would seem to require the cooperation of several banks. Barclays, UBS, and RBS have already been charged with criminal activity, but it is unknown at present if or how many other banks were involved. Even here, the extent of the coordination was more limited than in the German case. In the precrisis environment, it is unknown what sort of quid pro quo may have been provided in return for collaboration in fixing the LIBOR. During the crisis, the banks known to be involved – Barclays, UBS, and RBS – all were struggling and therefore would all stand to benefit from a lower LIBOR. UBS, while not a recipient of aid from the United Kingdom, had significant subprime exposure and received assistance from the Swiss state. Therefore, limited joint action such as this is not unsurprising, even in an atomized liberal system: all parties benefited directly, more than they would have by not cooperating, so there was no collective action dilemma. If one of the healthy banks had participated, that would be more indicative of corporatist-style joint action in the systemic interest. However, until investigations into the scandal by the United States, the United Kingdom, and Canada are complete, the full extent of the LIBOR scandal remains unknown.

This lack of a private alternative compelled the state to act, but also gave it the upper hand in dealing with failing banks that had to choose between state aid and failure. Policymakers laid out a clear hierarchy of preferred policy tools, designed to minimize costs to taxpayers. Aid conditions provided the state with control, a substantial share of the profits, or a mix of the two in any banks that it aided. The subsequent controversies over job cuts and foreclosures from state-owned Northern Rock and majority state-owned RBS illustrate reasons why the state may prefer a share of profits without control, to insulate elected officials from criticism over unpopular business decisions that may increase the likelihood and speed of repayment of the taxpayer assistance.

The UK political parties demonstrated a general consensus on the shape of state aid, agreeing that it should aim to minimize losses to taxpayers and carry an ownership stake to give the state a share in future profits. The parties chiefly differed over when the crisis reached a point requiring state action and whether to run the banks as state-owned enterprises or resolve them once they had been seized from shareholders. The Liberal Democrats argued for nationalization or part-nationalization of distressed banks earlier than Labour. The Conservatives argued that both Northern Rock and Bradford & Bingley should have been allowed to fail into administration instead of nationalized, to minimize longer-term risks to taxpayers. When the crisis reached a head in 2008, however, the Conservatives generally backed the Labour bank recapitalization plan. No party save the Scottish National Party advocated more generous terms for banks and their shareholders, and the SNP wanted to keep HBOS independent and private as part of their strategy for Scottish independence rather than concern for HBOS shareholders.

The patterns of response in the United Kingdom fit the predictions for a liberal financial system. Banks that failed found themselves with virtually no allies in the rest of the financial system, either economically or politically. Without a private source of aid, failing banks had no alternative to state aid, and without the healthy banks taking a hand in shaping the aid program, the state could adopt a stern line with the failing banks, requiring capital injections and only offering capital on punitively expensive terms. The state did pay above-market rates for the part-nationalization of RBS and Lloyds/HBOS, but only because the underwriting strategy used to encourage private participation backfired when the banks' share prices rapidly collapsed.

5 The United States and the 2007–2009 Crisis

The crisis in the United States was perhaps the most high profile in the 2007–2009 crisis, given the scale of the US financial system and the centrality of that system to global markets. Although the US federal system bears some similarities to Germany's, in its response to banking crises, the United States much more closely resembles the United Kingdom. Like the United Kingdom, the US financial system is dominated by stock market capital. Both large and small banks play a significant role, but provide a minority of capital to the economy. Also like the United Kingdom, the United States has a long history of both laissez-faire approaches to economic management in good times and heavy-handed and compulsory intervention when banks run into distress. Therefore, while Germany relied on voluntary plans and avoided state ownership, nationalizing only the massive and about-to-collapse Hypo RE, the United States, like the United Kingdom, relied heavily on compulsory nationalizations and part-nationalizations, on terms that were generally favorable to the state and onerous to the banks. Because of this, the United States would be the most successful of the three cases in recovering the money it contributed to financial rescues, avoiding losses or turning a profit on the majority of its rescue operations.

The US response to the crisis would be sharply criticized, especially by domestic actors, as being far too generous and lenient to the banks and bankers. However, closer analysis of the US response, especially in comparison with responses elsewhere, casts those programs in a far more favorable light. Most of the banks dealt with in the crisis were handled by the Federal Deposit Insurance Corporation (FDIC) in a relatively low-profile manner. This obscured the fact that 335 banks and \$2.65 trillion in assets were managed in a way that both protected the taxpayers and the broader economy from losses and imposed real costs on bankers with minimal moral hazard problems[1] (Federal Deposit Insurance

[1] \$646 billion was from standard resolution procedures, and \$635 billion from the FDIC-brokered nationalization and sale of Wachovia.

Corporation, 2013a). The programs outside of the FDIC, especially the Troubled Asset Relief Program (TARP), similarly imposed higher costs on bankers than were generally perceived. Moreover, despite the extremely high immediate costs, the US programs were structured in such a way that the taxpayers' money had largely been returned by 2012.[2] In contrast, the comparably sized British and German programs remain at a loss, with the British plan not likely to produce gains for some time and the German plan predicted to produce a net loss to taxpayers (Scally, 2008).

The United States was able to implement such a plan in large part because the banks played an extremely small role in the drafting and implementation of rescue policies. The failing banks were shut out of the policy process almost entirely, with bank management not even kept in the loop by Treasury or Federal Reserve officials as those policymakers negotiated the banks' terms of sale. The healthy banks, which largely kept their access to policymakers, displayed virtually no interest in assisting their failing peers, except in circumstances where they could secure a good deal to themselves. This meant that attempts to organize private rescues, which succeeded in Germany, fell flat in the United States. However, this also meant that policymakers had a free hand to draft and implement policies they felt best defended the interests of the US state, taxpayers, and broader economy. As such, the shape of US bank rescue policies reflected not the influence of banks and bankers but the internal policy preferences and debates of US policymakers in the regulatory agencies and Congress.

As in the United Kingdom, the limited role played by both healthy and unhealthy banks in the United States can be traced to the structure of its national financial markets. The United States, to an even greater extent than the United Kingdom, is an exemplar of a capital market–based financial system, with stock markets providing over 80 percent of capital to firms, and banks under 20 percent (Beck, Demirgüç-Kunt, and Levine, 2009). This is much higher than Germany's 1:2 stock market–bank capital ratio and higher even than the United Kingdom's 1:1 ratio (Beck, Demirgüç-Kunt, and Levine, 2009). This in turn means greater competition between US banks due to the pressures for short term, easily broken arrangements created by a capital market–based system. As such, US banking has long been extremely atomized, with very little interfirm

[2] The FDIC-managed procedures imposed no losses on taxpayers, while the other capital injection programs have almost all produced positive returns. The chief outstanding losses are from the nationalization of the GSEs (Fannie Mae and Freddie Mac) and the automotive bailout component of TARP (US Department of the Treasury, 2013).

cooperation and no significant banking associations. Lobbying groups such as the American Banking Association and the Financial Services Roundtable exist, but have significantly less clout than the individual banks and no ability to organize the banks around a common cause. At times, the major banks may even take opposite sides on an issue than the banking associations. When the FDIC debated changes to the funding rules for its bank-funded Deposit Insurance Fund, the American Banking Association and Financial Services Roundtable were opposed by several of the major US banks. In that instance, reflecting the clout of the banks over the banking associations, the banks won the day over the bank lobbies (Bair, 2012, pp. 23–24).

In addition to being intensely competitive with each other, US banks before the crisis were functionally divided as well. British banks divide by scale but are generally universal banks, combining both investment and commercial banking functions. From 1933 to 1999, the Glass-Steagall Act legally divided American banks between deposit-taking commercial banks and securities-managing investment banks. Commercial banks focused on retail deposits and lending but were legally prohibited from engaging in stock market speculation, a task left to investment banks. With Glass-Steagall's repeal in 1999, the legal barriers to a universal banking disappeared, but until 2008, a practical divide between commercial and investment banks persisted. With the exception of Citigroup, banks moved to a universal banking model only timidly. The commercial banks in some cases obtained a small investment banking arm but remained primarily focused on commercial banking activities. Similarly, no investment bank obtained or developed a commercial banking arm of any significant size.

The divided banking system in the US is matched by a similarly divided and patchwork regulatory regime. Although the Federal Reserve is given formal authority to regulate the entire banking system, in practice regulation is divided between half a dozen federal agencies, in addition to state-level regulators. As of 2007, regulation of the national commercial banks was divided between the Office of the Comptroller of the Currency (OCC) and the Office of Thrift Supervision (OTS), independent agencies housed within the Department of the Treasury. The OTS would be merged into the OCC in 2011. Additionally, the FDIC serves both as the manager of the national deposit insurance program and a "backup" regulator, with the power to second-guess the primary regulator's opinions. Investment banks were more lightly regulated, with responsibilities divided between the Federal Reserve and the Securities and Exchange Commission (SEC). The SEC, however, focused more on fraud prevention than systemic stability (United States Congress House Committee on Financial Services, 2011, p. 66). Because of the geographic concentration of investment banking on Wall Street, the Federal Reserve Bank of New York was especially prominent in Fed regulation of the investment banks. A final regulator relevant in the 2007–2009 crisis was the Office of Federal Housing Enterprise Oversight (OFHEO), overseeing the government-sponsored but privately owned and run Fannie Mae and Freddie Mac, major purchasers of mortgages and mortgage-backed securities. Beyond the federal level, state regulators were in charge of financial institutions without a national charter, though commonly took their lead from the national regulators and operated under Federal Reserve supervision.

This divided regulatory regime makes US crisis management almost inevitably a negotiation between various agencies claiming jurisdiction. In theory, this could make the US system more permeable to firm influence than Germany's single regulator model. Prior to their merger into a single agency in 2011, the OTS and the OCC, in particular, jealously guarded their prerogatives against each other and against the FDIC (Bair, 2012, pp. 32, 41, 77). In practice, however, the limited capacity of US firms for collective action means that firms play little direct role in shaping policy, responding to state proposals rather than helping to shape them.

Because of the divided nature of the US regulatory regime, there are substantially different policies and precedents in place when different types of financial institutions fall, reflecting the historical commercial investment bank divide. Prior to 2008, the United States adopted a laissez-faire attitude toward investment banks. Distressed investment banks were allowed to fail, and their customers were assumed to be "sophisticated investors," capable of understanding and managing the risks involved in stock market speculation (United States Congress House Committee on Financial Services, 2011, pp. 66, 555). Commercial bank customers, however, were not assumed to have such specialized financial risk management expertise. Unlike sophisticated investors, these general depositors are less capable of informing themselves of risks through an in-depth understanding of market signals and less able to insulate themselves from the risks of bank failure through diversified investments. General depositors, therefore, are both more vulnerable and, because of that vulnerability, more likely to engage in panic behavior. Such bank panics and runs can exacerbate problems and even cause healthy banks to fail on only the rumor of distress. Moreover, because general depositors are both more numerous and more likely to lose the vast majority of their savings in a bank failure, the collapse of a commercial bank could cause substantial economic catastrophe should those deposits be wiped out.

As such, the United States has long had in place a mechanism to resolve failed commercial banks through the FDIC. The FDIC guarantees that insured depositor accounts will be covered up to a set limit, $250,000 as of October 2008, insulating general depositors from fear of losses. To maintain this guarantee, the FDIC has a standing pool of money, prefunded by levies on insured banks, and statutory authority to temporarily nationalize insured banks. As such, bank failures, even of large institutions or of a large number of institutions, can be handled in a predictable procedure, relying on established protocols and resources. This has the added advantage of avoiding a scramble by regulators to develop an ad hoc solution, which will likely prove to be suboptimal given the time constraints of policymaking in a financial crisis.

The situation is quite different for the investment banks and other non–FDIC-insured financial firms. The dominant approach for SEC or Federal Reserve regulators assumed that the typical investment bank client was a "sophisticated investor," capable of understanding and absorbing the risks of financial speculation (United States Congress House Committee on Financial Services, 2011, pp. 66, 555). While aid to unsophisticated depositors is seen as necessary to prevent panics, aid to sophisticated investors would be problematic from a moral hazard perspective, insulating them from risks they should have understood and prepared for. Moreover, until the 1990s, investment banks tended to be considerably smaller than their commercial bank peers, meaning the potential for damage to the wider economy from their collapse was more limited (United States Congress House Committee on Financial Services, 2011, p. 73). For most of the period since the enactment of Glass-Steagall, US investment banks and other financial firms had no set procedures for dealing with failures. Rather, each failure was dealt with on an ad hoc basis. While the commercial banks were dealt with in a relatively straightforward fashion, regulators would scramble to find a solution to each individual investment bank or other financial firm in distress. This approach was largely sufficient from the Second World War through the 1980s, a period of relative financial stability in the United States and a period in which investment banks were considerably smaller and less interconnected than their commercial bank peers.

In the decades prior to the 2007–2009 crisis, however, the increasing size and interconnectedness of the non–FDIC-insured institutions grew more problematic, and regulators proved more willing to take more substantial steps to cushion the blow of their collapse. The 1990 collapse of Drexel Burnham Lambert, at the time the country's fifth largest investment bank, would be the last time until Lehman's failure in 2008 that US regulators would let an investment bank simply fall into bankruptcy. The Federal Reserve would step up to provide liquidity support to the other investment banks, such that they would not fail as a result of an inability to borrow in the panic surrounding Drexel's collapse, but no measures were taken to prevent Drexel's collapse (United States Congress House Committee on Financial Services, 2011, p. 73). The following year, investment bank Salomon Brothers also ran into difficulties, this time related to financial malfeasance and subsequent fines imposed by the SEC. Again, the United States did not intervene directly, and Salomon only avoided failure by selling itself to Travelers Group, an insurance company (Lowenstein, 2000, pp. 114–116). These two failures typified the twentieth-century approach to managing investment bank failure in the United States, with the banks either allowed to fail or pushed into mergers and the state playing a minimal role in managing those failures.

By 1998, however, US regulators abandoned their previous willingness to tolerate the failure of a major institution. Long-Term Capital Management (LTCM), a large hedge fund, was far smaller than Drexel or Salomon Brothers, but the Federal Reserve nevertheless put significant effort into organizing a rescue. Federal Reserve chairman Alan Greenspan judged that, because LTCM was highly interconnected, its failure would impose too severe losses on the major Wall Street firms (Bair, 2012, pp. 195–201; Lowenstein, 2000; United States Congress House Committee on Financial Services, 2011, p. 88). Therefore, the Fed broke from the sophisticated investor approach and organized a private consortium rescue of the ailing hedge fund. While such rescues are not uncommon in Germany, they are extremely rare in the atomized US financial system. LTCM's rescue was possible only because of three key factors. The major banks were exposed enough to LTCM that its failure would cost them significantly (Bair, 2012, pp. 194–195; Lowenstein, 2000; United States Congress House Committee on Financial Services, 2011, p. 88). At the same time, LTCM was small enough to not be a competitor to the major investment banks, such that the banks saw little opportunity to gain from its collapse (Lowenstein, 2000, pp. 207, 215). Even these two factors would likely have been insufficient without the Fed playing a strong coordinating role to overcome collective action problems.

Even as US regulators shifted away from tolerating losses to sophisticated investors, they simultaneously rolled back financial regulations. This seeming paradox illustrates the strength of US financial actors when healthy. Although little deregulation followed the 1999 repeal of the Glass-Steagall commercial/investment bank separation, regulators also declined to expand regulation to the increasingly important world of "shadow banking," unregulated financial actors paralleling the functions of the commercial banks. They also declined to regulate new financial instruments, such as Credit Default Swaps (CDS) and Collateralized Debt Obligations (CDOs), which purported to allow banks to lower their capital ratios by better distributing risks of losses (Stiglitz, 2010, p. 141; United States Congress House Committee on Financial Services, 2011 pp. 59, 60, 89; Wessel, 2010, p. 64). As these new unregulated institutions and instruments became increasingly important, an increasing portion of US financial activity was unregulated, even without the repeal of existing regulations.

Regulators were not bind to the dangers of systemic risk, but generally stymied in their attempts to address the problem. In 2006, the new Treasury Secretary, Henry Paulson, anticipated the threat of a financial crisis in the investment banks, though by his own admission neither the scale nor the proximate cause (Paulson, 2010, pp. 47, 94, 139; Sorkin, 2009, p. 83; Wessel, 2010, p. 176). Paulson, a former CEO of Goldman Sachs, sought to develop a systemic response plan for investment bank failure, hoping to give the Treasury as clear a wind-down authority for investment banks as the FDIC possessed for commercial banks. Despite initial support from Barney Frank, the Ranking Minority Member of the House Financial Services Committee, the difficulty of passing major financial reform without the pressure of a crisis meant that the plan never advanced beyond the hypothetical stage (Paulson, 2010, p. 139).

Therefore, when the United States entered the crisis, beginning in 2007, two very different response regimes were in place, depending on the type of institution in distress. For the commercial banks, a very clear regime existed under the auspices of the FDIC, with a large pool of money at the FDIC's disposal for just such an occasion, paid by a levy on the FDIC-insured institutions. Until the scale of the crisis became extremely large, the FDIC encountered relatively little difficulty in resolving those firms under its purview. The non–FDIC-insured institutions, however, had no such clear authority. Despite Paulson's proposal, the regulatory regime had not substantially evolved beyond where it was when Drexel failed in 1990 and reflected neither the increased size and interconnectedness of the investment banks nor the wider range of increasingly unsophisticated investors exposed to the consequences of investment bank failure. This would create, therefore, two very different dynamics of policy response between the two types of banks. Each can be evaluated separately, but since both responses were implemented simultaneously, a brief overview of the timeline of events in the US crisis is necessary.

Timeline

The first major US institution to run into trouble was Countrywide Financial, an FDIC-insured institution heavily invested in subprime mortgages. When those assets began to lose value, Countrywide fell into distress and was ultimately resolved by being purchased by Bank of America in January 2008 without the involvement of policymakers (Bair, 2012, p. 76). The next major institution to run into problems was Bear Stearns, the smallest of the five major investment houses. In March 2008, Bear would be sold to JP Morgan-Chase, a large commercial bank, in a deal in which $29 billion of Bear Stearns' anticipated losses from subprime assets would be absorbed by the Federal Reserve. The $29 billion deal, which came to be known as a "Jamie Deal" after JP Morgan CEO Jamie Dimon, was the only example of the US government directly subsidizing a sale and would complicate future rescues, as other would-be buyers would demand their own "Jamie Deals."

On July 14, IndyMac, a major commercial bank, would be resolved through the FDIC's temporary nationalization procedure. The following month, Fannie Mae and Freddie Mac, private firms with a quasi-public function in the mortgage industry, would be put into conservatorship, a form of nationalization, by their regulators. The crisis reached its apex in September, with the near-simultaneous distress of the third and fourth largest investment banks, Merrill Lynch and Lehman Brothers, and of a massive insurance company, American International Group (AIG). AIG would be part-nationalized; Merrill Lynch sold to Bank of America; and Lehman Brothers declared bankrupt, all in the same week. The last remaining major investment banks, Morgan Stanley and Goldman Sachs, would then reorganize themselves as bank holding companies, increasing regulatory oversight but allowing them to borrow from the Federal Reserve. Two more massive commercial banks would also fail with the next few weeks, as Washington Mutual ("WaMu") would be seized by the FDIC and sold to JP Morgan, and Wachovia would be sold to another major commercial bank, Wells Fargo, in a sale negotiated by the FDIC.

Following this tumultuous month, the United States organized a systemic response plan – the TARP – under which the United States made direct investment, or partial nationalization, in both investment and commercial banks. Partial nationalization was mandatory for the nine largest US banks and after that became a voluntary plan. Major firms to accept TARP injections after the initial announcement included

AIG, Citigroup, and Bank of America, as well as Chrysler and General Motors, two of the Big Three US automakers.

The Commercial Banks and the FDIC

Unsurprisingly, much of the attention given to US response policies in the 2007–2009 crisis focused on the ad hoc rescues of the investment banks and other major financial institutions. These rescues produced the greatest drama, given the scramble for policymakers to respond quickly and in unprecedented ways. They are also instances where policymakers could most credibly be accused of bending to financial interests or providing an undeserved bailout to the financial industry.

Overlooked in much of the discussion of the US responses to the banking crisis were the failures of the commercial banks and the role the FDIC played in resolving those failures. Although it did not get the attention of the other agencies, the FDIC oversaw the resolution of by far the majority of institutions in crisis and a significant portion of the assets involved as well, resolving 335 banks and $2.65 trillion in assets (Federal Deposit Insurance Corporation, 2013a). Among the banks that failed were several of systemic importance. Independent National Mortgage Corporation ("IndyMac"), with $30 billion in assets, was, at the time of its failure, the second largest bankruptcy in US history (Lowenstein, 2010, p. 144). WaMu held $307 billion in assets, making it comparable to Bear Stearns in size (Federal Deposit Insurance Corporation, 2013a). Wachovia, resolved through an FDIC-brokered sale to Bank of America rather than receivership, rivaled Lehman Brothers in size, with $635 billion in assets to Lehman's $639 billion (Federal Deposit Insurance Corporation, 2013b).

The FDIC resolved these banks on what is essentially a temporary nationalization model. If a member bank falls below a certain capital threshold and the judgment is made by the bank's regulators that the firm is no longer solvent, the FDIC puts that bank into conservatorship or receivership. The FDIC takes ownership of the bank, wiping out the existing owners' value and resolving the bank's assets and liabilities. The remaining property of the bank, including physical property and financial assets, are sold whole (in a conservatorship) or piecemeal (in a receivership) to other banks. Depositor accounts are, if possible, sold to another commercial bank, typically in a process arranged in advance of the nationalization to minimize market disruptions and the time the bank is in public hands (FDIC representatives, interview by author, 2011). In the absence of a buyer, depositors are paid up to a set amount on their accounts, $250,000 as of October 3, 2008. Debts to creditors are settled on the basis of seniority as in a bankruptcy proceeding. The capital needed to manage this process is drawn from the FDIC's Deposit Insurance Fund, which all insured banks pay into. Any profits realized from the resolution of a failed bank go back into the Fund.

This is a highly effective model for resolving the failure of commercial banks, solving a number of problems arising from bank failure. Because the resolution process has been established policy for decades, there is little uncertainty about what will happen when a commercial bank runs into problems, and little of the time-consuming and expensive debate and uncertainty that surrounds the failure of other financial institutions, which lack pre-set resolution plans and must be resolved on an ad hoc basis. Market investors react poorly to the uncertainty surrounding the distress of an American investment bank or a German universal bank, but can anticipate what will happen when an FDIC-insured bank fails (FDIC representatives, interview by author, 2011). Timely resolution also contains the costs of a bank failure. The longer a bank lingers in limbo, the greater the costs of resolving it, as more and more investors desert it. Acting quickly can avoid the most extreme of these losses. Most importantly, FDIC nationalization minimizes damage to the broader economy. Depositors are covered up to a set high amount, and other creditors can expect an orderly resolution of their situations. This is all done with a minimum of moral hazard, as bank owners still bear the costs of their firm's failure, receive at best a fraction of the firm's value. Because the nationalization is explicitly temporary, the FDIC rarely finds itself owning a bank for long (FDIC representatives, interview by author, 2011). Thus, the potential negative effects of state ownership of a portion of the financial sector are mitigated.

In the crisis, the FDIC proved adept at managing even the failure of large and systemically important institutions. Although it went largely unremarked at the time, the 335 banks with $2.65 trillion in assets resolved between 2007 and 2011 made up the vast majority of distressed institutions, and although exact asset values are difficult to calculate, a significant portion of the total assets were held by distressed institutions in the crisis (Federal Deposit Insurance Corporation, 2013a). The FDIC resolved these institutions with a minimum of moral hazard, given its approach of mandatory nationalization at minimal compensation. Due to its industry-funded Deposit Insurance Fund, these institutions were resolved at no cost to the taxpayer. Moreover, the disruptions caused by these resolutions were relatively minor, especially compared to the panic surrounding the major investment banks and nonbank financial institutions. Even IndyMac's closure caused relatively little concern and occurred with a minimum of politicking (Bair, 2012, p. 80; Sorkin, 2009, p. 190; United States Congress House Committee on Financial Services, 2011, p. 408). Only the largest two commercial banks to fail, WaMu and Wachovia, saw intense political pressure, and even then the FDIC showed a consistent focus on resolving with a minimum of moral hazard.

Washington Mutual

WaMu, with $307 billion in assets at the time of its closure, was the largest insured depository institution in United States to fail and comparable in size to Bear Stearns (Federal Deposit Insurance Corporation, 2013a; United States Congress House Committee on Financial Services, 2011, p. 408). Although it was 110 years old, WaMu had only in the last three decades evolved from being a small Seattle area community bank to one of the United States' largest financial institutions (Grind, 2012, p. 14). Much of its rapid growth came through its mortgage business, leaving the bank highly exposed to a collapse in the value of mortgage-backed assets. In the last quarter of 2007, WaMu took $1.9 billion in mortgage losses, with another $1.1 billion in losses in the first quarter of 2008 (United States Congress House Committee on Financial Services, 2011, p. 408).

Initially, the primary regulator, the OTS, sought to keep WaMu open and independent, declining to pressure WaMu into a sale to JP Morgan despite the urgings of the FDIC (Grind, 2012, pp. 188–189; United States Congress House Committee on Financial Services, 2011, p. 89). The OTS' support of WaMu, however, only lasted so long as WaMu could remain open without assistance. After the fall of IndyMac that July, and as WaMu's losses rose, the OTS joined the other regulators in pressuring WaMu to sell itself (Bair, 2012, p.91; Grind, 2012, p. 292). The FDIC began soliciting buyers for WaMu, both as an open bank under private ownership and as a closed bank, after an FDIC seizure to put it in receivership (Bair, 2012, p. 92; Grind, 2012, p. 284; Lowenstein, 2010, p. 239).

WaMu management refused to sell the bank, unwilling to accept the low prices offered by buyers, and petitioned the state for support to keep it open as an independent entity (Grind, 2012, p. 294). New WaMu CEO Alan Fishman admitted that his predecessors had mismanaged WaMu, but nevertheless petitioned for $20 billion in Treasury loans despite the moral hazard, in order to preserve systemic stability. Fishman argued that, despite the mess created by WaMu, "for the good of the country, these guys ought to be saved" (Grind, 2012, p. 294). These pleas fell on deaf ears at the Federal Reserve, Treasury, and FDIC, and plans were made to put the bank into receivership. JP Morgan, which had been rebuked by WaMu management in its efforts to buy the bank directly, gladly bought it out of receivership (Bair, 2012, pp. 90, 92; Grind, 2012, p. 246). The FDIC concealed that the other potential buyers – Santander, Wells Fargo, and Citi – declined to bid, so that JP Morgan would make a competitive offer. When CEO Jamie Dimon learned after the fact that JP Morgan was the only bidder for WaMu, he could only rue that, if he had known, he "would have bid a dollar" (Bair, 2012, p. 92; United States Congress House Committee on Financial Services, 2011, p. 485).

The resolution of WaMu demonstrated the strength of the FDIC resolution process. WaMu shareholders and management were wiped out, and the bank resolved at no cost to taxpayers, avoiding both moral hazard and perverse redistribution issues. However, unlike in a bankruptcy, WaMu's resolution was orderly and caused relatively minimal market disruption. Moreover, because the predetermined bid process enabled greater secrecy than ad hoc proceedings, the FDIC was able to prevent JP Morgan from realizing its potential leverage as the sole interested buyer. The WaMu resolution also illustrates the limits of a bank's influence. WaMu had the ability to keep the support of the OTS and resist FDIC pressures to merge so long as it could sustain itself without state support. Once WaMu's health declined, the OTS quickly shifted position to be in line with the FDIC and forced the bank to accept receivership. Would-be saviors, such as JP Morgan, chose to let the government resolution play out and buy WaMu out of receivership rather than petition for state aid to obtain the bank from its original private owners.

Wachovia

Shortly after WaMu's failure, Wachovia came under pressure. Through its acquisition of Golden West, Wachovia had exposed itself to the same toxic asset problems as WaMu and IndyMac before it (Bair, 2012, p. 95). However, Wachovia was substantially larger than even these two institutions, with twice as much asset value as WaMu and twenty times that of IndyMac (Federal Deposit Insurance Corporation, 2013a). Because of this, despite the success of the WaMu resolution, both Paulson and New York Federal Reserve President Timothy Geithner expressed concern about the FDIC process going forward (Sorkin, 2009, pp. 496–497; United States Congress House Committee on Financial Services, 2011,

p. 486; Wessel, 2010, p. 220). They feared that the losses to debtholders at Wachovia would be too great and that the takeover would disturb already nervous markets to an unacceptable amount. Therefore, they moved for an ad hoc emergency procedure. Even here, though, the FDIC showed a clear focus on minimizing moral hazard, resisting pressure for a subsidized sale.

Although the Federal Reserve, especially Geithner, wanted Wachovia to be sold rather than placed into receivership, Wachovia's toxic asset problems and the precedent of Bear Stearns' subsidized sale made it difficult to attract a buyer without government assistance (Sorkin, 2009, pp. 472, 495). Wachovia's own management opposed both receivership and subsidized sale and offered instead a proposal for Wachovia to raise its own capital and remain an independent institution. This proposal was not regarded as serious by anyone in the intraregulator debates and was dismissed accordingly (Wessel, 2010, p. 222). Although some in the debate, especially Geithner, wanted to keep Wachovia out of receivership, this was not due to pressure from Wachovia management or shareholders, who were ultimately largely shut out of the debate.

Instead, the FDIC would make the crucial decisions on the fate of Wachovia. Once support for a state-assisted sale was agreed to in principle, two offers remained, from Citi and from Wells Fargo. Citi offered $1 per share and wanted the FDIC to cover all losses on a $312 billion pool of toxic assets after an initial $42 billion in losses to Citi. Wells Fargo wanted loss protection for a smaller $127 billion pool, but with Wells only absorbing the first $2 billion and 20 percent of losses beyond that (Bair, 2012, p. 102; United States Congress House Committee on Financial Services, 2011, p. 489). Initially the FDIC favored the Citi bid, which was estimated to cost the FDIC nothing, while the Wells Fargo bid would cost the FDIC an estimated $5.6–$7.2 billion (Bair, 2012, p. 102; United States Congress House Committee on Financial Services, 2011, p. 489). Therefore, only the Citi offer was presented to the Wachovia board. Given a choice between a sale to Citi and receivership, and no chance of the state supporting Wachovia as an independent institution, the board accepted the Citi bid (Bair, 2012, p. 102; Paulson, 2010, p. 317; Wessel, 2010, p. 224).

However, before Citi and Wachovia could close the deal, Wells Fargo made a second offer. Having examined Wachovia's books in greater detail and seeing tax advantages in being able to use Wachovia's losses to reduce taxable income, Wells Fargo made a new offer of $7 per share with no state assistantship (Bair, 2012, p. 104; United States Congress House Committee on Financial Services, 2011, p. 490; Wessel, 2010,

p. 224). Sheila Bair, the FDIC chair, and Paulson strongly favored the new bid, which, by being wholly private, not only removed risk from the government but also removed the moral hazard problem of providing another subsidized merger (Bair, 2012, p. 105; Paulson, 2010, p. 327). Geithner had some reluctance, concerned about a loss of credibility if the government backed down from an all-but-completed deal and hoping to use the merger to help prop up Citi as well (Bair, 2012, p. 105; Paulson, 2010, p. 327; Wessel, 2010, p. 226). Citi, still wanting to purchase Wachovia, offered to raise its price to $7 per share, if it could keep the loss-sharing agreement (Bair, 2012, p. 105; United States Congress House Committee on Financial Services, 2011, p. 491). The FDIC demurred, not wanting to help Citi win a bidding war against a rival that did not need government assistance, and the rival offer was presented to the Wachovia board (Bair, 2012, p. 105). Given the choice between a $7 per share bid from Wells Fargo, a $1 per share bid from Citi, and a loss of all shareholder value in receivership, the Wachovia board voted unanimously to merge with Wells Fargo (Bair, 2012, p. 105).

Even though receivership was not used for Wachovia, its resolution nevertheless illustrates the advantages that a standing procedure gives policymakers in negotiations with firms. In contrast to the investment banks, which could threaten to go into bankruptcy and wreak massive economic damage, Wachovia's alternative to accepting the mergers the government presented to it was receivership, a procedure causing far less collateral damage. Unlike the investment banks, Wachovia was unable to bluff its way into a better deal. The same held for the would-be buyers, which knew that their threats to let the bank fall into receivership would be less motivating to policymakers than if the alternative was bankruptcy.

The Wachovia resolution also illustrates how limited the influence of bankers were on the political process. Wachovia itself had virtually no leverage in the process, with the FDIC ultimately making all the crucial decisions and then presenting the Wachovia board with choices for which the advantages of the FDIC-approved course were overwhelming. The would-be buyers also had relatively little leverage. Wells' first proposal, which would have introduced substantial moral hazard, was rejected in favor of Citi's more favorable proposal. Citi in turn lacked the ability to convince the FDIC to help it buy Wachovia once Wells underbid it, despite Geithner's fears that breaking the already negotiated deal would have real reputational costs for the United States. The FDIC, moreover, again illustrated its focus on moral hazard concerns and avoiding costs, resisting Geithner's pressures and opting to embrace the Well Fargo assistance-free plan.

Ad Hoc Rescues of the Investment Banks

Bear Stearns

The first of the five major US investment banks to run into trouble, Bear Stearns, also provided the first major break from precedent in dealing the collapse of an investment bank. While Drexel Burnham Lambert was allowed to fall into bankruptcy in 1990, and Salomon Brothers sold without subsidy in 1998, US regulators in 2007 decided early on that letting Bear go bankrupt would impose too great a cost on the broader economy (Lowenstein, 2010, p. 127). However, despite a growing recognition that letting investment banks fail now entailed too high collateral costs and Paulson's initial tentative steps to build a pre-established response capacity, the fall of Bear Stearns caught regulators off-guard (Kelly, 2009, p. 67; Paulson, 2010, p. 93). Lacking the legal authority to resolve the bank through state action other than bankruptcy and unable to find a buyer to take Bear Stearns without a state subsidy, US policymakers would ultimately subsidize the purchase of Bear by a large commercial bank, JP Morgan-Chase. The loss guarantee deal for Bear Stearns produced the most naked moral hazard in the US response, with the state providing a direct subsidy to a private bank to insulate it from losses. However, even this case illustrates the dynamics of atomized finance in the United States. The deal ultimately agreed to was good for the buyer, JP Morgan-Chase, but bad for Bear Stearns shareholders, who took heavy losses on the sale. JP Morgan, which remained healthy through the crisis, was able to take advantage of its continued influence and the disorganized response of US policymakers to Bear's failure to negotiate favorable terms for itself, even as it allowed heavy costs to be imposed on Bear shareholders.

Bear Stearns was the smallest of the US investment banks and also the most highly leveraged. In its bid for rapid growth, Bear took on $386 billion in debts and other liabilities, while holding only $11.6 billion in equity capital to service those liabilities (United States Congress House Committee on Financial Services, 2011, p. 18). This was well in excess of legal limits on capital ratios, limits that Bear eluded by disguising its balance sheets when it came time to make quarterly earnings reports to regulators and shareholders. Basically, Bear manipulated its capital ratio by selling assets with high liabilities just before earnings reports were due, temporarily increasing its equity and decreasing its liabilities to within legal limits. It then bought those assets back immediately after issuing its quarterly report (United States Congress House Committee on Financial Services, 2011, p. 374). Therefore, Bear's extremely high leverage was masked on paper. In order to service its massive liabilities in practice, Bear relied heavily on short-term lending, borrowing up to $70 billion in overnight lending, such that at close of business it was able to service its long-term debts, then paying that back the next morning only to borrow it again the following night (United States Congress House Committee on Financial Services, 2011, p. 18). These practices allowed Bear Stearns to grow rapidly, but left it extremely vulnerable and dependent on its short-term lenders. If one of its short-term lenders were to refuse to continue to lend, Bear Stearns would very quickly be unable to service its debts and be forced to close.

This is ultimately what happened to trigger Bear's demise. Goldman Sachs refused to serve as counterparty in a routine $5 million trade between Bear Stearns and Hayman Capital (United States Congress House Committee on Financial Services, 2011, pp. 383–384). A counterparty essentially guarantees that the parties involved will pay their obligations, so Goldman's refusal to serve as a counterparty for Bear Stearns sent a devastating signal to markets that Bear could no longer be trusted to honor its short-term obligations. Sixteen minutes later, Goldman relented and agreed to serve as counterparty, but the damage was done, and Bear found itself increasingly unable to get the short-term loans it needed to function (United States Congress House Committee on Financial Services, 2011, p. 384).

A combination of lax oversight by the SEC, Bear Stearns' primary regulator, and Bear's own quarterly chicanery meant that Bear's failure caught US policymakers off-guard and unprepared to respond. While in the past investment banks had been regarded as small enough that their failure could be absorbed by markets, the growth in their size and the number of counterparties that would suffer losses if Bear fell meant that US policymakers no longer felt that this was an acceptable course of action (Lowenstein, 2010, pp. 127, 175; Paulson, 2010, pp. 99, 109). Ben Bernanke, Chair of the Federal Reserve, feared that Bear Stearns' key role in the markets could have caused the collapse of the $2.8 trillion triparty repo market, a key part of the risk management strategy of financial institutions (United States Congress House Committee on Financial Services, 2011, p. 386). Paulson feared that the collapse of Bear Stearns would cause panicked investors to start a run on the next smallest investment bank, leading to the collapse of Lehman soon after (Paulson, 2010, p. 120; United States Congress House Committee on Financial Services, 2011, p. 388). Such an unexpected collapse, on the heels of Bear's already unexpected collapse, would have produced even greater disruption than Lehman's actual fall in September ultimately did. This was reinforced by panicked calls from other Wall Street actors, warning of potentially devastating consequences should Bear Stearns fail (Paulson, 2010, p. 106).

Policymakers, therefore, scrambled to find a solution. This process was marked by two key dynamics that shaped its outcome. The first was that Bear Stearns management and shareholders quickly lost their autonomy and voice in the process. In order to prevent Bear's collapse before a buyer could be found, the Federal Reserve issued the bank an emergency loan of $12.9 billion. Given that the loan was made on $14 billion in collateral and was paid back with $4 billion (31 percent) in interest after three days, this followed the Bagehot rule that central banks should lend freely on good collateral at a penalty rate of interest (Wessel, 2010, pp. 158–159). It also signaled the beginning of US policymakers taking over the process from Bear Stearns. The loan was formally a thirty-day loan, but when Bear CEO Alan Schwartz took that as a sign that he could take a more leisurely path toward selling his bank, he was sharply rebuked by the Federal Reserve. Schwartz was instructed to act immediately or his bank would be shuttered by regulators as insolvent (Kelly, 2009, p. 67; Paulson, 2010, p. 103). At this point, dependent on emergency aid from the Federal Reserve to remain open, Bear Stearns had little choice but to bow to Fed and Treasury demands.

The second key dynamic was the self-interest of the other banks, their unwillingness to act in the interest of broader systemic stability or of Bear Stearns, and their willingness to take advantage of the desperation of policymakers to find a solution. Despite Goldman CEO Lloyd Blankfein's stated fears of a financial "apocalypse" should Bear fall, he was unwilling to make an offer to purchase his failing rival, being more concerned with losses to his own bank than systemic stability (Paulson, 2010, p. 106). Paulson's attempts to convince Fannie Mae and Freddie Mac to play a role similarly met with disappointment (Lowenstein, 2010, p. 123). Ultimately, only two bidders emerged with an interest in providing a private solution to Bear Stearns: equity investor JC Flowers and commercial bank JP Morgan.

JP Morgan was an attractive potential savior for several reasons. It was large enough that, unlike with JC Flowers, a JP Morgan purchase of Bear Stearns could prevent the latter's failure without risking the stability of JP Morgan itself (Kelly, 2009, p. 164; Paulson, 2010, pp. 107, 127). It was also intimately familiar with Bear's operations already, having served as a major source of the short-term lending on which Bear sustained itself prior to the collapse (United States Congress House Committee on Financial Services, 2011, p. 386). Therefore, JP Morgan could research and make a decision on purchasing Bear much faster than other potential suitors. However, it was also the only viable candidate and, therefore, in a position to extract concessions from the United States by playing on policymakers' unwillingness to risk the systemic fallout from letting Bear fail. JP Morgan and its CEO Jamie Dimon, therefore, refused to make a purchase of Bear Stearns without state support.

This left US policymakers in a weak position. Caught unprepared to confront the failure of an uninsured institution of Bear Stearns' scale, they now had only three options: let Bear fail, which would have unknowable but likely high and possibly catastrophic consequences; extend loans to Bear Stearns in the unlikely hope that a suitor more willing to make an unsubsidized purchase would appear; or assent to JP Morgan's demands and subsidize the purchase. Direct purchase of Bear Stearns by the state, which could have saved Bear without subsidizing JP Morgan, was impossible in the time frame at hand, as neither the Federal Reserve nor the Treasury could make such a purchase with their existing legal authority, and Bear would not survive long enough to pass new legislation through the slow-moving US Congress (Wessel, 2010, p. 167). Given that an alternate purchaser seemed unlikely to emerge, the choices became between allowing Bear's failure and subsidizing the purchase. Unwilling to risk potentially catastrophic consequences, Treasury and Federal Reserve officials agreed to extend the subsidy.

The subsidy to JP Morgan, which became known as the "Jamie Deal," was a "backstop" on losses from a designated pool of Bear Stearns toxic assets, mostly mortgage-backed securities. As originally constructed, $29.97 billion of Bear Stearns assets were placed in a new legal entity, Maiden Lane LLC, funded by the Federal Reserve. As those assets matured, that money would be repaid to the Fed, though likely with high losses given their poor quality. The deal, therefore, essentially took $30 billion of risk away from JP Morgan (United States Congress House Committee on Financial Services, 2011, p. 386).

Although these terms were generous to JP Morgan, Paulson insisted that the terms to Bear Stearns shareholders be harsh, to limit the political fallout. Although JP Morgan was willing to offer $4 per share for its purchase of Bear Stearns, Paulson insisted on $2 per share, for shares valued at $172 per share a year prior (Kelly, 2009, pp. 9, 210; Paulson, 2010, pp. 111, 118; Sorkin, 2009, p. 37; United States Congress House Committee on Financial Services, 2011, p. 386). This would, therefore, at Paulson's insistence, impose severe losses on Bear shareholders (Kelly, 2009, p. 204; Lowenstein, 2010, p.128; Paulson, 2010, p. 111). Ultimately, those losses proved too severe for Bear shareholders, who, although shut out of policy deliberations to this point, still had the ability to refuse the deal and fall into bankruptcy. The difference between the negligible benefit of $2 a share and a total loss from bankruptcy would be only minor, so Bear shareholders refused to sell for less than $10 a share (Kelly, 2009, p. 208; Paulson, 2010, p. 119). This was acceptable to JP Morgan, but the Treasury balked, given Paulson's desire to impose pain on the Bear shareholders to limit the moral hazard of the deal. Paulson, therefore, threatened to withdraw the backstop, but this was in turn unacceptable to JP Morgan (Kelly, 2009, p. 215; Paulson, 2010, pp. 119, 120). Instead, the Treasury was able to modify the terms of the backstop, such that JP Morgan now contributed $1.15 billion to funding Maiden Lane, to be repaid only if the Federal Reserve received all of its money first. Therefore, in the final plan, JP Morgan would absorb the first $1.15 billion in losses on the Maiden Lane assets, with the Fed taking losses above that, up to $28.82 billion (United States Congress House Committee on Financial Services, 2011, p. 386). The merger went forward on March 16, 2008.

The Bear Stearns rescue illustrates the perils to the state of a voluntary rescue plan. The United States above all wanted to limit the systemic consequences of a Bear Stearns collapse, while JP Morgan was willing to risk systemic fallout unless it could get favorable terms. JP Morgan's greater tolerance for the consequences of a Bear collapse put the United States at a severe disadvantage. Without a rival bidder, JP Morgan could at any time threaten to walk away, while US threats to let Bear Stearns fall were not regarded as credible. This illustrates how US financial firms can continue to wield significant influence, so long as they are healthy. At the same time, the Bear Stearns case also illustrates how the influence of firms drops off considerably once they are in distress. Prior to the fall, Bear was an extremely powerful financial actor, but once it began to fail, and especially once it became reliant on Federal Reserve loans to survive, Bear management and shareholders were all but completely shut out of policy deliberations (Kelly, 2009, p. 102). The Fed and Treasury set the terms of any potential sale in negotiation with would-be buyers, and Bear management were put in the position of simply receiving those terms. The one bit of influence they had, increasing the sale price, was only possible because the initial price proposed, $2 a share, was close enough to bankruptcy that Bear could credibly threaten to simply take bankruptcy instead. Even here, Bear's intransigence managed to secure only a purchase price of 5.8 percent of its value a year prior, rather than 1.2 percent, only a slight improvement and still a substantial loss to Bear shareholders (Kelly, 2009, p. 6). JP Morgan was willing to acquiesce to this higher sale price, but only because it still represented a good deal to JP Morgan. JP Morgan initially proposed $4 a share, but gladly bowed to Treasury pressure for $2 a share, which was an even better deal. This illustrates that JP Morgan had little regard for Bear Stearns, except insofar as making the deal required the assent of the Bear Stearns Board of Directors.

The resolution of Bear Stearns was, therefore, a severe blow to Bear Stearns' shareholders, but a good deal for JP Morgan's, especially with the Maiden Lane loss backstop. In the short term, it could be seen as a good deal for the United States as well, as the costs of a Bear Stearns failure would have surely exceeded $29 billion (Paulson, 2010, p. 120; United States Congress House Committee on Financial Services, 2011, pp. 387, 388; Wessel, 2010, p. 175). The losses to Bear shareholders preserved some market discipline for failing firms. However, the precedent of the "Jamie Deal" would haunt US policymakers in the later stages of the crisis, as other healthy banks attempted to leverage their position to extract similar concessions. The desire to remove the precedent set by the Jamie Deal would be cited as a major reason for letting Lehman Brothers fall six months later.

Lehman Brothers

The failure of Bear Stearns cast doubt on the next two smallest investment banks, Lehman Brothers and Merrill Lynch, both of which would fail by September 2008. Lehman Brothers would declare bankruptcy, while Merrill Lynch would sell itself to Bank of America to avoid a similar collapse. Their resolution, and the relationship of the two banks with policymakers, demonstrates both the way in which political influence declines with fiscal health and the commitment of US policymakers to avoid moral hazard problems. Merrill Lynch, which was the stronger of the two banks, retained enough clout to preserve its autonomy and negotiate its own sale, though not enough clout to secure state assistance. Lehman Brothers lost even the ability to negotiate its own resolution, and instead its management was sidelined while US officials attempted to broker a sale and a private consortium rescue. When those attempts failed, the United States chose to let Lehman Brothers fall rather than provide a direct subsidy to the failing bank or any would-be purchaser. This precipitated massive financial crashes globally, but decisively erased the precedent of the Bear Stearns bailout, illustrating a strong commitment by the US government to avoid moral hazard issues.

Both Merrill Lynch and Lehman Brothers had difficulties stemming from subprime assets before Bear Stearns' collapse, but the unexpected fall of the smallest of Wall Street's Big Five investment banks put substantial pressure on Merrill and Lehman, the third and fourth largest of the remaining investment banks. Absent a deposit insurance provision, investors looking to protect themselves from losses must pull out their investments before the firm loses value. This withdrawal in turn causes the firm to lose value, making projections of decline a self-fulfilling prophecy. Nervous investors, taken off-guard by the fall of Bear, assumed that others would look askance at the next smallest institutions (United States Congress House Committee on Financial Services, 2011, pp. 397, 433). They therefore began to withdraw their investments and, in doing so, caused Lehman and Merrill to decline from an already vulnerable position. Investors' fears were compounded when both banks failed stress tests imposed by the Federal Reserve and the SEC in late spring 2008 (United States Congress House Committee on Financial Services, 2011, p. 397). Lehman contested these results, claiming the bank passed their own internal stress tests with liquidity to spare, but this did little to assuage doubtful investors, and pressures increased (United States Congress House Committee on Financial Services, 2011, p. 398).

By August, Treasury and Federal Reserve regulators began to worry that Lehman Brothers was already insolvent, masking its insolvency by refusing to fully acknowledge the decline in the value of its assets (United States Congress House Committee on Financial Services, 2011, p. 432). Lehman management maintained that the bank was solvent and suffering only from liquidity pressures caused by "naked shorts," (Sorkin, 2009, pp. 96–100; United States Congress House Committee on Financial Services, 2011, p. 435).[3] Lehman CEO Dick Fuld would maintain even after the bank's collapse that the problem was always liquidity pressure from unfounded rumors, and not mismanagement by the bank itself (Sorkin, 2009, p. 507; United States Congress House Committee on Financial Services, 2011, p. 435). However, such claims were treated skeptically, given Lehman management's desire to make a case for state assistance by painting their problems as external. This created a private information dilemma for regulators, who could neither trust Lehman's own statements nor compel it to reveal its true position without potentially triggering a run that would sink the bank regardless of its solvency. Because of this, planning for a Lehman collapse needed to remain only roughly sketched out, without access to specific figures (United States Congress House Committee on Financial Services, 2011, p. 438).

The first preference of policymakers was to sell Lehman Brothers to another bank, a move that would potentially save the bank without

[3] A naked short is in essence a bet that a given asset, such as Lehman Brothers stock, would fall in value. Although such a short does not require the purchase of Lehman stock, the number of investors betting against Lehman Brothers increased pressure on the bank by decreasing confidence in its stability and discouraging other financial actors from lending to it.

imposing a cost on the state (Paulson, 2010, p. 130). This was contrary to the wishes of Lehman management, which sought to preserve the bank as an independent institution. Lehman, therefore, pressed for direct liquidity and capital support from the Federal Reserve (Lowenstein, 2010, p. 149). These petitions, however, found little positive reception at the Federal Reserve or the Treasury. A proposal by Fuld to reclassify Lehman Brothers as a bank holding company, and thus be regulated by the Federal Reserve and able to borrow directly from the Fed's Discount Window, was rejected by all relevant regulators. New York Fed President Timothy Geithner described the proposal as "gimmicky" (United States Congress House Committee on Financial Services, 2011, p. 437). When it became clear that Lehman Brothers would need capital support, and not just liquidity support, Fuld pressed the Federal Reserve to find a way to make a direct capital injection into Lehman Brothers (United States Congress House Committee on Financial Services, 2011). Fed Chair Ben Bernanke refused, arguing that he lacked the authority to do so.

Policymakers spent the first weeks of September attempting to broker a sale or capital injection from a private bank to Lehman. Lehman, however, balked at the fire sale prices those institutions offered and continued to hope for direct assistance from the US government. Fuld sabotaged discussions with Korea Development Bank over a potential capital injection by insisting on an above-market purchase price and that the Koreans take some of Lehman's toxic assets (Sorkin, 2009, pp. 116, 215). Negotiations with JP Morgan never even reached the point of Fuld's involvement. JP Morgan negotiators dubbed the representatives Lehman sent to talks the "Junior Varsity" and took it as a sign that Lehman was not serious about negotiations (United States Congress House Committee on Financial Services, 2011, p. 440). Lehman representatives retorted that JP Morgan was just using the negotiations as cover to probe Lehman's confidential records and plans, which would enable them to better poach Lehman's clients and to profit at Lehman's expense (United States Congress House Committee on Financial Services, 2011, p. 440).

Lehman's intransigence in negotiating sales increased the pressure on the bank, as each failed negotiation caused market investors to lose more faith in Lehman Brothers. In contrast to Germany, where the healthy banks organized consortium rescues for the ailing ones, US banks increased the pressure on Lehman to protect their own positions. JP Morgan, Citi, and Bank of America all demanded additional collateral from Lehman Brothers, or they would refuse to continue providing essential interbank lending (United States Congress House Committee on Financial Services, 2011, p. 439). Lehman, therefore, posted an additional $3.6 billion in collateral from its dwindling capital reserves to maintain the interbank lending it needed to survive. Fuld continued to press for a direct injection from the Federal Reserve (United States Congress House Committee on Financial Services, 2011, p. 440). US policymakers continued to refuse, but grew increasingly frustrated with Fuld. As such, by September 10, when only Bank of America and Barclays remained as potential buyers of Lehman, policymakers would eliminate Fuld's role entirely (Sorkin, 2009, p. 270). When Bank of America CEO Ken Lewis complained of Fuld's resistance to a sale, Treasury Secretary Paulson replied that it "doesn't matter what Fuld thinks" and that he was "in no condition to make any decisions" (Sorkin, 2009, p. 303, 319). By this point in the process, Lehman management was not only excluded from debates but was no longer even kept informed as to the status of negotiations, unable to get their telephone calls returned as the sale of Lehman Brothers was negotiated (Sorkin, 2009, pp. 306, 328).

Negotiating a final sale with either Bank of America or Barclays would remain complicated even with Fuld removed, however, due to the precedent set by the "Jamie Deal" the Federal Reserve provided in JP Morgan's purchase of Bear Stearns. Both potential buyers, in addition to offering only fire sale prices for Lehman Brothers, insisted that no deal could take place without state support. Both demanded that the United States provide $40 billion in loss guarantees (Sorkin, 2009, pp. 282, 319). In doing so, the banks not only looked out for their own self-interest but bet that policymakers would rather repeat the moral hazard–creating precedent from Bear Stearns than deal with the consequences of Lehman's collapse. Policymakers, however, refused to consider another Jamie Deal. In addition to the political cost, another loss backstop would cement the precedent set by Bear Stearns, meaning that any further brokered sale would likely contain a similar provision. The pressure for another such backstop would be felt immediately, as both Merrill Lynch and giant insurance company AIG were distressed and seeking buyers at the same time.

Unwilling to provide state assistance, policymakers instead attempted to organize a consortium of private banks to provide the necessary loss backstop, essentially attempting to create a privately funded Jamie Deal, similar to the 1998 rescue of LTCM. This would be good for the United States, which would avoid deepening the Bear Stearns precedent, but also potentially good for the banks, given that the alternative, a Lehman collapse, could be expected to impose high and unpredictable costs on all other banks in the ensuing panic. Four key factors, however, distinguished the LTCM rescue from the situation with Lehman Brothers. First was the scale. While the potential costs of a Lehman failure would also be higher than those of an LTCM failure, the direct cost to banks to rescue Lehman was significantly higher. Bank of America and Barclays insisted on a $40–$50 billion loss backstop to purchase Lehman Brothers, compared to a $3.6 billion consortium rescue for LTCM (Lowenstein, 2000, p. 207; Sorkin, 2009, p. 282).

Second was that policymakers' statements that no government money would be forthcoming in any circumstance were not regarded as credible (Sorkin, 2009, p. 282). Although Paulson told the assembled bankers that not a penny of government assistance would be provided, Lehman Brothers' lawyer, Roger Cohen, maintained that this was a bluff. In his words, the government was playing "a game of chicken" and that policymakers were unwilling to let Lehman fall regardless of the success or failure of the liquidity consortium (United States Congress House Committee on Financial Services, 2011, p. 445). The United States had not let a major financial actor fall into bankruptcy since Drexel Burnham Lambert in 1990 and had provided support for a Bear Stearns sale only months earlier. This caused bankers to reasonably suspect the Fed would do so again for the larger and more systemically important Lehman Brothers.

Third, Lehman Brothers and its would-be rescuers were direct competitors. In a cooperative system like Germany's, subsidizing a peer institution is less problematic, as lower interbank competition and greater interdependence decreases the long-term costs of supporting a peer while also raising the costs of letting a peer fail. In a liberal system, however, any aid to either Lehman or its would-be purchaser would eventually result in the supported bank directly competing with its saviors. Several bank representatives at the Lehman consortium meetings raised this as their chief objection (Paulson, 2010, p. 192). Moreover, concerns that some partners in the consortium would contribute more, or benefit more, further divided the investment bankers from the commercial bankers (Paulson, 2010, p. 202). In a corporatist system, strong private bank associations could help to organize the banks and avoid the danger that a single bank will refuse to participate, free-riding on the others' willingness to spend to prevent systemic crisis. No such institution existed to play a comparable role in the United States, however.

Finally, saving Lehman Brothers would not even guarantee that a broader panic would be contained, given that both AIG and Merrill Lynch were under pressure (Paulson, 2010, p. 192). A failure by either of these larger institutions would have even greater consequences than a collapse of Lehman. As such, the planned liquidity consortium failed to produce an agreement in the time Paulson had allotted them, and Bank of America removed itself as a potential buyer (Paulson, 2010,

p. 350; United States Congress House Committee on Financial Services, 2011, p. 442). Barclays remained interested, hopeful that a consortium would yet emerge to absorb $40–$50 billion of Lehman's bad assets (United States Congress House Committee on Financial Services, 2011, p. 446). However, executing a merger of that size requires a shareholder vote under UK law, and Barclay's UK regulator, the Financial Services Authority (FSA), refused to grant a waiver allowing a more rapid sale (Sorkin, 2009, p. 343; Paulson, 2010, p. 188; United States Congress House Committee on Financial Services, 2011, p. 446). UK regulators, wary of importing the United States' "cancer" and leery of the viability of a consortium rescue, were unwilling to approve, in large part because Barclays itself was already in distress (Darling, 2012, pp. 123–124; Sorkin, 2009, p. 348). Should Lehman drag down Barclays, UK taxpayers would bear the costs for the failure of both banks. The FSA, therefore, refused to grant a waiver unless the US government, not a private consortium, provided the loss guarantee (United States Congress House Committee on Financial Services, 2011, p. 447). This would have both deepened the Jamie Deal precedent and left the United States potentially with tens of billions in losses and ownership of Lehman Brothers if Barclays ultimately backed down from the merger (United States Congress House Committee on Financial Services, 2011, p. 447). With neither the United States nor the United Kingdom willing to take on the direct costs of a Lehman Brothers collapse, the Barclays deal fell through.

With both Bank of America and Barclays out of the running, no bank remained as a potential buyer for Lehman Brothers. This left US policymakers with three unpalatable options (United States Congress House Committee on Financial Services, 2011, p. 441). The first was to provide another Jamie Deal, enabling Barclays or Bank of America to make a purchase; the second was direct state assistance to Lehman Brothers; and the third was to let the bank fail and declare bankruptcy. Another Jamie Deal, up to 70 percent larger than the one for Bear Stearns, could have prevented Lehman's collapse, but only at the cost of reinforcing the moral hazard problems created by the first such deal (United States Congress House Committee on Financial Services, 2011, p. 446). Moreover, Paulson's repeated statements to the public and the banks that no state support for Lehman would be forthcoming meant that providing public assistance after all would have severely reduced his credibility in future negotiations (Paulson, 2010, pp. 184–187). This would almost immediately be an issue, given that Merrill Lynch and AIG were also under pressure (Lowenstein, 2010, p. 176). This was the option favored by the other banks, as it contained the crisis at no cost to themselves, and with a subsidy to the purchasing bank. The banks, however, had no direct role in advising US policymakers on the fate of Lehman and so had limited ability to push their favored policy.

The second option, direct aid to Lehman Brothers, had practical, legal, and moral hazard issues. Because the bank was insolvent, even a massive government loan could delay but not prevent the bank's failure unless some other source of capital could be found to restore its balance sheets. A state-provided injection of capital that kept the bank in private hands, as favored by Lehman CEO Dick Fuld, created severe moral hazard problems. Keeping Lehman private but injecting sufficient state capital would have required the price the state charged for its injection to be well below market value, a substantial subsidy to Lehman shareholders. If that subsidy were to be avoided, Lehman would need to be nationalized, either by fiat or by taking a controlling stake through capital injections. This was the most palatable direct aid option for policymakers and received serious consideration from Paulson, Bernanke, and Geithner (Lowenstein, 2010, p. 196; Wessel, 2010, p. 21). It also would have been the worst option for Lehman shareholders other than bankruptcy, as they would take heavy losses, either through expropriation at something close to the virtually nil market value or heavy dilution through the state taking an overwhelming majority stake. However, since early in September, representatives from Lehman had been almost entirely shut out of the policy process (Sorkin, 2009, pp. 303, 319).

The bigger issues with nationalization were legal and normative. Bernanke was willing to contemplate nationalization, though only with the support of Paulson (Wessel, 2010, p. 21). Geithner had strong normative opposition to state-owned banks, arguing that preserving a privately owned financial system should be a central state goal (Conaway, 2009). Paulson, for his part, argued that nationalization could not be done under existing legal authorities. It would require an act of Congress, and Lehman would not survive the time it would take to pass such an act (Lowenstein, 2010, p. 169; Paulson, 2010, p. 224). The Federal Reserve was expressly prohibited from any capital support. The only agency legally able to provide capital injections of any kind was the FDIC, and it could only do so for commercial banks already seized by the FDIC (Bair, 2012, p. 75). Nationalizing Lehman, therefore, would require an act of Congress (Paulson, 2010, p. 224; United States Congress House Committee on Financial Services, 2011, p. 453). This would be virtually impossible to obtain, especially on the short notice required. Opposition to state aid for Lehman Brothers was both fervent and bipartisan (Lowenstein, 2010, p. 169). Some key members of Congress, especially Jim Bunning on the Senate Banking Committee, went even further than Geithner, opposing not only state ownership but any state aid as "creeping socialism" (Sorkin, 2009, p. 246). Direct aid, therefore, could only be provided on terms that would have introduced severe moral hazard problems and essentially subsidized Lehman losses.

Thus, letting Lehman fail was the last available option for US policymakers, an extremely risky and costly option that nevertheless offered certain benefits. Perhaps the clearest benefit was a definitive refutation of the precedent set by Bear Stearns' Jamie Deal. New York Fed Senior Vice President Patricia Mosser argued that a Lehman bankruptcy would be a "mess on every level, but fixes the moral hazard problem" (United States Congress House Committee on Financial Services, 2011, p. 441). By letting an institution even larger than Bear Stearns to collapse into bankruptcy, the United States would effectively restore the old Drexel precedent of no support for investment banks nearing bankruptcy.

There were also some reasons to think that the fall of Lehman Brothers would not be catastrophic. Bear Stearns' failure caught market actors and regulators by surprise, meaning that they had little time to prepare for the fallout of its collapse. This increased the potential for disastrous consequences and motivated policymakers to implement the Jamie Deal despite the moral hazard problems. Lehman Brothers, by contrast, had been in clear distress since at least July, giving market actors months to brace themselves for a collapse. Because of this, Paulson believed that the contagion effects of Lehman Brothers might be relatively small, larger than those from Drexel, but still manageable (Sorkin, 2011, pp. 230, 307; United States Congress House Committee on Financial Services, 2011, p. 454; Wessel, 2010, p. 25). Members of the Fed's Federal Open Market Committee even argued that the benefit from restoring this precedent would offset the costs of Lehman's collapse (United States Congress House Committee on Financial Services, 2011, p. 454).

Ultimately, however, the potential costs of letting Lehman fall were unknowable in advance. The largest previous investment bank collapse, Drexel, was smaller than Lehman and in a less interconnected market that was not already reeling from the failure of other institutions in both the United States and Europe. Estimates of the consequences ranged from relatively minor, as Paulson anticipated, to catastrophic. The actual effects of letting Lehman fall proved closer to the latter, though there is some reason to think that, as UK Liberal Democrat Shadow Chancellor Vince Cable argued, the fall of Lehman was the "Franz Ferdinand" moment of the crisis (Thomas and Gallagher, 2009). The assassination of the heir of the Austro-Hungarian Empire started a chain of events that culminated in the First World War, but given the high tensions and irresolvable conflicts of interest in Europe in 1914, some other event would have triggered the war if Ferdinand's assassination had not. Similarly, per Cable, increasing tensions across Europe and the United States left markets ready to panic, and Lehman Brothers' collapse was "the trigger not the cause" (Thomas and Gallagher, 2009).

Cable was not alone in giving grudging support for the decision. Jamie Dimon, CEO of JP Morgan, agreed with Cable's assessment, arguing that "the crisis would have unfolded along a different path, but it probably would have unfolded" (United States Congress House Committee on Financial Services, 2011, p. 455). US President George W. Bush expressed support, glad that the Lehman bankruptcy signaled that the United States would not bail out private investors (Sorkin, 2009, p. 374). Others were far more critical and far more willing to see the subsequent crisis as preventable, if only the United States had rescued Lehman Brothers. Some argued even that Paulson's inconsistencies exacerbated the crisis, as bailing out Bear Stearns signaled to markets that Lehman would also be saved, causing market actors to not anticipate that Paulson would let Lehman fail. One European Central Bank executive board member captured this sentiment memorably, declaring that "we don't let banks fail. We don't even let dry cleaners fail. It never occurred to us that the Americans would let Lehman fail" (Wessel, 2010, p. 22). ECB President Jean-Claude Trichet would privately argue that letting Lehman fail was a mistake (Wessel, 2010, p. 22).

At the same time, while US policymakers undoubtedly underestimated the fallout from a Lehman bankruptcy, that bankruptcy made both Lehman Brothers and US policymakers convenient scapegoats. If Cable and Dimon are correct that Lehman was simply the proximate cause of a crisis that was bound to erupt inevitably, letting Lehman go bankrupt made the US government a convenient scapegoat for both other banks and other governments, which could argue that needed assistance and unpopular bailouts were necessary because of US actions, and not their own failure to plan for a crisis.

Merrill Lynch

Merrill Lynch, the third largest American investment bank, ran into difficulties roughly in parallel with Lehman Brothers. Both failed the late spring 2008 Federal Reserve/SEC stress tests, with inadequate liquidity to survive a Bear Stearns–comparable level of market pressure (United States Congress House Committee on Financial Services, 2011, p. 397). That being said, Merrill Lynch was in a somewhat better position than Lehman Brothers. Although both were vulnerable to liquidity pressures, few market observers thought that Merrill had the solvency issues suspected at Lehman Brothers (Paulson, 2010, p. 123). That greater value meant that Merrill's management could more easily borrow money and could potentially sell the bank whole or in part to raise additional capital. It also meant that Merrill Lynch management retained a greater measure of political clout than Lehman Brothers. The bank retained the autonomy to negotiate its own terms of sale, if not the influence to win state aid or other favorable government treatment.

Merrill did come under pressure from Paulson to take a large step to ensure its solvency, but while the Treasury Secretary urged CEO John Thain to complete a deal in the interest of systemic stability, at no point was state aid offered to Merrill, either directly or as a subsidy for a sale (Paulson, 2010, p. 211). Thain, believing that Lehman would fall and Merrill would be next, contacted both Goldman Sachs and Bank of America to negotiate a sale, ultimately opting to sell Merrill entirely to Bank of America (Paulson, 2010, p. 176; United States Congress House Committee on Financial Services, 2011, p. 445). Merrill Lynch, therefore, would be the investment bank resolved in the manner most closely resembling the pre-LTCM precedents, brokering a private sale with minimal government involvement not unlike the resolution of Salomon Brothers.

Morgan Stanley and Goldman Sachs

The largest two major US investment banks and the only ones to survive 2008 as independent institutions were Morgan Stanley and Goldman Sachs. They also were the two in the best position when the crisis struck, having passed the Federal Reserve/SEC stress tests and with no speculation that they may be weak in themselves (United States Congress House Committee on Financial Services, 2011, p. 397). Nevertheless, both would be subject to market pressures, under the "domino" theory that drove investors to focus on Lehman Brothers and Merrill Lynch after Bear Stearns' fall, and then look to Morgan Stanley and Goldman Sachs after Lehman failed and Merrill sold itself to Bank of America (Sorkin, 2009, p. 464; United States Congress House Committee on Financial Services, 2011, p. 447). Within days of Lehman's failure, some European banks stopped accepting Morgan Stanley as a counterparty for derivatives trades, until directly pressured by Morgan's treasurer (United States Congress House Committee on Financial Services, 2011, p. 477).

The resolution of Morgan Stanley and Goldman Sachs also illustrates how closely bank health is linked to the autonomy and ability to negotiate the terms of rescue in the United States. Unlike the smaller investment banks, Morgan Stanley and Goldman Sachs only came under serious pressure once the crisis reached its apex and received the most favorable treatment from policymakers of any of the investment banks. Even this, however, did not take the form of direct capital support, but only regulatory relief, giving Morgan Stanley and Goldman Sachs the same privileges and restrictions as other bank holding companies. However, while the management of the other investment banks was shut out of policymakers' deliberations, both Morgan Stanley and Goldman Sachs were able to propose potential solutions.

Both banks had expectations of more generous state relief, assuming that, because of their systemic importance, the United States could ill-afford to let them fail. As advisor Eugene Ludwig argued to the Morgan Stanley board, "if we go, Goldman goes. And then GE will go" (Sorkin, 2009, pp. 463–464). The collapse of GE, which was vulnerable because of its GE Capital division, would cause substantial damage to the real economy, so even massive sums of money to stop the dominos from falling with Morgan Stanley, and Goldman Sachs could be justified.

Both banks, however, would be thwarted in their attempts to secure generous rescue terms. Goldman Sachs proposed a merger with Wachovia, with a government subsidy modeled on JP Morgan's "Jamie Deal" for Bear Stearns (Paulson, 2010, p. 276). This would have given Goldman the support of Wachovia's depositor base and saved Wachovia from closure, while the taxpayer would have absorbed the losses. However, Paulson, Bernanke, and Geithner refused to support this plan, which would have both extended the moral hazard precedent set by Bear Stearns and left Morgan Stanley, as the last remaining independent investment bank without a depositor base, even more vulnerable to market pressures (Paulson, 2010, p. 276).

Morgan Stanley similarly tried to save itself through mergers, though no suitors offered an acceptable price without government support. Secretary Paulson initiated talks with Chinese Vice Premier Wang Qishan on Morgan Stanley's behalf, hoping to secure a sizeable investment from the China Investment Corporation, a Chinese state-owned bank (Sorkin, 2009, p. 469). Qishan balked, insisting that the US government explicitly guarantee the Chinese investment. Paulson refused, and without a government guarantee, China Investment Corporation would not invest.

The United States also pursed a JP Morgan–Morgan Stanley merger, though both parties balked at this. Morgan Stanley was pressured by Paulson, Bernanke, and Geithner to accept whatever offer JP Morgan put forth, even if for only a dollar (Lowenstein, 2010, p. 234; Sorkin, 2009, pp. 480–481). JP Morgan, however, was reluctant to take on Morgan Stanley even for free, arguing that such a merger would cost JP Morgan

$50 billion plus job losses (Sorkin, 2009, pp. 478–479). As the United States lacked the ability to compel either bank, merger talks collapsed.

Ultimately, Goldman Sachs and Morgan Stanley together proposed reclassifying their firms as bank holding companies. Prior to the crisis, all five of the major investment banks had been regulated as independent broker dealers, which did not provide access to borrowing from the Federal Reserve Discount Window but meant that the firms were only lightly regulated by the SEC. Bank holding company status, by contrast, allowed borrowing from the Discount Window for up to ninety days on good collateral, but meant that the firms would be under more stringent regulatory oversight of the Federal Reserve. Prior to the crisis, all the investment banks regarded this as undesirable, a move that would solve liquidity problems but would lower the banks' market value in the long term (Sorkin, 2009, pp. 442, 448, 450).

However, after attempts to secure more favorable terms of assistance failed, Blankfein would propose bank holding company status as a possible solution for Goldman Sachs. He would urge John Mack at Morgan Stanley to do so as well to contain the panic (Lowenstein, 2010, p. 227; Sorkin, 2009, p. 448). With unsubsidized mergers unlikely to materialize, US policymakers came to see a shift to bank holding company status, coupled with a modest private capital injection for each bank, as the most viable solution going forward (Sorkin, 2009, pp. 450, 466). With the understanding that both would seek additional private capitalization, Paulson and Geithner accepted their applications and pressed the Federal Reserve to approve them immediately, rather than taking the customary review for several weeks (Lowenstein, 2010, p. 230; Paulson, 2010, p. 276). Goldman Sachs would ultimately receive a capital injection from Warren Buffet, and Paulson, Bernanke, and Geithner helped persuade the Japanese bank Mitsubishi UFJ to take a stake in Morgan Stanley (Lowenstein, 2010, pp. 265–267; United States Congress House Committee on Financial Services, 2011, p. 481).

Goldman Sachs and Morgan Stanley, therefore, emerged from 2008 as the only two of the Big Five investment houses to survive as independent firms, though not without accepting the additional regulatory oversight of bank holding company status. They also retained considerably more autonomy in their dealings with the US government than Bear Stearns, which was forced into a merger with JP Morgan, Lehman Brothers, which policymakers let fail rather than assist, or Merrill Lynch, which was directed to find a merger partner or fail. This greater autonomy followed from their relatively healthy economic position. Although both Goldman Sachs and Morgan Stanley faced a risk of collapse, neither firm's fall was imminent and both still had substantial value. While

Goldman Sachs and Morgan Stanley failed in their attempts to secure state subsidies or guarantees to make mergers on favorable terms, they retained enough health to refuse state pressures to merge at any price.

They were also able to obtain bank holding company status, whereas Lehman Brothers' similar proposal to shift regulatory status was dismissed by Geithner as "gimmicky" (United States Congress House Committee on Financial Services, 2011, p. 437). This again reflects the superior health and access of Goldman and Morgan Stanley. Because they were healthier, the liquidity support of bank holding company status could do more to help them than it could do for insolvent Lehman Brothers. Moreover, their ability to survive, at least temporarily, without accepting whatever terms policymakers offered them meant that they were still able to negotiate with policymakers, while Lehman management were shut out of debates over the bank's fate and forced to accept whatever terms were offered. Thus, both Goldman and Morgan Stanley could still propose a solution of their own devising, even if it was not their first choice.

Ultimately, while the expedited approval of the change in status for Goldman Sachs and Morgan Stanley demonstrated the willingness of policymakers to prioritize steps to save the two banks, the change in status itself was not a significant extension of state aid. Both banks had considered and rejected the option of a change in status in good times, preferring the lighter regulation by the SEC that came with independent broker dealer status to the more invasive Federal Reserve oversight that came with the Discount Window access of bank holding company status. Moreover, bank holding company status was not an emergency provision providing unusually generous terms of access to Federal Reserve borrowing but an existing regulatory option. Since Discount Window borrowing was well collateralized, the risk of losses to the Federal Reserve was minimal. Because the liquidity access gained was not extraordinary and because the increased regulatory burden was high, bank holding company status was not in itself a radical improvement. The systemic importance of the two banks, and the political autonomy that followed from that, enabled them to secure rapid approval of a reclassification while Lehman Brothers was rejected, but the reclassification itself was not exceptionally generous. Indeed, it was seen by management at both banks as a move of desperation and a last resort option, after efforts to secure more generous assistance failed.

Nonbank Financial Institutions

In addition to the commercial and investment banks, several other institutions of systemic importance to the US financial system also came under pressure in 2008. The dynamics in the resolution of these institutions were broadly similar to those in the investment banks. These large nonbank institutions had significant political clout when they were healthy, but lost it rapidly once their economic position worsened. As with the investment and commercial banks, healthy institutions showed no interest in helping Fannie Mae and Freddie Mac or AIG. As such, policymakers had a free hand to implement whatever policies they thought appropriate. As with the investment banks, however, no clear resolution authority existed for the nonbank financial institutions, necessitating ad hoc decisions on the part of policymakers. Unlike the investment banks, however, policymakers chose to respond to the failure of these institutions with nationalization, and Fannie Mae, Freddie Mac, and AIG all ended up wholly or majority owned by the United States by the end of 2008.

Fannie Mae and Freddie Mac

Fannie Mae and Freddie Mac, the so-called government-sponsored enterprises (GSEs), are a crucial case demonstrating how rapidly even the most connected American firms can lose their clout in a crisis. Prior to the crisis, Fannie and Freddie were regarded as the most politically connected US financial firms. Despite their structural importance and political clout and the widespread belief that they operated with the implicit backing of the US government, both firms would be taken into conservatorship, a temporary and compulsory nationalization without compensation for shareholders, in early September 2008.

The two GSEs had significant precrisis political influence, through a combination of history, structural importance, and deliberately cultivated political connections. All of these factors relate ultimately to the two firms' role as private companies with a public mission. Fannie and Freddie existed to create a "secondary mortgage market," buying mortgages from banks in order to increase the ease with which people could get mortgages (Lowenstein, 2010, pp. 8–9; United States Congress House Committee on Financial Services, 2011, p. 412). The essential problem with mortgages from a bank's perspective is that they present an enormous sunk cost: money lent out all at once to fund a real estate purchase is paid back only slowly, conventionally over a thirty-year period and with a not insignificant risk of default. Because this ties up so much of a bank's money, they would normally be reluctant to issue significant numbers of mortgages, or at least want to charge a substantial amount and only offer them to the most creditworthy borrowers, to minimize the opportunity costs and risks to the bank. The secondary mortgage market, allowing bankers to sell mortgage-backed securities, made issuing mortgages more attractive for bankers, as issuing mortgages no longer meant tying up substantial liquidity. Mortgages could be issued and then sold to third parties to bear the risk and the sunk costs. It was for this public function that Fannie Mae was created in 1938 as a state-owned enterprise. It would be privatized thirty years later, though with the same public function, and its sibling organization, Freddie Mac, would be created by Congress as a private firm in 1970 to avoid monopoly concerns by providing a competitor to Fannie Mae in the secondary mortgage market.

In part because of their origin and public function, and in part as a corporate strategy, both GSEs had long cultivated close ties with Congress, especially with Democrats (Lowenstein, 2010, p. 11). Between 1999 and 2008, the two firms spent over $164 million on lobbying, including $15 million directly to election campaigns (United States Congress House Committee on Financial Services, 2011, p. 80). They were consequently regarded by the Wall Street firms as having a distinct competitive advantage. This was reflected in their regulatory treatment, which was among the lightest of any American financial institutions. The GSEs' regulator, the OFHEO, had less authority over its subjects than any of the bank regulators (United States Congress House Committee on Financial Services, 2011, pp. 78, 80). The GSEs' capital requirements were substantially lower, being required to hold in capital only 0.45 percent of the value of their mortgage-backed securities and 2.5 percent of the value of their directly held mortgages (United States Congress House Committee on Financial Services, 2011, p. 76). In contrast, banks and thrifts were required to hold a minimum of 4 percent of the value of any mortgage assets they held to absorb any potential losses (United States Congress House Committee on Financial Services, 2011, p. 76). Moreover, the GSEs' legal definition of what counted as capital reserves was looser than that for the banks, leading the Wall Street banks, and Secretary Paulson, to refer to the GSEs' reserves as "bullshit capital" (United States Congress House Committee on Financial Services, 2011, p. 412). The GSEs were able to maintain such low capital ratios without investors losing faith, in part because the two were widely believed to have an implicit guarantee from the Federal government. Fannie and Freddie bonds, despite the thin underlying capital, were regarded as virtually as safe as US Treasury bonds (Paulson, 2010, p. 56). This in turn allowed the two firms in good times to borrow at lower rates than they otherwise could have done.

These structural and political advantages did little to help the GSEs when they ran into trouble, however. They were already under pressure from the Bush administration, which had fewer close links with the GSEs than the Democrats who, at the time, controlled the US Senate and House of Representatives (Paulson, 2010, p. 5). The new OFHEO director, James Lockhart, from the beginning of his term in 2006 showed concern as to the stability of the GSEs and lobbied for an increase in his regulatory authority (United States Congress House Committee on Financial Services, 2011, p. 248). One key area of concern was resolution authority: the OFHEO had the authority to put the GSEs in conservatorship, a form of temporary nationalization, but lacked the funds to do so, making the power essentially unusable (United States Congress House Committee on Financial Services, 2011, p. 415). Resistance from the Democratic-controlled Congress, however, blocked his initial moves to increase the viability of this authority.

Once Fannie and Freddie actually started running into difficulties, however, their support from Congress would fade. As early as the collapse of Bear Stearns, their weaknesses became apparent. Paulson was forced to abandon an early plan to push the GSEs to save Bear once it became clear that they were too fragile to play a constructive role (Lowenstein, 2010, p. 123). Once Bear collapsed, both GSEs would come under increased pressure. Of the two, Freddie Mac was in a worse position, but since investors treated them as essentially identical, Freddie Mac's problems would increase Fannie Mae's problems as well (Paulson, 2010, pp. 10–11). Their initial appeals for regulatory relief, for a lowering of capital requirement, met with resistance from Lockhart (United States Congress House Committee on Financial Services, 2011, p. 414). Lowering capital requirements would have let the GSEs to increase their borrowing without increasing their capital reserves, by loosening their restrictions on the maximum ratio of borrowing to capital reserves. Thus, it would have increased their ability to borrow without improving their actual position. Instead, Paulson and Lockhart pressured the GSEs to solve their problems by increasing their capital reserves with capital from new investors, allowing temporarily lower capital reserves on the promise that the reserves would be increased above the legal requirements immediately thereafter (Sorkin, 2009, p. 183; United States Congress House Committee on Financial Services, 2011, pp. 418–419). Fannie Mae would keep this promise, raising $7.4 billion in preferred stock (United States Congress House Committee on Financial Services, 2011, p. 419). Freddie Mac, however, did not, claiming that existing capital stock was sufficient and any raise would unacceptably dilute existing shareholders (United States Congress House Committee on Financial Services, 2011, pp. 419–420). Lockhart countered that Freddie Mac was simply attempting to put a brave face on its inability to find investors willing to buy into the troubled institution (United States Congress House Committee on Financial Services, 2011, p. 420).

In contrast to their close relationship with politicians in good times, the GSEs found their relationships with regulators in bad times to be considerably cooler. Once regulators beyond the toothless OFHEO became involved, the two institutions' problems were revealed to be considerably worse than previously thought. Federal Reserve and OCC audits found the reserves of Fannie and Freddie to be significantly lower than the OFHEO had believed (United States Congress House Committee on Financial Services, 2011, p. 421). At this point, it was clear that the two institutions required a significant capital injection to survive. Rather than pursue options that would keep Fannie and Freddie going as private institutions, which would have required a Bear Stearns–like subsidy to find a willing partner, Paulson instead began pressing Congress to grant the Treasury wind-down authority for the two GSEs (Paulson, 2010, p. 143; Sorkin, 2009, pp. 187, 196). The increase in regulatory oversight involved supplanting the OFHEO with a more powerful newly created replacement, the Federal Housing Finance Agency (FHFA) (United States Congress House Committee on Financial Services, 2011, p. 421).

Chief among the new FHFA's powers was an expanded conservatorship authority. The struggle over establishing this authority itself illustrated the reach of the GSEs' influence. Paulson wanted authority to put the two institutions in receivership, which would allow the FHFA to break up the GSEs and sell their component parts (Paulson, 2010, p. 162). The Democratic Chairs of the House and Senate Financial Services Committees, Barney Frank and Chris Dodd, respectively, resisted this, and Paulson was forced to accept conservatorship, which allowed the Treasury to seize the failing institutions but required them to be kept whole (Paulson, 2010, p. 164). Paulson was, however, able to secure an $800 billion increase in the debt ceiling, giving the Treasury access to the funds necessary to make conservatorship viable (United States Congress House Committee on Financial Services, 2011, p. 422).

Once Paulson had conservatorship authority, he immediately moved to seize the two institutions. This process would still take three weeks, due to resistance from the FHFA, which still hoped to preserve the institutions as private firms (United States Congress House Committee on Financial Services, 2011, p. 423). As the two firms' problems became more apparent, however, both the FHFA and the GSEs' previous defenders in the Congress came to support a government seizure of the institutions. Both Barney Frank and Chris Dodd would bless Paulson's actions as driven by necessity (Paulson, 2010, p. 12). Finally, on September 6, 2008, the FHFA acted, placing the two firms under state control, with the Treasury taking warrants for 79.9 percent control of each firm, plus injecting $1 billion in preferred stock paying a high 10 percent dividend (United States Congress House Committee on Financial Services, 2011, p. 428). This move essentially wiped out the value of all existing preferred and common stock holders, though by leaving a portion of the firms in private hands, the Treasury avoided a legal obligation to wipe out bondholders as well. Bondholders were spared, however, because of international concerns, not domestic pressure. Global investors had long assumed that the US government provided an implicit guarantee of GSE debt and treated them as equivalent to Treasury bonds. This created two difficulties in taking a harsh line with bondholders. The first was that investors would continue to regard GSE bonds as equivalent to Treasuries, only now regarding a default on GSE bonds as a signal that Treasuries were also not as secure as previously thought. This could substantially increase the cost of future US borrowing, including borrowing necessary to roll over the national debt. The second was that the global GSE bondholders included important foreign states, which shared the general market view on GSE bonds being as safe as Treasuries (Lowenstein, 2010, p. 143). China, in particular, held a significant portfolio of GSE bonds, and Chinese officials voiced their concerns to US policymakers over potential losses (Lowenstein, 2010, pp. 143–144; Stiglitz, 2010, p. 12). A default on GSE bonds, therefore, risked both raising doubts about US creditworthiness generally and offending major foreign powers.

The resolution of the GSEs illustrates both the tremendous influence American financial firms can hold in good times and how quickly they can lose that influence. When they were strong, the GSEs managed to secure more favorable treatment than any other US firm, including an implicit guarantee that ultimately forced policymakers to choose between insulating bondholders from losses or risk threatening the United States' own credit rating. Despite this, the GSEs would ultimately be dealt with as harshly as any firms outside of the reach of the FDIC. Their influence managed at best to delay their resolution, but ultimately even their allies in the OFHEO, its successor the FHFA, and Congress all came around in support of a compulsory nationalization. Those terms would be harsh to the firms' shareholders, and the generosity to bondholders had little to do with the firms' lobbying strength. Rather, it reflected the ability of foreign sovereign creditors, especially China, to pressure the United States.

American International Group

The other major nonbank financial institution to run into trouble in 2008 was AIG, an insurance company that had moved into the business of insuring stock market deals through CDS (Lowenstein, 2010, p. 55). A CDS is basically a bet against a stock's performance, designed to minimize losses if an investment underperforms by providing a compensatory payout. As such, they serve a countercyclical function for investors, diminishing the losses from a market downturn. They are, however, strongly procyclical for CDS issuers, which collect fees when the stock gains in value but must pay out when it falls. They, therefore, profit from investments succeeding in good times but lose out in bad times, when many stocks fall in value. Such operations are customarily the province of hedge funds, which are small enough that their failure cannot precipitate systemic crises. Regulated banks have restrictions from taking on such risk. AIG, however, as an insurance company was free of these restrictions on banks and took advantage of this loophole to function as an enormous hedge fund (Wessel, 2010, p. 194). The insurance company's financial division, AIG Financial Products, took on some $300 billion in counterparty risk, from many of the largest banks both in the United States and internationally (Sorkin, 2009, p. 395). The vast majority of this risk was to insure CDOs, a form of financial derivative, and those CDOs were largely based on the collapsing subprime mortgage market.

The enormous scale of AIG's operations created significant problems for regulators. Much as with investment banks, the old regulatory approach to hedge funds was to rely on market discipline and let them fail when they ran into trouble. However, AIG's fall would be far greater than that of a conventional hedge fund, dwarfing even LTCM. Its counterparties included many of the largest and most vulnerable investment institutions, meaning that the collapse of AIG would increase the losses to these institutions, threatening systemic stability (Lowenstein, 2010, p. 215; Sorkin, 2009, p. 395). Moreover, several of AIG's major counterparties were European banks, meaning foreign states, especially France and Germany, also wanted to avoid an AIG collapse (Sorkin, 2009, pp. 391, 394). At the same time, the same regulatory gap that let AIG take on so much procyclical risk also hindered the ability of the Federal Reserve and Treasury to act on the failing institution. As a nonbank institution, AIG could not access either the conventional or emergency liquidity programs of the Federal Reserve without a specific invocation of emergency authority (United States Congress House Committee on Financial Services, 2011, p. 460). This delayed the ability of AIG to access liquidity, as the insurance company needed to reach a level of distress that could justify extraordinary measures, while banks could seek smaller Fed loans earlier and, in doing so, stave off larger problems later.

These circumstances essentially produced a game of chicken between AIG and policymakers. AIG management, knowing the systemic importance of their institutions, argued that the Federal Reserve should exercise its emergency lending provision to allow them to borrow directly from the Fed. AIG's problem was one of liquidity, not solvency. AIG's other operations remained profitable but illiquid, and the problem was that AIG Financial Products needed to pay out a lot of CDS immediately. Therefore, AIG management argued that a $40 billion bridge loan would allow AIG to survive and even pay back the Federal Reserve (Paulson, 2010, pp. 218, 229). This, however, created significant moral hazard problems, as the Federal Reserve's extraordinary lending would essentially allow AIG to escape the consequences of its severely misplaced gamble that its CDS would turn out in their favor, or at least not go bad all at once. Policymakers, therefore, again showed their first preference for a private solution and pressed AIG to perform a private capital raise (Sorkin, 2009, pp. 375, 380). Geithner even took steps to broker such an injection, from a banking syndicate led by private equity firm JC Flowers and German insurance company Allianz. The proposed merger would inject $10 billion in equity capital, transfer control of AIG to Allianz, and, because of Allianz's regulatory status, allow the newly merged institution to tap Fed financing as a bank (United States Congress House Committee on Financial Services, 2011, p. 465). AIG management, however, refused to even negotiate with JC Flowers or Allianz, dismissing the offer immediately as not a "serious effort." Like Lehman, AIG management instead held out hope that the Federal Reserve would aid them directly (United States Congress House Committee on Financial Services, 2011, p. 465).

The collapse of Lehman Brothers altered the dynamics of this struggle considerably. The increasing pressure on their own balance sheets caused the partners in the proposed rescue syndicate to withdraw their offer and focus on their own problems, leaving the Federal Reserve as the only viable savior for AIG. It also increased pressure on policymakers from their French and German counterparts, concerned that the collapse of AIG would increase the capital needs of their own banks and thus deepen the crisis in Europe (Paulson, 2010, p. 233; Sorkin, 2009, p. 394). These developments strengthened AIG's campaign for Fed assistance, as no private alternative remained for the Fed to press AIG to accept, and AIG now had allies in the French and Germans, who wanted to avoid contagion from the insurer's collapse. On the other hand, the post-Lehman downturn increased AIG's liquidity needs, which more than doubled to $85 billion. AIG could no longer play a waiting game, as it would run out of money within days (Paulson, 2010, p. 240; Sorkin, 2009, p. 400; United States Congress House Committee on Financial Services, 2011, p. 466). Moreover, having shown their willingness to let

Lehman Brothers fall, policymakers could credibly threaten to let AIG go as well.

Policymakers took advantage of this position to offer assistance to AIG on punitive terms. The Federal Reserve extended $85 billion in credit that AIG was in no position to refuse, but offered it in the classic Bagehot formula of abundant liquidity at punitive rates backed by good collateral. The rate, the benchmark Federal funds rate plus 8.5 percent, was extremely high and imposed a heavy loss on the company (Lowenstein, 2010, p. 210; Sorkin, 2009, p. 402). It was also basically comparable to what risk-conscious and self-interested JP Morgan offered in liquidity support to Goldman Sachs. As collateral, the Federal Reserve took 79.9 percent of AIG stock, essentially wiping out AIG's private shareholders in a move comparable to that taken with the GSEs (Sorkin, 2009, p. 401). In the words of Treasury advisor Dan Jester, "the important point was that AIG shareholders would be punished" (Lowenstein, 2010, p. 210). Unlike the FHFA with the GSEs, however, the Federal Reserve lacked the ability to compel AIG to accept its terms. In that light, the terms were arguably as harsh as could credibly be offered. Like Bear Stearns, AIG's board debated bankruptcy, feeling that the difference between bankruptcy and the losses from accepting the Fed's offer would be only slight (Sorkin, 2009, p. 404). However, unlike with Bear Stearns, AIG was unable to win any concessions, and policymakers remained resolute that this would be the only offer AIG would receive. The AIG board accepted the terms, and the Federal Reserve became the majority owner of the firm (Sorkin, 2009, p. 206).

A subsequent lawsuit by AIG shareholders argued that these terms, much harsher than any other non-FDIC institution faced in the crisis, were excessive. They would win an essentially meaningless victory, however, as a judge ruled that the government was unduly harsh, but that since AIG would have been worthless without state action, AIG shareholders were entitled to no damages (Pearlstein, 2015).

Although their hands were tied by lack of regulatory oversight over AIG, US policymakers nevertheless took a hard line, refusing to offer any state aid until all private alternatives had dissipated, and even then offering aid on harsh, market-conforming terms. Although AIG managed to escape regulatory oversight while healthy, once in distress, it was unable to win favorable terms. The case of AIG also illustrates the lack of allies for firms in crisis. The private syndicate of buyers faded away almost immediately after Lehman fell, being far more concerned with their own balance sheets. Even AIG's interconnectedness with other banks won them no allies in the crisis to lobby on their behalf, though the atomized US system also meant that no LTCM-style rescue could be organized with the speed and on the scale required. The only significant advocates for preserving AIG with clout in negotiations were the French and German governments, and their concern was entirely with limiting their own banks' exposure, and not over the terms of US rescue. Both states were satisfied with the United States taking a hard line with AIG, so long as the risks to their own markets were contained.

Systemic Responses

In contrast with the United Kingdom and Germany, which only turned to systemic solutions relatively late in the crisis, US policymakers began considering systemic response plans as early as 2006. Efforts prior to TARP, however, would be stymied by the need to rely entirely on liquidity-based solutions. Prior to October 2008, no federal agency had the authority to inject capital into banks except the FDIC (Bair, 2012, p. 75). Even the FDIC, however, could only inject capital into commercial banks, and only into commercial banks it had already nationalized unless given a "systemic risk exception" by the Federal Reserve. State capital injections beyond those narrow conditions would require congressional approval. In a precrisis environment, such an extension of regulatory authority was unlikely, given the political clout of healthy US investment banks and their desire to resist an FDIC-style moral hazard–containing resolution authority, especially one funded by a levy on the insured institutions. Therefore, despite considering capital injections earlier than the United Kingdom or Germany, the United States would adopt such a plan only after the United Kingdom had already unveiled its own systemic response.

Prior to the enactment of TARP, therefore, US policymakers were forced to rely only on liquidity solutions from the Federal Reserve and private market capital solutions. The latter would prove difficult to organize. The subsidization of JP Morgan's purchase of Bear Stearns, and the failures to find buyers for Lehman Brothers and AIG, showed the limits of case-by-case capital-raising solutions, but systemic solutions were also difficult to come by. Early in his tenure as Treasury Secretary, Henry Paulson had sketched out a "Break the Glass" plan, a recapitalization plan based on a bad bank model. Essentially, the plan called for the United States to establish a facility to buy toxic assets from struggling banks, to return them to solvency (Paulson, 2010, p. 131; Sorkin, 2009, p. 83; Wessel, 2010, p. 176). Such a plan, as with all bad bank plans, carried with it moral hazard issues. Those issues would lead to the United States scrapping TARP's initial bad bank approach. Paulson, however, never got that far with Break the Glass, as congressional opposition blocked any major regulatory reforms (Paulson, 2010, p. 139; Wessel, 2010, p. 179). Absent a systemic capital support system, until the crisis reached a point of panic, the only systemic responses were liquidity programs, which the Federal Reserve had broad authority to implement at its own discretion. The Federal Reserve became increasingly concerned about liquidity at the investment banks, which lacked the ability to borrow from the Federal Reserve discount window, and that commercial banks were hoarding cash rather than lending it to either the investment banks or the broader economy. Initial attempts to encourage commercial banks to increase their liquidity, and thus their lending to the investment banks and the real economy, by lowering the overnight bank borrowing rate failed to significantly affect markets (United States Congress House Committee on Financial Services, 2011, pp. 343, 366). Borrowing directly from the Fed discount window carried a stigma, signaling to markets that the borrowing bank could no longer secure private lending. Therefore, prior to the Bear Stearns panic, the Fed launched two programs aimed at expanding lending. The Term Auction Facility aimed to reduce the stigma of using the discount window by releasing liquidity at auction. Such auctions ensured that the Fed would get a good price for its money, but also avoid signaling weakness on the part of the borrowing banks. This met with some success, with $40 billion in borrowing by the end of 2007, but did not sufficiently increase lending to the broader economy, as the banks instead continued to hoard the cash in anticipation of liquidity problems (United States Congress House Committee on Financial Services, 2011, p. 367). Therefore, the Fed embarked on a more ambitious program to lend directly to investment banks, the Term Securities Lending Facility (TSLF). The TSLF would provide Treasuries at an above-market rate to be backed by very high-quality collateral, thus minimizing the risk to the Fed and charging a penalty rate in the classic Bagehot formula (United States Congress House Committee on Financial Services, 2011, p. 382). Following the collapse of Bear Stearns, the TSLF would be supplemented with the Primary Dealer Credit Facility (PDCF), which would lend overnight cash, not Treasuries, to the investment banks (United States Congress House Committee on Financial Services, 2011, p. 392). This, therefore, gave the investment banks a way to borrow overnight from the Federal Reserve comparable to the access held by commercial banks. As with the commercial banks, above-market fees encouraged the investment banks to use the PDCF only as a facility of last resort. This, however, discouraged the use of PDCF for reasons beyond the higher cost, as using the expensive facility would signal weakness, potentially triggering a loss in confidence by investors. As such, it saw much less use than the TSFL until the peak of the crisis (United States Congress House Committee on Financial Services, 2011, p. 393).

All of these Federal Reserve programs followed the Bagehot formula and thus fulfilled the Federal Reserve's lender-of-last-resort function without significantly increasing moral hazard problems. Moreover, the required collateral meant that such lending, though reaching massive scales, never presented a significant risk of losses to the Fed, or the taxpayer. The PDCF, for instance, was specifically only offered after Bear Stearns failed, so that it would be a measure to preserve banks in future panics, and not a moral hazard–creating life preserver for Bear (United States Congress House Committee on Financial Services, 2011, p. 392).

Following the collapse of Lehman Brothers, however, it became clear that liquidity programs and private market capital were insufficient. Borrowing from the PDCF and TSLF reached nearly $300 billion in the ten days after Lehman's bankruptcy, increasing the Federal Reserve's balance sheet by 67 percent (United States Congress House Committee on Financial Services, 2011, p. 492). Moreover, liquidity solutions could only buy time for banks with solvency issues. Such issues could only ultimately be addressed by new sources of capital. The government's decision to let Lehman Brothers fall made it clear that another Jamie Deal-style government subsidy of a private rescue would not be forthcoming. However, it also meant that private investors under pressure would be more reluctant to provide capital to failing banks if government loss guarantees would not be offered. Therefore, by mid-September, both Federal Reserve and Treasury officials turned to debates over a capital injection plan.

The debates over what would ultimately become the TARP essentially broke down into a debate between whether it should take the form of a bad bank or direct share purchase. Apart from Republican Senators Richard Shelby and Jim Bunning, none of the major participants in the debate favored a laissez-faire approach, though they disagreed, at times bitterly, over the form capital injections should take (Paulson, 2010, pp. 261, 275, 283). The relatively convoluted US legislative process meant that the debate over the US systemic plan was both lengthier and involved more actors than in the United Kingdom. However, like in the United Kingdom but unlike in Germany, the banks themselves were shut out of the policy debate. Debates over the form of TARP, therefore, were driven by politicians' and policymakers' preferences, and not the self-interest of the banks.

The substance of the TARP debates reflected this lack of voice for the banks. Those with the closest links to the financial industry showed no inclination to protect it. The strongest advocate for preserving private ownership was New York Federal Reserve President Timothy Geithner, a career civil servant without close links or a personal stake in the financial industry (Conaway, 2009; Johnson and Kwak, 2010, p. 178). Federal Reserve Chair Ben Bernanke was the most comfortable with the state taking direct ownership stakes, even up to full nationalization, being vocally more concerned with the economic consequences than the political or ideological implications of state ownership of the financial system (Paulson, 2010, p. 323; Sorkin, 2009, p. 510). The members of the House and Senate Financial Services Committees, despite substantial campaign donations from financial actors, insisted that bank shareholders and management bear substantial pain (Paulson, 2010, pp. 259, 304). Republicans Richard Shelby and Jim Bunning argued against any capital injections at all (Paulson, 2010, pp. 261, 275, 283; Sorkin, 2009, p. 418). Bunning especially rejected any state aid to the banks as "socialism" and dismissed concerns about broader economic consequences (Paulson, 2010, pp. 275, 283). The Democrats were more receptive to an active state role, but acutely aware of the need to impose costs on the banks, both as a matter of good policy, to limit moral hazard, and as a matter of good politics, to limit voter backlash. House Financial Services Committee Chair Barney Frank proved especially caustic in remarking on the disconnect between banks' previous support for deregulation and current petitions for state aid, asking "how are all of the these free-market people going to feel about letting the markets work?" (Paulson, 2010, p. 220). Frank would be the strongest voice arguing for the need for compensation restrictions and other forms of punishment for the banks. His Senate counterpart Chris Dodd and Speaker of the House Nancy Pelosi both focused on the need to limit the political backlash by providing other measures to help struggling mortgage holders (Paulson, 2010, p. 261).

The crucial actor in the actual drafting of TARP was Treasury Secretary Henry Paulson. Paulson, a former Goldman Sachs CEO, shared Geithner's philosophical opposition to state ownership of the financial system but, despite his stronger links to the financial community, showed a greater concern with avoiding problems of moral hazard than with ideological concerns over state ownership (Paulson, 2010, pp. 332, 337). Paulson would also prove to be the key debate player whose position evolved the most, eventually supporting state ownership stakes as the moral hazard problems of other solutions became apparent. Paulson's original proposal for TARP was for a bad bank based closely on the never implemented Break-the-Glass plan (Paulson, 2010, p. 248).

This original bad bank vision of TARP would have preserved private ownership, but posed significant moral hazard problems: overpaying for assets would help the banks but subsidize their bad decisions, while underpaying would inflict costs on the banks but not do much to prevent their failure. Paulson initially proposed to evade this problem through a "reverse auction," in which the banks would bid to sell their assets to the bad bank, driving down the price the Treasury would pay (Paulson, 2010, p. 267). This plan fell apart upon closer inspection, however, as the various toxic assets were not comparable enough to make this approach viable (Sorkin, 2009, p. 500).

In addition to the increasingly apparent impracticality of this approach, two events moved Paulson closer to accepting direct capital injections. The first was the failure of the first bill authorizing TARP in the House. In part, this was because TARP become entangled in the politics of the ongoing presidential election campaign. Democratic candidate and ultimate victor Barack Obama cautiously supported the bill and heeded Paulson's request to avoid further complicating the already fraught negotiations (Paulson, 2010, p. 278). His Republican rival, John McCain, however, was trailing in the polls and sought to harness anti-bailout sentiment by publically inserting himself into TARP debates (Lowenstein, 2010, p. 243; Paulson, 2010, p. 294). This politicization broke the congressional leadership's ability to hold their coalitions together in support of the bill. Once right-wing Republicans, upset about the intervention of the state in markets, started following McCain's lead and challenging TARP from the right, left-wing Democrats, who had concerns about redistribution to bankers, similarly broke from congressional leadership. This splintering, coupled with the general unpopularity of any bailout and concerns about the lack of details in the open-ended, sixteen-page original legislation, led to the bill's initial defeat in the House of Representatives (United States Congress House Committee on Financial Services, 2011, p. 493). In order to win passage of the bill on a second vote, Paulson needed to address some of the concerns of legislators who had voted it down. Provisions for oversight and enhanced depositor protections were added, and the focus shifted to buying direct stakes, which the Democrats generally supported more strongly than Paulson (Paulson, 2010, p. 367; Sorkin, 2009, p. 500; United States Congress House Committee on Financial Services, 2011, p. 494). The second event moving Paulson toward direct injections was the implementation of the UK systemic response plan, which involved substantial direct ownership stakes (Sorkin, 2009, p. 510; Wessel, 2010, p. 229). The initial successes of the UK plan in stabilizing British markets convinced both

Paulson and congressional Democrats of the viability of a systemic response based on direct injections.

Paulson did retain his reservations about politicizing financial markets by taking controlling stakes, however; so he opted instead for a plan based on preferred shares (Lowenstein, 2010, p. 270; Paulson, 2010, pp. 337–338; United States Congress House Committee on Financial Services, 2011, p. 495). This was broadly moral hazard equivalent, as it diluted shareholders a comparable amount. Moreover, because preferred shareholders were senior in any payment of dividends or bankruptcy payout, holding preferred shares reduced the risks of losses to the Treasury (Paulson, 2010, p. 338). Preferred shares also avoided giving the Treasury controlling interest in supported institutions. With these changes, TARP secured passage in the Senate on October 1 and in the House on October 3 (United States Congress House Committee on Financial Services, 2011, p. 494).

The next challenge was implementation. Unlike the UK plan, TARP was formally a voluntary plan, creating a problem of negative signaling. Institutions that accepted TARP money risked signaling to markets that they were in distress, potentially causing a run by investors and obviating any advantage gained from TARP participation. The similarly voluntary German SoFFin plan would address this problem by offering assistance on such generous terms that any costs of sending a negative signal about firm health were offset (Dempsey, 2008; Dougherty, 2009). In the United States, where the banks had less organizational strength and no role in the drafting of the state response plan, the problem was addressed by making TARP functionally mandatory for the top nine US financial institutions.

On October 13, Paulson summoned the heads of the top nine US financial institutions to the offices of the Treasury in Washington (Paulson, 2010, p. 359; Sorkin, 2009, p. 519; United States Congress House Committee on Financial Services, 2011, p. 495). Those banks were Citi, JP Morgan, Wells Fargo, Bank of America, Merrill Lynch (not yet merged with Bank of America), Morgan Stanley, Goldman Sachs, and clearing banks BNY Mellon and State Street (United States Congress House Committee on Financial Services, 2011, p. 495). Once assembled, the heads of these banks heard from Paulson, Bernanke, OCC Chair John Dugan, and FDIC Chair Sheila Bair (Lowenstein, 2010, p. 270; Sorkin, 2009, p. 521). Paulson informed them that each would be required to accept a capital injection from TARP at a specific value (Lowenstein, 2010, p. 271; Sorkin, 2009, p. 524). Citi, JP Morgan, and Wells would each take $25 billion, Bank of America $15 billion, plus $10 billion to Merrill Lynch, $10 billion each to Morgan Stanley and Goldman Sachs, $3 billion to BNY Mellon, and $2 billion to State Street (Sorkin, 2009, p. 524; United States Congress House Committee on Financial Services, 2011, p. 495). These injections would be nonvoting preferred shares, to avoid the appearance of a government takeover of the financial sector, but would be for nonnegotiable terms. Those terms included a 5 percent annual dividend for the first five years, which would subsequently rise to 9 percent per year thereafter (Swagel, 2009, p. 52; United States Congress House Committee on Financial Services, 2011, p. 495). The banks had the ability to refuse, but were informed that if any of them did so, none of them would receive capital on the terms presented and any subsequent application for aid would be on much harsher terms (Paulson, 2010, p. 365). Coupled with this was a threat that the banks' regulators would closely audit any banks that refused the injections to determine their continued viability (Sorkin, 2009, p. 525). If found to be undercapitalized, the government could force them to accept recapitalization, but Paulson indicated he wanted voluntary consent (Lowenstein, 2010, p. 270). Confronted with these alternatives and unable to negotiate for better terms, the bankers ultimately all agreed to accept the terms offered. Because TARP recipients now included all of the most high-profile financial actors, the stigma was removed for future voluntary participation by smaller and less visible actors.

This strategy was successful for two reasons. The first was the ability of policymakers to play off the disorganization of the US banks. The struggling banks needed the capital, were in too weak a position to refuse the terms offered, and could not count on the healthy banks to advocate for more generous terms on their behalf in the future. The healthy banks did not need or want the injections, which carried additional oversight and diluted existing shareholders. However, even if concerns over collective action and relative gains prevented them from acting directly to support systemic stability, they had a clear interest in limiting the growing financial panic. This was acknowledged most clearly by JP Morgan CEO Jamie Dimon, who maintained that he did not need or want the support and that it was "asymmetrically bad for JP Morgan" but was willing to act in the interest of systemic stability (Sorkin, 2009, p. 527). In his own words, "we [JP Morgan] shouldn't stand in the way" (Sorkin, 2009, p. 527). The CEOs of Morgan Stanley and Goldman Sachs would echo this position (Sorkin, 2009, p. 527). Refusing to participate would have further destabilized the markets, causing the panic to grow, potentially threatening even the healthiest institutions. US policymakers, therefore, were essentially able to threaten even the healthiest banks to cajole them into accepting the terms of the deal.

In this they were also helped by the terms offered, which were relatively generous at first, charging a relatively low dividend for the first five years, but then rising to a penalty rate thereafter. In effect, this was market-priced capital for the healthy banks with little risk of failure, but initially below-market for the failing banks. This is why Vikram Pandit, CEO of the highly distressed Citi, described the initial TARP injection as "cheap capital"; it was for his struggling bank because of the risks, but not for the healthier banks (Paulson, 2010, p. 365). Assistant Treasury Secretary Phillip Swagel described this initial rate as "the opposite of the 'Sopranos' ... a deal so attractive that banks would be unwise to refuse it" (Swagel, 2009, p. 52). This was true only for the first five years, however. Distressed banks unable to repay within five years would still be paying dividends when the rate rose to penalty levels in 2013. The healthy banks, however, would be able to repay the Treasury sooner, prior to the penalty rate kicking in. This had the added advantage to the United States of having the healthy banks essentially subsidize the failing ones. Injections in the healthy banks presented relatively little risk and could be counted on to yield a positive return. This compulsory positive return to the United States would help offset losses from those banks that accepted TARP capital but either failed anyway or could not repay for a long time.

TARP in practice looked very similar to the UK systemic response plan. Both were ultimately mandatory plans that part-nationalized the respective national financial systems. Moreover, both were drafted without the input of the banks and implemented by using the disorganization of the banks against them, turning the healthy banks into allies against the failing ones. Both plans were also drafted with an eye toward minimizing moral hazard and maximizing the chances of a positive return, though the specific strategies varied. The UK plan relied on punitive rates for the distressed banks, while the US plan involved roping the healthy banks into shouldering some of the burden as well. Crucial to evaluating TARP is the recognition of the lack of role played by the banks in its drafting. This left policymakers free to draft whatever policies they thought best. This still captured a variety of policy positions, from Bunning's free market fundamentalism to Bernanke's ambitious state ownership plans. However, the politically isolated failing banks had no ability to shape the policymaking process, and the healthy banks no incentive to do so. This meant negotiations were driven by the ideologies and electoral calculations of the executive and legislative branch agents, which, despite some arguments for avoiding state control, nevertheless consistently favored limiting moral hazard as a chief goal alongside restoring systemic stability.

Post-TARP Rescues

Once TARP was in place, it became the chief vehicle for the distribution of assistance to failing institutions. Three financial institutions in particular are worth analyzing, as all were of systemic importance: AIG, Citigroup, and Bank of America. Moreover, all would be cited by critics of the US response as prime examples of US generosity to the financial sector.

AIG under TARP

Even after falling into majority government ownership and receiving an $85 billion line of credit from the Federal Reserve, AIG continued to struggle, requiring an additional $27 billion to pay off its outstanding CDS (United States Congress House Committee on Financial Services, 2011, p. 498). This would prompt additional state support in three components. The first was a $40 billion injection of preferred stock from TARP, while the second and third, known as Maiden Lane II and III, were loans to address AIG's outstanding obligations (United States Congress House Committee on Financial Services, 2011, p. 498). Maiden Lane II was a $19.8 billion loan from the New York Fed to allow AIG to purchase mortgage-backed securities from its life insurance company subsidiaries, essentially preventing an escalation of losses on that front. Maiden Lane III was designed to address AIG's outstanding CDS problems (Johnson and Kwak, 2010, p. 169; United States Congress House Committee on Financial Services, 2011, p. 499).

The TARP injection and Maiden Lane II were relatively unproblematic from a moral hazard standpoint, as the injection got relatively good terms and Maiden Lane II was well collateralized. Maiden Lane III, on the other hand, attracted considerably more controversy, as it was used to buy back CDOs from AIG-FP's counterparties. The value of these CDOs had been guaranteed by AIG-FP's CDS, so their collapse in value threatened to drag down all of AIG. While the buyback was necessary to limit AIG's exposure, Maiden Lane III controversially paid 100¢ on the dollar for CDOs, effectively insulating all counterparties from risk (Johnson and Kwak, 2010, p. 169; United States Congress House Committee on Financial Services, 2011, pp. 499–500). This lack of burden-sharing by AIG counterparties would be roundly criticized not only by outside observers such as Clinton-era Treasury Secretary Larry Summers and former IMF Chief Economist Simon Johnson but also by Special Investigator General for TARP Neil Barofsky, the program's independent overseer (Barofsky, 2012, p. 180; Johnson and Kwak, 2010, pp. 169, 174). Treasury officials would counter that they had no leverage to renegotiate, as the counterparties had legal claim over AIG assets if AIG defaulted on its obligations. This meant that the creditors would have been legally entitled to full repayment, and the Treasury and Federal Reserve left with a substantial loss on their investments in AIG (United States Congress House Committee on Financial Services, 2011, p. 500). Therefore, there was little space to negotiate a more favorable offer, making the alternative a bankruptcy in which counterparties receive only a fraction of their value but with much broader systemic consequences. The CDO buyback was a good deal for the bank counterparties and again illustrates the political clout of US banks when healthy, as, apart from their AIG exposure, most of the relevant banks were in no danger of collapse. Importantly, since AIG was majority-owned by the United States at this point, there were relatively few moral hazard problems in the United States supporting AIG shareholders. Because AIG was nationalized, aid to AIG essentially was simply a transfer of funds from one government account to another, and not a transfer to private citizens.

Citigroup

Despite $25 billion in capital injections from TARP, Citi continued to struggle into 2009. Citi was in a unique position in American finance, being the only true universal bank in the United States. Although universal banking, combining investment and commercial banking in one institution, had been legalized with the repeal of Glass-Steagall in 1999, most US banks remained primarily focused on one function or the other. The large investment houses may have owned small commercial banks, but their investment operations dwarfed their deposit-taking ones. Similarly, the large commercial banks that branched out into investment banking generally kept their investment arms relatively limited. Until 2008, when JP Morgan obtained Bear Stearns and Bank of America took Merrill Lynch, Citi alone had both substantial commercial and investment banking operations (Bair, 2012, p. 121; United States Congress House Committee on Financial Services, 2011, p. 138). In addition to Citibank, Citi's large commercial bank, Citi had acquired Salomon Brothers' investment bank operations by merging with Salomon's buyer, Travelers

Insurance, in 1998[4] (United States Congress House Committee on Financial Services, 2011, pp. 96, 354). This meant that Citi also had a substantial investment bank within its operations. Therefore, the collapse of Citi had greater potential to wreak havoc than other comparably sized institutions and that existing resolution procedures were limited in their reach. Different regulators had responsibility for different arms of the bank, such that neither of the bank's primary regulators – the Federal Reserve and the OCC – had a clear picture of what was going on in other parts of the bank, though problems in one division could bring down the whole edifice (Bair, 2012, p. 121; United States Congress House Committee on Financial Services, 2011, p. 404). The FDIC could put Citibank, the commercial banking arm, into receivership, letting the rest of Citigroup fall into bankruptcy. This would not, however, protect the FDIC from taking losses on Citibank as a result of losses from the investment bank or other divisions, making receivership an unattractive option that would both fail to contain the crisis and impose high losses on the FDIC's Deposit Insurance Fund (Bair, 2012, p. 173). This complexity also meant that managing the bank was more difficult. CEO Vikram Pandit came out of the investment banking world and was regarded by regulators, especially Sheila Bair at the FDIC, as being outside of his competence managing a commercial bank (Bair, 2012, p. 2).

Citi, therefore, presented significant and unique risks and was a high priority for US policymakers. Citi was highly exposed to subprime assets, up to $55 billion, from its investment banking arm and had been in a precarious position for most of 2008 (United States Congress House Committee on Financial Services, 2011, pp. 346, 353). Citi attempted to address its weaknesses by acquiring Wachovia with federal loss guarantees, which could have potentially used Wachovia's deposit base to plug Citi's own holes. This move backfired, however, and publically losing a bidding war with Wells Fargo for Wachovia rattled investor confidence in Citi, leaving the bank in a worse position than before (United States Congress House Committee on Financial Services, 2011, p. 501). Citi became heavily dependent on state aid, taking $25 billion in TARP capital injections, $25 billion in liquidity assistance, and $32 billion in senior debt guarantees from the FDIC (United States Congress House Committee on Financial Services, 2011, p. 504). Nevertheless, the bank continued to teeter, weighed down by its increasingly worthless

[4] This merger, prior to Glass-Steagall's repeal, was possible because existing law allowed such mergers so long as either the commercial or investment banking activities were spun off within five years. The repeal of Glass-Steagall the following year made this spin-off unnecessary.

toxic assets. Moreover, the bank's lack of sufficient remaining collateral and fears that any new liquidity would immediately be drained by panicked investors meant that the Federal Reserve balked at expanding Citi's liquidity support (United States Congress House Committee on Financial Services, 2011, p. 504).

It became clear to policymakers that Citi would either need to solve its toxic asset problem or fail. Only Citibank could be taken into receivership by the FDIC, leaving a significant portion of its operations to fall into Lehman-style bankruptcy. Moreover, the costs of resolving Citibank threatened to drain the FDIC's Deposit Insurance Fund, handicapping the agency's ability to resolve future commercial bank failures (Bair, 2012, p. 123). Therefore, senior policymakers, especially Geithner and Paulson, resisted use of the FDIC receivership process and rejected any plan to let Citi fail (Bair, 2012, p. 123; Lowenstein, 2010, p. 278; Paulson, 2010, p. 411).

If failure and receivership were not viable, this meant that Citi needed to contain the losses on its toxic assets. A bad bank remained problematic for both moral hazard and practical reasons, meaning that policymakers turned to a "ring fence" approach not unlike the loss backstop provided to JP Morgan in the Bear Stearns purchase. Citi and the Treasury together identified $306 billion in problem assets to be put under loss-sharing protection (Bair, 2012, p. 125; Paulson, 2010, p. 410; United States Congress House Committee on Financial Services, 2011, p. 505). Citi would absorb the first $39.5 billion in losses, the estimated most likely depreciation of the assets, while the government and Citi would split losses on the remaining assets, with the United States taking 90 percent and Citi 10 percent of all further losses (Bair, 2012, p. 125; United States Congress House Committee on Financial Services, 2011, p. 505). Reflecting Citi's sprawling reach and multiple regulators, the costs were divided among various government agencies. The Treasury would absorb the first $5 billion in losses, the FDIC the next $10 billion, and the Federal Reserve any losses above that (United States Congress House Committee on Financial Services, 2011, p. 505). In order to further improve market confidence in Citi, an additional $20 billion in new preferred stock was issued (Bair, 2012, p. 125; Paulson, 2010, p. 414; United States Congress House Committee on Financial Services, 2011, p. 505). This new preferred stock was not on the relatively generous 5 percent dividend terms of the first injection, but carried a higher 8 percent dividend (United States Congress House Committee on Financial Services, 2011, p. 504). This improved Citi's capital position and increased the cost to the Treasury, but also further diluted shareholders and improved the Treasury's terms of capital injection. Once again, Bernanke pushed for expanded common stock purchases, but Paulson resisted, not wanting to become a majority shareholder in Citi (Paulson, 2010, p. 413).

Thus, the arrangement as structured aimed to expose Citi to the most likely actual losses while limiting investor panic at the prospect of broader losses. It, therefore, was moral hazard–limiting if estimates of losses were correct, though undeniably created moral hazard if losses exceeded $39.5 billion. On the other hand, Citi private shareholders saw their equity further diluted, as the Treasury was now one-third owner of the bank (Lowenstein, 2010, p. 278). Moreover, the terms of preferred stock that Pandit had described as "cheap capital" were now altered, replaced with terms that were market value, further diminishing the position of Citi's private shareholders. Citi's terms of repayment would worsen further in February 2009, when the original $25 billion of preferred stock, with more generous terms, would be converted into common stock, eliminating the "cheap capital" advantages of the original injection (Bair, 2012, p. 167).

Ultimately, the ring-fence and injections worked to stabilize Citi. Furthermore, though, at $45 billion, Citi took more in TARP capital than any other institution, it was ultimately either repaid or sold at a profit by the Treasury by the end of 2010 (United States Congress House Committee on Financial Services, 2011, p. 505). The Citi ring-fence would also serve as a model for the United Kingdom's own asset protection plan, as a solution to toxic assets that minimized the moral hazard issues of a bad bank (Comptroller and Auditor General National Audit Office (UK), 2010a, pp. 20–21).

Bank of America

Citi's ring-fence would also attract the attention of Bank of America, which was struggling with its purchase of Merrill Lynch (Bair, 2012, p. 127). Following third-quarter losses of $5.1 billion, estimated fourth-quarter losses for Merrill Lynch climbed from $5 billion to $12 billion by December 2008 (United States Congress House Committee on Financial Services, 2011, p. 506). It became increasingly clear that Merrill Lynch was insolvent, and not merely illiquid (Bair, 2012, p. 114). Merrill's outgoing CEO, John Thain, claimed that Bank of America was aware of Merrill's position at the time of purchase, but Bank of America CEO Ken Lewis disagreed (United States Congress House Committee on Financial Services, 2011, p. 507). More problematically for policymakers, Lewis began suggesting he would invoke a "material adverse change" clause in the Bank of America–Merrill Lynch merger contract to exit from the agreement (Paulson, 2010, p. 429; United States Congress House Committee on Financial Services, 2011, p. 507). In taking this position, Lewis attempted to use Bank of America's remaining political clout, pressing to either break the merger or get government assistance to back the merger.

Bank of America's position had deteriorated both legally and economically, however, and with it the bank's political influence. Legally, invoking the material adverse change clause was by no means guaranteed to succeed, leaving Bank of America potentially irrevocably tethered to Merrill Lynch's losses. Even without Merrill weighing down Bank of America, the commercial bank was coming under increasing market pressure. Just as the fall of Bear Stearns put pressure on Lehman Brothers, so too did Citi's distress cause investors to look askance at the other commercial banks. Of the remaining major commercial banks, Wells Fargo, with its West Coast focus and lack of ties to Wall Street, was seen as outside the crisis, while JP Morgan was regarded as perhaps the sturdiest financial institution in the United States (Bair, 2012, p. 331). That left Bank of America as the most prominent target after Citi for investors nervous about distress in the commercial banks.

Policymakers took advantage of both of these factors to put pressure on Bank of America. Paulson and Bernanke both informed Lewis that invoking the material adverse change clause "was not a legally reasonable option" (United States Congress House Committee on Financial Services, 2011, p. 507). Paulson moreover argued that the collapse of the deal would demonstrate a "colossal loss of judgment" by Bank of America, weakening Bank of America as well as Merrill Lynch (United States Congress House Committee on Financial Services, 2011, p. 508). Paulson reminded Lewis that pursuing a "destructive" strategy on "no reasonable legal basis" would give the Federal Reserve pretext to exercise its legal authority to replace both the Bank of America board and management (United States Congress House Committee on Financial Services, 2011, p. 508). Bernanke, for his part, supported Paulson by promising Lewis that Bank of America would receive no government assistance of any kind unless the Bank of America–Merrill Lynch deal went through (Paulson, 2010, p. 427; United States Congress House Committee on Financial Services, 2011, p. 508). Given that investor confidence in Bank of America would be rattled by the collapse of the Merrill deal, policymaker resistance threatened to put Bank of America in a devastating position. These naked threats worked, and the Bank of America–Merrill Lynch merger was completed without renegotiation or direct subsidy on January 1, 2009 (United States Congress House Committee on Financial Services, 2011, p. 509).

Once Citi won its ring-fence protection, however, Bank of America petitioned for a similar plan. Having decided that ring-fences were a superior method than bad banks to provide supplemental support, the Federal Reserve and FDIC negotiated an equivalent plan for Bank of America (Bair, 2012, p. 126). $118 billion in assets, mostly from Merrill Lynch, would be identified, with Bank of America taking the first $10 billion in losses, then burden-sharing losses on the same 9:1 split with the government that Citi received (United States Congress House Committee on Financial Services, 2011, p. 509). Because the majority of assets were not from commercial banking, the FDIC's exposure was less, with the first $10 billion of government losses split 75 percent/25 percent between the Treasury and FDIC, and the remaining losses taken by the Federal Reserve (United States Congress House Committee on Financial Services, 2011, p. 510). In addition, the Treasury would use TARP to purchase an additional $20 billion in preferred stock, carrying the same high 8 percent divided as the second Citi injection (United States Congress House Committee on Financial Services, 2011, p. 509). As with Citi, the plan was designed for Bank of America to absorb all likely losses and the government to absorb extraordinary losses above that. However, by May, Bank of America came to believe that losses would be below $10 billion, making maintaining the ring-fence arrangement expensive and unnecessary. It, therefore, negotiated an exit from the program, but not before paying a $425 million termination fee to cover the benefit it received from four months of coverage (United States Congress House Committee on Financial Services, 2011, p. 510).

State policies toward Bank of America again demonstrate the willingness of policymakers to take a hard line with weak banks. Although Bank of America had been a valuable partner in helping policymakers broker a private solution for Merrill Lynch, once Bank of America itself was in distress, it was dealt with as harshly as any other failing bank. Paulson and Bernanke nakedly threatened Lewis with both legal action shattering confidence in the bank and with withholding of state aid to prevent its failure unless Bank of America fulfilled its obligations and completed the Merrill Lynch merger. Once again, the Lehman Brothers precedent proved valuable, by demonstrating the willingness of policymakers to allow the failure of a major institution. Moreover, since Bank of America was FDIC-insured, the threat gained additional credibility. A Bank of America receivership would have been costly to the FDIC Deposit Insurance Fund, but a legal mechanism already existed to make the fall of Bank of America softer than that of Lehman Brothers. This gave policymakers an even stronger negotiating position to compel Bank of America to commit to its private rescue of Merrill, even as the profitability to Bank of America declined. Subsequent aid, moreover, ultimately would be declined by Bank of America as imposing greater costs on the bank than going forward without aid would do.

Conclusion

Ultimately, the financial crisis and its responses in the United States is a story not of political weakness of the financial sector generally but of disorganization and self-interest, producing a scenario where the healthy firms retain considerable clout while the failing firms have little choice but to accept whatever offers policymakers or other firms present them with. The clout of healthy firms in the United States is readily demonstrated before the crisis, with the Glass-Steagall repeal and the successful campaign against derivatives regulation, and also during the crisis, especially in JP Morgan's ability to secure a generous subsidy for its purchase of Bear Stearns. However, when banks fail, they fall both far and fast. Their representatives are largely shut out of policy negotiations, and their proposals for relief generally disregarded, as seen in the immediate rejection of proposals by Bear Stearns, Lehman Brothers, and Wachovia for terms of state assistance. Not only are the banks themselves shut out, but they lack the healthy bank allies and strong organizational support found in Germany. The healthy banks in the United States neither played a lobbying role on behalf of the failing ones nor provided any direct support. The one attempt to organize a consortium rescue, for Lehman Brothers, failed to produce a result, and purchase offers for failing banks were made only at fire-sale prices. In some cases, successfully for Bear Stearns and unsuccessfully for Lehman Brothers, healthy banks attempted to secure state aid to benefit the buyer, but not the distressed bank. Even at the height of the crisis, failing banks saw the healthy banks as rivals, potentially looking to poach valuable clients rather than potential saviors.

US banking associations played even less of a role than their British peers. The British Banking Association had no organizational role, but at least remained a high-profile and vocal critic of state policies. The major US organizations, the American Banking Association and the Financial Services Roundtable, played no such role and certainly came nowhere close to the active role of the German associations, which not only organized private and public–private rescues directly but also were active participants in the policy debates on the terms of state rescues.

As a result, US policymakers were unencumbered by pressures from the banking sector, and the key determinants of policy outcomes were the policy preferences of the relevant policymakers. These proved diverse in the US case, from Senator Bunning's willingness to let the banks fail no matter the consequence rather than involve the state to Fed Chair Bernanke and FDIC Chair Bair's strong support for temporary nationalization. Apart from New York Fed President Geithner, the vast majority of voices preferred taking a hard line with the banks, even if it meant failure or state ownership. Even here, it is hard to see a clear influence of the financial sector. Geithner was a career civil servant, without direct links to Wall Street, and therefore more likely swayed by ideology rather than political influence. By contrast, Treasury Secretary Paulson, a former Goldman Sachs CEO with the clearest links to Wall Street of any of the major players, would be one of the strongest advocates for defending the principle of limiting moral hazard, supporting a Lehman bankruptcy and mandatory capital injections on punitive terms for the others.

The results of this political configuration were a range of resolution policies that broadly conform to the principles of minimizing moral hazard and perverse redistribution. The US experience also illustrates the value of a predefined resolution authority. By far, the most successful rescues, in terms of limiting both broader panic and moral hazard, were the FDIC resolutions, which proved capable of resolving even large banks such as Countrywide and WaMu on good terms for taxpayers. Resolution authority was not used in the cases of Wachovia and Bank of America, but was a useful credible threat to force the banks into accepting alternate rescue programs. A compulsory legal authority also enabled the resolution of Fannie Mae and Freddie Mac with a minimum of negotiation.

Where no preexisting authority existed, state responses depended largely on the amount of leverage the state possessed over the affected banks. JP Morgan was able to secure a favorable subsidy for its purchase of Bear Stearns because it could more credibly threaten to walk away from the merger than the United States could credibly threaten to allow Bear Stearns to fall. Even here, though, JP Morgan used its clout in its own interest, and not in the interest of Bear Stearns. A desire to reject the precedent set with Bear Stearns drove the United States to then let Lehman Brothers fall, in order to restore the credibility of US threats to let a major institution go into bankruptcy. A lack of leverage also forced the United States to accept a 100 percent payout for AIG's CDOs, as the counterparty banks could insist on full repayment, which would produce an AIG bankruptcy without state support but would be unlikely to bring down the counterparties. Since this was an unacceptable outcome to the United States and policymakers lacked either the legal authority or the leverage to compel compromise, they had little choice but to accept these terms.

When the state did possess leverage, however, it was quick to use it. Both Bear Stearns and Lehman Brothers, which were reliant on state support to survive, found that they virtually all influence in the policy process, while the GSEs and AIG had plans presented to them on a "take it or leave it" basis, forced to choose between majority state control and bankruptcy. Even the strongest of the investment banks, Morgan Stanley and Goldman Sachs, could not win exceptionally favorable treatment, only able to gain regulatory reclassification and not direct state support.

This dynamic is found in the TARP plan as well. In order to eliminate the stigma of accepting state aid, which forced the Germans to offer aid on extremely generous terms, US policymakers chose to make TARP injections mandatory for the top nine financial institutions. This required striking a balance between imposing harsh terms on failing banks and convincing healthy banks to accept assistance that they could not be legally compelled to take. This was accomplished by a combination of playing off of the healthy banks' systemic fears, making it an all-or-nothing proposal, and offering assistance on terms that were generous at first but would become punitive later. Doing so won the support of the healthy banks while providing cover for the weaker ones. These terms would be more generous than any future TARP support, however, which would carry a moral hazard–limiting 8–10 percent dividend, at or higher than the rate a market investor would charge.

The cases of chief criticism similarly reflect the United States attempting to minimize moral hazard within the limits of its ability. The most naked state aid, the subsidy of JP Morgan's purchase of Bear Stearns, reflected the influence of the healthy JP Morgan and benefited JP Morgan but not Bear Stearns. The greatest losses to the taxpayer in the crisis would come from Fannie Mae and Freddie Mac, but even here the actual terms of intervention wiped out existing shareholders in a compulsory nationalization. The failure of the GSE rescue to produce a positive return reflect not the terms of the rescue but the deep fiscal hole the two institutions were able to dig themselves thanks to decades of kid-glove treatment by regulators in the time when their political clout was unrivaled. Finally, Citi, the case where Bair, among others, saw the softest treatment by the state, did ultimately produce a positive return for the state and in less than two years. Indeed, excluding the automotive industry bailout component, TARP would produce a positive return for the United States, reflecting terms that defended taxpayer interests.

The US experience, therefore, shows policymakers consistently taking as hard a line as possible against the failing firms, in contrast to the soft line of the Germans. In some cases, such as the bankruptcy of Lehman Brothers and the FDIC nationalizations, the United States would take a harder line than the United Kingdom. At the same time, however, the healthy US institutions continued to demonstrate considerable influence. While the United States can impose a hard line against the failing firms, it has limited ability to prevent banks from engaging in risky behavior or to develop an FDIC-style prefunded resolution authority for the investment banks. This in turn increases the importance of imposing harsh costs on failing banks, as the threat of market discipline remains the most effective tool US regulators possess to limit the excesses of its investment banks.

6 Conclusion

Examining state responses to financial crises reveals a seeming paradox: states with a tradition of laissez-faire economic policies adopt crisis response policies that both rely heavily on an expansion of state ownership and involve the state taking a hard line with private interests, while states with a tradition of state management through organized capitalist systems respond with a far lighter state intervention, through generous assistance that minimizes state ownership and relies heavily on the voluntary compliance of private interests. Through an examination of the interests of healthy banks and banking associations and the political positions they take in times of crisis, this seeming paradox can be resolved. Liberal, capital market–based financial systems produce atomized interbank relationships, such that when banks run into distress they have little influence and few allies, enabling the state to take a hard line and adopt policies that minimize moral hazard and perverse redistribution while maximizing the likelihood of the state recovering its money. By contrast, in corporatist, private bank–based financial systems, greater interdependence means failing banks have allies in other banks and in private governance associations. This means that private banks and their associations are more willing both to contribute their own money toward rescuing their peers and to use their political influence to shape state responses to be more favorable to the banks.

This understanding of the comparative dynamics of banking crises across advanced capitalist states carries important lessons for understandings of financial power and the ability of financial systems to resist convergence pressures, which will be discussed following an examination of the validity of the argument in comparative perspective and a discussion of relevant alternate explanations. Finally, although significant structural differences exist between the liberal and corporatist financial systems, a series of policy lessons may be gleaned that are applicable in both contexts and will be discussed at the close.

Comparing State Responses to Banking Crises

The Role of Financial Systems

Looking at state responses to banking crises comparatively reveals clearly divergent patterns of state response. Those states in which stock markets dominate the provision of capital have a markedly and statistically significantly greater propensity toward state intervention through ownership stakes or nationalization than those with a private bank–dominated national financial system. Moreover, the former are also significantly more likely to recover the money they invest in rescuing their financial systems in times of crisis. An examination of responses in Germany, the United Kingdom, and the United States reveals that this divergence can be traced to the tighter and more cooperative interbank relationships in private bank–based systems, which produces stronger private governance networks and both greater willingness and greater ability for healthy banks to intervene to secure more favorable treatment. In their absence, policymakers in states with capital market–based systems can more easily implement policies that minimize moral hazard and perverse redistribution while maximizing the chances of the state recovering its money. Private rescues are also more common in states with private bank–based systems and that the terms of public intervention are harsher for banks in states with capital market–based systems.

In Germany, private banks dominate the provision of capital, providing approximately twice as much capital to firms as the German stock markets. In the United Kingdom, this ratio is closer to 1:1, while in the United States, stock markets provide over four times the capital of private banks. Because of the longer-term nature of bank–client relationships when private bank capital dominates, banks in such systems are in less direct competition with each other and more likely to form interdependent relationships and stronger private governance systems. In the three pillars of German banking, banks are highly interdependent, with extensive cross-shareholding and strong private governance networks. In the highly competitive British and American systems, interbank relationships are far more at arm's length. Interbank lending is only done at risk-sensitive rates and on good collateral, cross-shareholding is extremely limited, and sectoral associations are extremely weak. In contrast to the strong German associations, which even run private deposit insurance schemes, the British and American banking associations are merely industry lobbies, which cannot stop their members from working at cross-purposes. These differences would be reflected in how both the banks and the states managed the 2007–2009 crisis.

In Germany, private banks played a key role in organizing and funding rescue efforts, especially initially. Initial rescues of IKB, SachsenLB, and Hypo RE contained significant private components, negotiated by the banking associations and funded by contributions from their members. Such privately funded rescues were virtually unheard of in the United States and the United Kingdom. The British government organized a small private consortium to support Bradford & Bingley, but only with significant effort by policymakers to extract a relatively meager contribution. In the United States, attempts to organize a private consortium to rescue Lehman Brothers collapsed entirely. The only private bank involvement in resolving failing banks in the United States and the United Kingdom were "fire sale" purchases: buying the assets of a distressed peer at a bargain price. In some cases, such as the purchase of Bear Stearns by JP Morgan or the proposed purchase of Northern Rock by Virgin, even the fire sales would only be contemplated with a subsidy by the state. The German banks, therefore, showed a consistently greater willingness to contribute to rescues in the interest of systemic stability than their Anglo-American peers. Diminished interbank competition in Germany made systemic stability more important than gaining a marginal advantage over other banks and made private governance associations stronger. Stronger private governance associations, in turn, made it easier to act in the interest of systemic stability by rapidly organizing private consortium rescues.

The shape of the financial system also played a key role in shaping public rescues. In the absence of private rescues, the United States and the United Kingdom needed to intervene in relatively small cases such as the FDIC-insured institutions and Northern Rock. The quantitative data reflects this as well, as the state in capital market–based systems generally intervened more readily than in private bank–based systems. Not only the extent but also the form of state intervention would be determined by the role played by the healthy banks and the banking associations. Since failing American and British banks found no support from healthy banks or banking associations, they had little choice but to accept whatever terms the state issued. This enabled policymakers in both the United Kingdom and the United States to shape rescues that came at a high cost to failing banks. In Germany, the banks and banking associations played a key role in shaping state responses. Representatives of the banking associations and the major private banks helped draft not only the rescue of Hypo RE but also the SoFFin systemic rescue plan and its later modifications. These banks even included Commerzbank, one of the institutions seen as highly likely to need to participate in these rescues. This access reflected not only the interest of the still powerful healthy banks but also the importance of the private governance associations as regulatory partners of state authorities. The banks and banking associations used their position to promote plans that treated the failing banks more favorably. This is nowhere more clearly illustrated than with the bad bank, which was a component of the second round revision of SoFFin, a plan that was based largely on one developed and promoted by the BdB, the commercial banks' association, and that helped insulate banks from losses on their toxic assets.

As a result of the differing ability and willingness of the healthy banks and their governance associations to shape rescues, the outcomes in the three cases were substantially different. In the United States, the rescue efforts were broadly successful at limiting a broader financial system collapse at a relatively small net cost, both containing the crisis and minimizing losses to taxpayers. This was accomplished by a reliance on full- and partial-nationalizations. Terms were either compulsory, as with the FDIC-insured banks and the GSEs, or effectively compulsory or nonnegotiable, as with AIG and the TARP recipients. The terms were structured in a way to minimize net costs to the United States, and indeed, by 2012, the United States had turned a profit on its state aid.

The British story is similar. State aid was on harsh terms, with the full nationalization of Northern Rock and Bradford & Bingley on *de minimis* terms and the compulsory capital injections into the larger banks carrying a high dividend on preferred shares and a low price on common stock. The United Kingdom has yet to show a profit on its rescue investments, but policymakers remain optimistic that they will ultimately recover all of their money. This reflects in part the larger scale of the crisis in the United Kingdom, relative to the GDP.

The German outcome was significantly worse in terms of recovery of investment. Although the banks contributed to early rescues, the ultimate state-funded plan was considerably more generous than in either the United States or the United Kingdom. The German plan was anticipated to ultimately operate at a loss, a prediction that proved accurate. Because Germany made state aid voluntary, the state was forced to incentivize banks to take up aid by making the terms attractive. The Germans, moreover, were extremely reluctant to engage in compulsory nationalization, favoring share purchases over expropriation, which also increased costs.

These patterns in the cases are broadly reflected in the quantitative analysis. Although the quantitative analysis cannot capture the specific terms of state aid, it does show that states with capital market–based systems were both more willing to use state ownership and more likely to recover their funds. As demonstrated in the cases, this divergence can be traced to the willingness of healthy banks and their governance associations to use their political access to shape state responses in ways more favorable to the failing banks and the banking sector generally.

Alternate Hypotheses

Several alternate hypotheses have been suggested to explain state policies in banking crises, though the statistical analysis and cases studies suggest that none of them were determinative. Party policies would seem to be an obvious potential factor, with left parties seen as more likely to take a harder line with the banks than right parties, which are less comfortable with state intervention and more likely to count financial interests as part of their base. Both the statistical analysis and the cases studied, however, show very little effect of party. Within the cases, there was much more consensus than division between parties over state responses to the crisis. Lack of division is somewhat unsurprising in Germany, which was governed by a center-right/center-left CDU-CSU/SPD (Christian Democrat/Social Democrat) Grand Coalition into 2009. However, the noncoalition parties also raised relatively few objections as well, and when the SPD moved into opposition in 2009, it remained quiet on bank assistance. In the United States, Democratic and Republican party leadership worked together to push TARP through, and opposition came primarily from the further left elements of the Democrats and the further right elements of the Republicans. This opposition, however, rather than arguing for more favorable terms for the banks, argued for even harsher terms, letting the banks fail even at the risk of systemic crisis. Parties in the United Kingdom disagreed somewhat more, but chiefly over whether the state should prioritize either minimizing the state's outlay of assistance, and thus risk of losses, or maximizing the likelihood of recovering investment, even if that meant taking large stakes at punitive terms in the banks. Neither the incumbent Labour Party nor the opposition Liberal Democrats and Tories favored more generous terms to the banks. The lone exception was the Scottish National Party, which favored more generous terms toward HBOS. Even this, however, was driven not by a desire to protect the bankers per se but rather out of a desire to keep HBOS independent of London banks and thus make a stronger case for Scottish secession. In all of these cases, therefore, state aid to the banks was therefore largely depoliticized and framed as a technical question rather than one to be addressed through party conflict.

A second factor to be examined in some detail is the role of international institutions in managing the conflict. The most prominent of these institutions to play a role in the crisis was the European Union, and especially the Competitiveness Directorate of the European Commission (EC). Obviously, the EC played no significant role in non-EU members, including the United States, but even in the United Kingdom, its role was fairly small, generally approving of UK rescue plans with only slight modifications. It played a much more important role in Germany, where it was routinely critical of German rescue plans, frequently flagging the German state for excessive state aid and insisting at times on substantial modifications to German policies or divestment of large portions of state-assisted German banks. This therefore fits the prediction that international integration creates pressures to limit competition-distorting, moral hazard–creating policies. The EC formed, in essence, an upper limit of how generous state aid to the banks could be. In the United Kingdom, where the failing banks had little influence, policymakers had no incentive to be generous, when such generosity would run the risk of greater state losses and political fallout from angry voters. As such, British aid routinely fell short of the maximums set by the EC. In Germany, by contrast, where the healthy banks and banking associations pressed for more generous aid, the state routinely pressed up against EC limits. The German assistance would have been even more generous without the EC to rein it in.

A final alternate argument is that dynamics should be different in federal states, where the banks will have more potential channels of influence. Federalism is not found to be a statistically significant predictor of state policy, and the two federal cases diverge in the role the federal system played. In the United States, the federal states played no real role in managing the crisis, with all assistance and thus all key policy debates, conducted by representatives of the federal government. In Germany, however, the Länder would play key roles in the response, at times serving as an alternate and more generous source of aid to the banks, especially the Landesbanken. There are some important differences between German and American federalism, including significantly that the US states operate under a hard budget constraint, barring them from running deficits and diminishing their ability to provide substantial assistance.[1] More important, however, is the extent of state ownership at the subnational state level in the two cases. The US states have virtually no ownership stakes in the banks, especially the national banks, and therefore little incentive to not simply let the federal government manage the crisis. The Länder, however, are large shareholders in the Landesbanken, meaning that they have a direct stake in the terms the Landesbanken

[1] This barrier to running deficits is found in the state constitutions of forty-nine of the fifty US states, with Vermont, not a major banking center, the lone exception.

receive. This in turn may give the Länder an incentive to provide an alternate source of assistance, rather than accept less desirable terms from the federal government. That ownership stakes, and not the hard budget constraint, is the key difference may also be indicated by the fact that the Länder only provided aid to the Landesbanken, and not to any distressed commercial banks in their territory.

Changes and Continuity in National Financial Systems

This analysis hinges on an understanding of how the structure of the domestic financial system affects the power resources and interests of banks in crisis and thus the degree to which they are capable of influencing policymakers. It therefore focuses on the political influence of financial actors, and not the economic functionalism that drives Hall and Soskice's *Varieties of Capitalism*. A logic of economic functionalism would suggest that states with a private bank–based system would consider a wholly different slate of options than those with a capital market–based system, but that does not bear out in practice. The menu of policy options was broadly the same in all three cases, but the choices made were different. The Germans considered mandatory plans and substantial capital injections, but ultimately rejected them, while the Americans and the British attempted private consortium rescues with little success. This is more adequately explained through a political theory of comparative capitalisms than one of economic functionalism. The German banks had political resources to shape the terms of the response more than their American or British counterparts, and this provides a more compelling explanation of the differences in outcome than the logic of economic functionalism. Moreover, similarities between the American and British financial systems precrisis means that economic functionalism is a poor explanation of why the outcomes of the two cases look more liberal in the American case and more statist in the British case. Again political explanations, especially a greater tolerance for state-owned enterprises among British policymakers, prove more credible.

The German case in comparison to the United States and the United Kingdom shows a clear difference that can be traced to the presence of private governance institutions in German finance. Conceiving of corporatism as a system in which private governance structures shape the direction of economic actors allows for a clear explanation of the greater political clout of the financial sector in times of crisis in corporatist systems, as the weaker actors have the support of the private governance institutions and the stronger actors, producing a better ability to shape the political process.

These power dynamics also explain why – despite a shock that weakened both the political strength of status quo actors and the legitimacy of the current system – neither the capital market nor the private bank–based systems saw significant reform or restructuring. In Germany, the crisis prompted some bank consolidation, both within the Landesbanken and the commercial banks, but the three-pillar structure remains intact and the state has not significantly changed its relationship with the banking sector. Only one bank was fully nationalized, and that bank, Hypo RE, was nationalized only to facilitate an orderly wind-down. State stakes in the other banks were kept as small as possible and with an eye toward selling them as soon as possible. The state's stake in IKB, which it obtained before the crisis, was even sold at a loss due to pressures from the banking industry to withdraw state ownership. This return to the status quo was thanks in no small part to the willingness of the healthy German banks and the banking associations to take steps to preserve that system, both through privately funded rescues, as in SachsenLB, and through a willingness on the part of the healthy banks to push for state aid that was generous and hands-off. The institutions of corporatist finance, bank interdependence, and private governance structures, therefore, worked as factors pushing toward the perpetuation of the corporatist structures.

The United States retained the essentially liberal orientation of its precrisis financial system, though with some significant changes. Most obviously, the US government now owns Fannie Mae and Freddie Mac, giving it a key position at the heart of the mortgage finance system. As of 2015, debate continues as to whether these firms should be held, sold off whole, sold off partially while retaining a public stake, or wound down and sold off in pieces. A second change is that, fifteen years after the repeal of Glass-Steagall, the United States is finally developing true universal banks. Bank of America's purchase of Merrill Lynch and JP Morgan's purchase of Bear Stearns means that these institutions now join Citigroup in having investment arms comparable in size to their commercial banks. Meanwhile, with Goldman Sachs and Morgan Stanley converted to bank holding companies, no large institutions remain chartered as independent investment banks. Ultimately, however, US finance remains dominated by stock market capital and largely free of state ownership.

The structure of the UK financial system is somewhat more changed than in the United States. While both states relied heavily on nationalization in the crisis, the United States largely either took preferred shares or quickly sold off its state-owned banks. The United Kingdom, however, emerged from the crisis as the sole owner of the now merged Northern

Rock and Bradford & Bingley, the majority shareholder of RBS, and a significant minority shareholder in Lloyds/HBOS. This is a significant move toward state-dominated banking. Politicians have repeatedly declared their intent to reprivatize the banks once the state can make a profit on its stake. However, there have been significant calls, both from outside groups and from members of Parliament, to manage these banks not just as profit-maximizing firms but with the aim of furthering state goals such as increasing credit to the economy and diminishing the impact of the postcrisis recession.

Unlike in Germany, however, differing structural developments in the United States and the United Kingdom are driven by choices made by state actors, and not of structural barriers to the transformation of the system. In the United States, Henry Paulson and his successor as Secretary of the Treasury, Timothy Geithner, both retained a strong ideological commitment to a privately owned financial system and therefore chose a model of state intervention that minimized state control and prioritized returning nationalized financial firms to private hands. In the United Kingdom, policymakers were more comfortable with longer-term state-owned banking. This choice was driven not only by ideology but also because rapid privatization would have imposed certain and high losses on the state, which might be ameliorated by delaying a sale until the banks recover. In neither case, however, were banks and banking associations the chief barriers to structural change.

The contrast between the two liberal systems and Germany is telling. In the German case, the institutions of private governance of finance served as barriers to systemic transformation. The healthy banks and banking associations were willing to use their political influence to block any move to a statist or liberal system. The preferences of state policymakers were thus only one factor determining whether the precrisis status quo would be preserved. This therefore furthers the argument that, while corporatist systems are hard to dislodge thanks to their self-perpetuating institutions, national financial systems can more easily transition between liberal and statist models, as the determining force pushing in one direction or the other is control of the state.

Policy Implications

In addition to the implications for the comparative capitalisms and multilevel governance literatures and the greater understanding of the dynamics of banking crises, the cases examined here also provide several lessons for policymakers, both in planning for managing banking crises and in devising policies in the midst of crises. The broader implication of this study focuses on the implications of structural features of national financial systems in shaping the politics of financial crises and as such may be of relatively little direct impact for policymakers. After all, the broad structural orientation of a national financial system will change only with immense effort, and one of the strengths of the comparative capitalisms literature is that it emphasizes the resilience of national financial systems. Therefore, changing the orientation of a national financial system will not be a viable option for policymakers, save perhaps in contemplating a broad overhaul of the national economy generally and in the long term. Nevertheless, there are several smaller policy implications that may be gleaned from comparing the responses of Germany, the United Kingdom, and the United States in the 2007–2009 crisis, especially for policymakers looking to take state action to limit moral hazard and maximize the chance of recovering state investment in banking rescues. Although the greater political clout of the banks in times of crisis in private bank–based systems may preclude their implementation in times of crisis, in principle all of the below prescriptions could be implemented as part of long-term crisis planning in economic good times, when the strength of the banks in a corporatist system is less clearly greater than that of those in a liberal system. Therefore, these prescriptions may be as valuable in either context.

Mandatory Plans Lower Costs to the State by Eliminating the Space for Banks to Negotiate Terms

Perhaps the chief reason why the German SoFFin plan consistently produced state intervention on better-than-market terms for the banks was that the German state lacked a mechanism to compel the banks to accept assistance. This created a space for banks to negotiate for more favorable terms, wagering that the state would sooner make the terms of aid more favorable than either risk letting a bank fail or risk letting a bank survive by contracting lending and cutting off credit to the broader economy. Without the ability to compel banks to accept money on state-determined terms, the state's unwillingness to risk damage to the broader economy gave banks leverage to extract above-market terms of assistance. Similarly, in the United States, because regulators lacked the legal authority to resolve Bear Stearns without the consent of both Bear Stearns and would-be purchaser JP Morgan-Chase, both Bear and JP Morgan representatives could extract favorable terms from the United States. JP Morgan, which could refuse to complete the purchase, leaving the United States no recourse other than to let Bear fall, used this leverage to extract a $29 billion subsidy of losses from the Federal Reserve.

Bear Stearns, meanwhile, successfully leveraged the potential damage of a Bear collapse to raise the sale price from the Treasury-directed $2 to $10 a share. If the United States had held the authority to compel an injection, Bear could not have refused the terms and would have lacked the ability to, in essence, hold the rest of the economy hostage in order to extract an increase in sale price.

By contrast, in cases in the United States and the United Kingdom where the state had the authority to compel the banks to accept assistance, they consistently were able to impose higher costs on the banks. The nationalization of the FDIC-insured banks and the GSEs in the United States and of Northern Rock and Bradford & Bingley in the United Kingdom came at *de minimis* compensation to shareholders. Similarly, the UK capital injections into RBS and Lloyds came at a higher price than the banks would have accepted if they had the authority to refuse. This was possible because the state possessed the legal authority to compel the banks to sell, meaning the banks had no opportunity to leverage the threat of refusal and failure to extract greater assistance.

Mandatory assistance, therefore, substantially increases the ability of the state to impose terms that best further its goals of minimizing moral hazard and maximizing the recovery of the state's investment. Although the German banks were able to block the imposition of mandatory terms of aid, the difficulties of the United States with Bear Stearns and the United Kingdom before it gained statutory authority to nationalize Northern Rock illustrate that voluntary assistance is problematic in liberal systems as well. Therefore, in both cases, pressing for mandatory aid may be a key element in the state's ability to maximize its goals.

Predetermined Response Plans Increase the Speed of Response and Thus Lower the Cost of Assistance Required

The FDIC approach, in addition to being a mandatory response plan, also had the virtue of being a predetermined response plan, drafted years in advance and executed according to a well-documented set of procedures. This produced several advantages. The first is minimizing market disruptions. FDIC procedures for managing a failing bank are well known by market actors, eliminating the uncertainty of investors: small depositors and senior debtholders can be reasonably assured of recovering their assets, while uninsured depositors, junior debtholders, and shareholders can assume they will lose out and plan accordingly. Although losses are imposed, they are known in advance and therefore produce less panic than in an ad hoc rescue. They also avoid suboptimal investment strategies for private investors. For instance, hedge funds SRM and RAB

Capital invested substantially in Northern Rock after its distress became public but prior to nationalization, assuming that they would be treated generously if the state intervened. Instead, both lost virtually their entire investment, increasing the uncertainty about investing in other institutions showing signs of weakness.

Predetermined plans are also faster to implement, enabling the state to act while the costs of intervention may be relatively low, before investors have fully deserted an ailing institution. The UK nationalization of Bradford & Bingley came at a lower cost to the state than that of Northern Rock, because the United Kingdom already possessed compulsory nationalization authority and could act as soon as it was clear that such a course of action would be necessary. In the Northern Rock case, UK officials delayed until it became clear that nationalization would be necessary and until the Parliament granted the Treasury nationalization authority. In the meantime, Northern Rock was propped up with expensive liquidity support, and investors deserted the bank, increasing the amount of state money needed to prop it up once in state ownership. At a further extreme, US policymakers' options were sharply limited for investment banks pre-TARP. Lacking a preexisting authority to inject capital, the state could only either let banks fail or subsidize private purchases. The slow-moving US legislative process meant that gaining new statutory authority was not possible in the time before major banks would collapse with potentially catastrophic effect. This forced policymakers to choose between a generous subsidy for purchasing banks, as in the Bear Stearns sale, or letting major institutions fail, as with Lehman Brothers.

Additionally, a predetermined process allows for longer deliberation over optimal policy choices in a precrisis environment. One common feature of crisis policymaking in all three cases discussed is that the time crunch required for policy action forced policymakers to "satisfice," adopting the first viable solution rather than debating at length the merits of various alternatives. This not only makes suboptimal policymaking more likely but gives greater clout to organized interests, which can present readily actionable plans that may be less advantageous than others. Since financial actors are generally more organized than, for instance, academics or public interest groups, this gives an advantage to bank-friendly policies.

A final advantage of predetermined plans is that they can potentially be prefunded. The FDIC-insured institutions imposed no costs on the American taxpayers in part because the rescues were paid for out of the FDIC Deposit Insurance Fund, filled by a precrisis levy on insured banks that gave the FDIC the resources to provide rescues without imposing new costs on taxpayers. By contrast, even the most moral hazard–limiting and expensive ad hoc plans in the United Kingdom and elsewhere in the United States necessarily imposed costs on taxpayers, whether ultimately paid back or not. Moreover, a prefunded system is fairer, by imposing some of the costs of the rescue on the banks that fail. Even if the costs of a non-prefunded rescue are ultimately covered by new taxes on the financial sector, as it has partially been in the United Kingdom, these are taxes on the banks that did not fail and did not require assistance. The banks that failed are in essence able to escape the tax by ceasing to exist before it is imposed. While the surviving banks still benefit from the containment of contagion, this is less fair than a prefunded levy, which enables burden-sharing even among the banks that fail to survive the crisis.

State Part-Ownership Gives Leverage to Banks to Extract More Generous Assistance from the State Because the State Will Feel Losses Directly

The broad disadvantages from state ownership of banks have been long debated in the literature. Critics of state ownership frequently highlight how the state may direct investment in suboptimal ways, to reward political allies or advance economically undesirable policy goals. Defenders of state ownership, meanwhile, highlight how state ownership of banks may allow for superior development policies and challenge the notion that state-owned banks are necessarily less successful than private banks. In times of crisis, however, state ownership presents additional issues, which are worth considering in drafting state response policies.

The first effect can be seen with the German Landesbanken, which are part-owned by the various German Länder. The distressed Landesbanken, especially HSH Nordbank and BayernLB, were able to use this to their advantage in a crisis, to extract assistance from the Länder in addition to or on more favorable terms than that available from the central government. These Landesbanken could leverage the costs their failure would impose directly on the Länder to extract additional support. Similarly, once RBS and Lloyds/HBOS were part-owned by the British state, the state had further incentive to keep them operational beyond issues of systemic stability, as the collapse of either would now prevent the state from recovering its investment and thus impose substantial costs on the state itself.

Preferred Stock Ownership Maximizes the Likelihood of Early Repayment by Minimizing Politicization of Firm Decision Making

A second effect of state ownership is that it politicizes operational decisions for the firm. The United Kingdom would be sharply criticized by the public for its management of its fully and partially nationalized firms, which embarked on a series of branch closures and layoffs. These contractions were part of a strategy to return the overextended firms to profitability by reducing operational expenses and thus increase the ability of the state to recover its investment. However, the affected customers and employees complained bitterly, creating a political conundrum for British politicians. They were forced to choose between a policy that would maximize profits to the state and repay assistance and one that would minimize the suffering of people affected by bank retrenchment. UK politicians would further be pressured to use their state-owned banks to provide relief to small businesses suffering from the credit crunch, which again would win political support but decrease the ability of the banks to repay state assistance.

Temporary ownership sidesteps these problems, assuming a willing buyer can be found. If the state can recover its investment immediately through a sale, as in the FDIC procedure, the state can avoid the political repercussions of state ownership. Preferred stock ownership offers some relief here as well. AIG's postcrisis policies were massively unpopular, but while the United States held 80 percent of AIG stock, it was in the form of preferred stock, meaning the United States lacked operational control of AIG. This did not relieve policymakers of all accountability, but it did enable them to pass blame onto AIG's common stockholders and management. AIG management adopted procedures that maximized repayment of the state's stake, but at a cost to laid-off employees and customers forced to pay higher rates.

The state may chose, of course, to use its position as owner or part-owner of financial institutions to provide crisis relief through more generous lending policies and avoiding redundancies, at a cost of a decreased speed with which it can extract itself from state ownership at a profit. However, if it takes ownership stakes with a goal of maximizing return on investment, this creates great political vulnerability. Therefore, if the goal is rapid repayment, and not to use the banks for policy objectives, an ownership structure that minimizes state control may be superior. This allows other shareholders and management to "play the heavy," taking the blame for unpopular decisions. This in turn insulates policymakers from political fallout and increases the ability of state-owned banks to undertake unpopular and painful decisions that increase the likelihood of rapid repayment.

Final Thoughts

The bailout of the banks remains highly contentious politically, over half a decade after the crisis began. Public resentment over government assistance continues to linger. However, the actual impact of bailouts on both state finances and the structure of national financial systems varied substantially across cases in ways that attracted relatively little public attention. In the United States, the state made a profit on its rescue, while the financial system retained its essentially liberal, private, and capital market–focused orientation, even as the move toward universal banking was accelerated by a wave of mergers. In the United Kingdom and Germany, the state took a loss on its rescue, though the effects on the structure of financial systems varied considerably. The German system remained fundamentally unchanged, and the German state has little chance of recovering its aid money. In the United Kingdom, the state is now an owner or significant shareholder in several major banks, which both alters the underlying dynamic of the financial system and creates a possibility of the state eventually recovering its funds upon reprivatization. The British, therefore, hope to reach the same point as the Americans, with state aid repaid and the liberal, private, and capital market–based system preserved. Perhaps as important are the precedents created for how to expect the state to respond to future crises. In the United States and the United Kingdom, shareholders in failing banks faced harsh terms, while healthy banks largely came out of the crisis in a better position than they entered it. In Germany, state aid was much more generous to shareholders, but the costs of the rescue were spread across both healthy and failing banks. This therefore creates incentives for US and UK banks to worry about their individual stability. Their German equivalents, however, should have less fear of needing state aid, but a more general concern for systemic stability.

These patterns demonstrate how, despite global pressures toward convergence, distinctive national financial systems play key roles in shaping the influence of banks and the ability of states to respond to financial crises. Moreover, those distinctive patterns of response mean that financial crises preserve national distinctiveness, rather than creating greater pressure toward convergence. Given the greater likelihood of financial crises from greater financial integration and the immense potential costs to both states and private actors, these are important dynamics to understand and to anticipate for the next financial crisis.

Appendix

Chapter 2 presents the results of a quantitative analysis of the use of several forms of financial intervention. In addition, tests were run with several additional variables, which are presented here. Additional discussion may be found in Mitchell (2016).

The first set of measures, regulatory responses, involves those measures that neither directly nor indirectly commit state funds to a rescue effort. The measures presented here are *Asset Freezes* and *Bank Holidays*. In an *Asset Freeze*, customers' access to their deposits is temporarily restricted until a panic passes, preventing a bank run and attendant liquidity crisis by preventing depositors from depleting the bank's liquidity reserves. The hope is that the panic will pass, people will regain faith in the health of the bank, and the freeze can be lifted. A *Bank Holiday* uses the same essential logic of restricting banking activity until the panic passes, but freezes activity more generally, encompassing all banking activities, limiting the ability of both depositors and creditors to make claims and the ability of the bank itself to make more loans.

The second set of measures involves those interventions aiming to increase a bank's ability to solve liquidity problems, either by supporting its ability to access private interbank lending or by lending directly to at-risk banks. In *Guarantees* of bank liabilities, the state attempts to restore a bank's ability to access private sources of liquidity by promising to pay any of the bank's debts the bank itself is unable to cover. Doing so potentially solves a bank's liquidity problems without directly involving state funds, by enabling the distressed bank to again access private sources of liquidity. Of course, the state can also provide *Direct Liquidity* support directly, by lending to the bank either from the central bank or state treasury.

Finally, in addition to the measures of capital support presented in Chapter 2, several additional forms of capital support are considered. *Direct Recapitalization* captures those instances where the state provides capital in return for a partial ownership stake, leaving the bank at least

Table A.1 *Regulatory Responses and Liquidity Support*

	Asset Freeze	Bank Holiday	Guarantees	Direct Liquidity
Financial system (0 = bank-based, 1 = market-based)	–0.180 (0.547)	–0.668 (0.684)	0.832* (0.435)	0.345 (0.431)
Trade as percentage of GDP	–0.016 (0.010)	0.013 (0.011)	7.75E–03 (5.70E–03)	1.41E–03 (6.63E–03)
Central bank independence	–1.907 (1.659)	–2.702 (2.237)	1.134 (0.983)	2.901** (1.238)
IMF program	1.011* (0.600)	–0.229 (0.599)	0.529 (0.501)	1.101** (0.544)
Political system (0 = pres., 1 = mixed, 2 = parl.)	0.742 (0.453)	–1.243** (0.528)	0.243 (0.270)	0.038 (0.266)
Federal/central state (0 = federal, 1 = mixed, 2 = central)	0.631 (0.460)	1.405* (0.826)	–0.333 (0.312)	–0.508 (0.401)
Executive party (0 = left, 1 = center, 2 = right)	0.323 (0.258)	0.424 (0.310)	0.393** (0.198)	–1.49E–03 (8.67E–03)
Legislative majority party (0 = left, 1 = center, 2 = right)	1.60E–03 (0.012)	–5.17E–04 (0.011)	1.96E–03 (0.017)	–8.65E–04 (6.43E–03)
GDP per capita (constant USD)	1.24E–04** (6.9E–05)	1.12E–05 (3.23E–05)	7.22E–05** (2.48E–05)	1.39E–05 (2.34E–05)
Constant	–0.739 (1.239)	–2.619 (1.603)	–3.103** (0.941)	–0.487 (0.877)
Observations	66	66	68	65
Pseudo-R^2	0.3941	0.3559	0.4401	0.2529

$^{*}p < 0.1$, $^{**}p < 0.05$, $^{***}p < 0.01$.

partially in private hands. There are also a series of measures to capture state attempts to support banks by purchasing distressed assets, in so-called "bad bank" measures. *Asset Buy* captures whether the state engages in distressed asset purchases of any type, while *Bad Bank* captures

Table A.2 *Other Forms of Capital Support*

	Asset Purchase	Bad Bank	Central Bad Bank	Guarantees	Direct Recapitalization
System	0.512	–0.067	–0.012	0.832*	–0.105
	(0.371)	(0.486)	(0.497)	(0.435)	(0.403)
Trade as percentage of GDP	0.00173	1.12E–03	4.28E–03	7.75E–03	0.013**
	(4.06E–03)	(5.28E–03)	(5.75E–03)	(5.70E–03)	(5.91E–03)
Central bank independence	0.748	–0.276	–2.109*	1.134	0.661
	(0.850)	(1.126)	(1.258)	(0.983)	(1.019)
IMF program	0.033	–0.887*	–0.424	0.529	9.85E–03
	(0.409)	(0.467)	(0.471)	(0.501)	(0.449)
System (0 = pres., 1 = mixed, 2 = parl.)	–0.180	0.288	0.253	0.243	–0.487*
	(0.225)	(0.320)	(0.337)	(0.270)	(0.278)
Federal/central state (0 = federal, 1 = mixed, 2 = central)	–0.128	0.194	–1.63E–03	–0.333	0.125
	(0.255)	(0.367)	(0.389)	(0.312)	(0.295)
Executive party (0 = left, 1 = center, 2 = right)	–0.147	–0.544	0.023	0.393**	–0.428
	(0.294)	(0.462)	(0.260)	(0.198)	(0.492)
Legislative majority party (0 = left, 1 = center, 2 = right)	0.394	0.476	2.22E–03	1.96E–03	0.819
	(0.299)	(0.463)	(0.011)	(0.017)	(0.506)
GDP per capita (constant USD)	–1.5E–06**	–1.4E–05**	–2.7E–05*	7.22E–05**	6.05E–05**
	(1.78E–05)	(2.28E–05)	(2.44E–04)	(2.48E–05)	(2.65E–05)
Constant	–1.231	0.092	0.480	–3.103**	–1.801
	(0.689)	(0.937)	(0.963)	(0.941)	(0.871)
Observations	67	42	42	68	67
Pseudo-R^2	0.1105	0.1638	0.1468	0.4401	0.2627

$^*p < 0.1$, $^{**}p < 0.05$, $^{***}p < 0.01$.

whether those asset purchases involve setting up a separate institution to manage those distressed assets. *Central Bad Bank* captures whether the state pools its newly acquired distressed assets in a central institution or keeps them in separate bad banks.

Bibliography

Abdelal, Rawi 2007. *Capital Rules: The Construction of Global Finance*. Cambridge, MA: Harvard University Press.

Albert, Michel 1993. *Capitalism vs. Capitalism: How America's Obsession with Individual Achievement and Short-Term Profit Has Led It to the Brink of Collapse*. New York: Four Walls Eight Windows.

Aldrick, Philip 2008. "Taxpayer's Rock Risk 'Disguised' Government Accused of Trickery over Bank Nationalisation Plan Amid Growing Fears of Damage to Public Funds. Philip Aldrick Reports." *The Daily Telegraph (London)*, January 15, sec. CITY; CREDIT CRISIS.

2009. "Germany Edges Closer to Hypo Nationalisation." *The Daily Telegraph (London)*, April 10, sec. CITY.

Aldrick, Philip and Griffiths, Katherine 2008. "Bail-Out to Change Face of Banking." *The Daily Telegraph (London)*, October 14, sec. CITY; STATE CONTROL.

Allen, Franklin and Gale, Douglas 2000. *Comparing Financial Systems*. Cambridge, MA: MIT Press.

Allen, Matthew M. C. 2006. *The Varieties of Capitalism Paradigm: Explaining Germany's Comparative Advantage?* New York: Palgrave.

Armitstead, Louise, Aldrick, Philip, and Griffiths, Katherine 2008. "Inside Story of Brown's Rescue Mission to Save British Banks; the Taxpayer-Funded Rescue of Three High Street Banks Represents Gordon Brown's Biggest Gamble. Louise Armitstead and Philip Aldrick Report on an Unprecedented Bail-Out." *The Sunday Telegraph (London)*, October 19, sec. CITY.

Arnone, Marco 2012. "Central Bank Law," sites.google.com/site/marcoarnone/centralbanklaws, accessed August 3, 2012.

Aronson, Bruce E. 2010. "The Financial Crisis One Year Later: Proceedings of a Panel Discussion," *Creighton Law Review* 43(2): 275.

Askeland, Erikka 2008. "Banks Now 'Bulletproof' and Must Start Lending-Sants." *The Scotsman*, October 16.

Bagehot, Walter 1892. *Lombard Street: A Description of the Money Market*. New York: Charles Scribner's Sons.

Bain, Simon 2008. "Revolt against Freeze on Bank Dividends Gaining Momentum; UKSA Urges Government to Amend Bailout Conditions." *The Herald (Glasgow)*, October 20, sec. BUSINESS.

Bair, Sheila 2012. *Bull by the Horns: Fighting to Save Main Street from Wall Street and Wall Street from Itself.* New York: Free Press.

Barnes, Eddie 2008. "Salmond Seeks HBOS Review First Minister Believes GBP 37bn Rescue Deal Can Allow Bank to Remain Independent." *Scotland on Sunday*, October 19.

Barofsky, Neil M. 2012. *Bailout: An Inside Account of How Washington Abandoned Main Street while Rescuing Wall Street.* New York: Free Press.

Barrow, Becky 2008. "Bank Bail-Out Costs UK Taxpayer Billions." *Daily Mail (London)*, September 29.

BBC Monitoring Europe 2008a. "German Chancellor Defends Financial Market Rescue Package." *BBC Monitoring Europe – Political Supplied by BBC Worldwide Monitoring*, October 13.

2008b. "German Finance Minister Says Crisis Not over Yet." *BBC Monitoring Europe – Political Supplied by BBC Worldwide Monitoring*, October 27.

2008c. "German Government Plans to Rush Bank Rescue Package through Parliament." *BBC Monitoring Europe – Political Supplied by BBC Worldwide Monitoring*, October 12.

2008d. "German Lender Hypo Granted First Liquidity Aid Amounting to 15bn Euros." *BBC Monitoring Europe – Political Supplied by BBC Worldwide Monitoring*, October 31.

2008e. "Germany Working on Plan B for Bank Rescue Plan Based on UK Model." *BBC Monitoring Europe – Political Supplied by BBC Worldwide Monitoring*, November 3.

2009a. "German Business Leaders Warn Chancellor Not to Harm Competition." *BBC Monitoring Europe – Political Supplied by BBC Worldwide Monitoring*, March 17.

2009b. "German Cabinet Approves Bill Enabling Nationalization of Beleaguered Banks." *BBC Monitoring Europe – Political Supplied by BBC Worldwide Monitoring*, February 18.

2009c. "German Upper House Approves Bank Expropriation Law-News Agency." *BBC Monitoring Europe – Political Supplied by BBC Worldwide Monitoring*, April 3.

2009d. "Shares in German Mortgage Lender Surge as Government Unveils Rescue." *BBC Monitoring Europe – Political Supplied by BBC Worldwide Monitoring*, March 30.

BdB, Bundesbank and Foreign Ministry representatives, interviews by author, 2011

Beck, Thorsten 2002. "Deposit Insurance as Private Club: Is Germany a Model?," *Quarterly Review of Economics and Finance* 42(4): 701–719.

Beck, Thorsten, Demirgüç-Kunt, Asli, and Levine, Ross 2009. "Financial Institutions and Markets across Countries and over Time-Data and Analysis." World Bank Policy Research Working Paper Series.

Beck, Thorsten, Clarke, George, Groff, Alberto, Keefer, Philip, and Walsh, Patrick 2001. "New Tools in Comparative Political Economy: The Database of Political Institutions," *The World Bank Economic Review* 15 (1): 165–176.

Becker, Joseph 1976. "International Insolvency: The Case of Herstatt," *American Bar Association Journal* 62(10-01): 1290.

Becker, Uwe 2009. *Open Varieties of Capitalism: Continuity, Change and Performances*. Basingstoke, NY: Palgrave Macmillan.

Behrmann, Neil 2008. "RBS Nationalised as Part of Rescue Deal; Britain to also Take Major Share in Merged HBOS-Lloyds; Bonus Culture to Go." *The Business Times Singapore*, October 14.

2009. "RBS Posts Biggest Loss in UK Business History; It Parks [GBP]325b in Asset Protection Scheme; Will Sell Some Operations." *The Business Times Singapore*, February 27.

Belfast Telegraph 2008. "Germany in Euro 50bn Rescue of Lender." *Belfast Telegraph*, October 6.

2009. "Taxpayer Will Own Half of 'Super-Bank.'" *Belfast Telegraph*, January 12.

Bello, Walden 1999. "The Asian Financial Crisis: Causes, Dynamics, Prospects," *Journal of the Asia Pacific Economy* 4(1): 33–55.

Bentley, Daniel 2012. "Northern Rock Bank Run Could Have Been Avoided, Says Hector Sants." *The Independent (London)*, June 13.

Bernanke, Ben 2002. "Remarks by Governor Ben S. Bernanke at the Conference to Honor Milton Friedman, University of Chicago, Chicago, Illinois November 8, 2002 on Milton Friedman's Ninetieth Birthday." The Federal Reserve Board.

Beyer, Jürgen and Höpner, Martin 2003. "The Disintegration of Organised Capitalism: German Corporate Governance in the 1990s," *West European Politics* 26(4): 179–198.

Bhattacharya, Sudipto and Gale, Douglas 1987. "Preference Shocks, Liquidity and Central Bank Policy," in Barnett, William A. and Singleton, Kenneth J. (eds.), *New Approaches to Monetary Economics: Proceedings of the Second International Symposium in Economic Theory and Econometrics*. Cambridge, UK: Cambridge University Press.

Birmingham Post 2007. "High Street Giants Turn Backs on Crisis-Hit Northern Rock." *Birmingham Post*, September 24, sec. BUSINESS.

Blackhurst, Chris 2008. "The Bankers' Banker Who Put Safety First and Came Out Ahead; Profile: Mike Geoghegan's HSBC Used to be Seen as a Plodder But He Didn't Get His Knuckles Rapped by Ministers and It Doesn't Need Our Money. Its Rivals Are Still Smarting." *The Evening Standard (London)*, October 22.

2009. "Is this the Man Who Sold Barclays Down the River?; A Rescue Deal Hailed Only Months Ago Seems Set to Put the Bank in the Hands of Arab Investors after a Run on Shares. Now CEO John Varley Is Being Blamed for the Humiliation." *The Evening Standard (London)*, January 22.

Block, Melissa 2014. *NPR All Things Considered: For Geithner, Financial Crisis Was Like Landing a Burning Plane*. May 12 (Radio).

Blyth, Mark 2013. *Austerity: The History of a Dangerous Idea*. Oxford, UK: Oxford University Press.

Board, Laura 2008a. "Germany Revives Hypo Real Bailout." *Daily Deal/The Deal*, October 6.

2008b. "HBOS Falls to Lloyds TSB." *Daily Deal/The Deal*, September 19.

Boles, Tracey 2008. "Don't Let Greed Drive a Sell-Out to the Sheikhs." *Sunday Express*, November 2.

Bonatti, Luigi and Andrea, Fracasso 2015. "The German Model and the European Crisis," *Journal of Common Market Studies* 51(6): 1023–1039.

Börzel, Tanja A. and Karen, Heard-Lauréote. "Networks in EU Multi-Level Governance: Concepts and Contributions," *Journal of Public Policy* 29(2): 135–151.

Boyd, John H., Kwak, Sungkyu, and Smith, Bruce D. 2005. "The Real Output Losses Associated with Modern Banking Crises," *Journal of Money, Credit and Banking* 37(6): 977–999.

Boyer, Robert 1996. "The Convergence Thesis Revisited: Globalization But Still the Century of Nations?," in Berger, Suzanne and Dore, Ronald Philip (eds.). *National Diversity and Global Capitalism*. Ithaca, NY: Cornell University Press.

Boyes, Roger 2008. "Every Country for Itself as European Unity Collapses in an Attack of Jitters." *The Times (London)*, October 6, sec. HOME NEWS.

Braude, Jonathan 2008. "Germany, Sweden Detail New Bailouts." *Daily Deal/ The Deal*, October 21.

2010. "BayernLB Ends WestLB Merger Talks." *Daily Deal/The Deal*, November 4.

Bristol Evening Post 2008. "Bradford & Bingley Facing Nationalisation," September 29.

Brogan, Benedict 2008. "Rock's Investors Line Up to Block a State Takeover." *Daily Mail (London)*, January 14, sec. 1ST.

Brogan, Benedict and Chapman, James 2007. "£55billion; Taxpayers' Bill to Support Northern Rock Outstrips the Education Budget." *Daily Mail (London)*, December 19, sec. 1ST.

Brummer, Alex 2007. "A Real Failure of Leadership." *Daily Mail (London)*, August 31, 2007, sec. 1ST.

2008. "The Banks Must be Forced to Save the Rock." *Daily Mail (London)*, January 16, sec. 1ST.

Bryant, John 1980. "A Model of Reserves, Bank Runs, and Deposit Insurance," *Journal of Banking & Finance* 4(4): 335–344.

Buergin, Rainer 2007. "German Minister Suggests Sale of Stake in IKB." *The International Herald Tribune*, August 9, sec. FINANCE.

Bulkeley, Andrew 2007a. "German Banks Save Subprime Victim." *Daily Deal/ The Deal*, December 14.

2007b. "Subprime Crisis Claims German Bank." *Daily Deal/The Deal*, August 28.

2008a. "BayernLB Calls for State Funding." *Daily Deal/The Deal*, October 23, 2008.

2008b. "German Bank Rescue Delayed." *Daily Deal/The Deal*, February 8.

2008c. "German Government Bails Out Hypo." *Daily Deal/The Deal*, September 30.

2008d. "HSH Takes Lehman-Related Write-Down." *Daily Deal/The Deal*, September 25.

2009a. "Berlin Injects More Capital into Hypo Real Estate." *Daily Deal/The Deal*, November 5.

2009b. "Commerzbank Considers Asset Sales." *Daily Deal/The Deal*, March 12.

2009c. "Commerzbank to Tap Rescue Fund Again." *Daily Deal/The Deal*, January 9.

2009d. "Critics Challenge German Bank Bailout." *Daily Deal/The Deal*, February 19.

2009e. "Dresdner Looks to Rescue Fund." *Daily Deal/The Deal*, January 7.

2009f. "Germany Launches Hypo Buyout." *Daily Deal/The Deal*, April 10.

2009g. "Germany May Take Majority of Hypo." *Daily Deal/The Deal*, January 29.

2009h. "Germany Reels in Hypo RE." *Daily Deal/The Deal*, March 31.

2009i. "HSH Awaits Government Bailout." *Daily Deal/The Deal*, February 24.

2009j. "Hypo Gets New State Aid." *Daily Deal/The Deal*, February 12.

2009k. "Path Cleared for Hypo Nationalization." *Daily Deal/The Deal*, May 7.

2010. "Seven European Banks Fail Stress Test." *Daily Deal/The Deal*, July 23.

2011a. "Germany Offers Three Restructuring Options for WestLB." *Daily Deal/The Deal*, February 16.

2011b. "WestLB Will Break into Two Lenders." *Daily Deal/The Deal*, June 24.

Burnham, Peter 2010. "Class, Capital and Crisis: A Return to Fundamentals," *Political Studies Review* 8(1): 27–39.

Callaghan, Helen 2009. "Insiders, Outsiders, and the Politics of Corporate Governance How Ownership Structure Shapes Party Positions in Britain, Germany, and France," *Comparative Political Studies* 42(6): 733–762.

2010. "Beyond Methodological Nationalism: How Multilevel Governance Affects the Clash of Capitalisms," *Journal of European Public Policy* 17(4): 564–580.

Callaghan, Helen and Höpner, Martin 2012. "Changing Ideas: Organised Capitalism and the German Left," *West European Politics* 35(3): 551–573.

Cameron, Martin 2008. "Salmond: New HBOS Rescue Plan Will Save Jobs; First Minister Backs Finance Chiefs' Bank Bid." *Daily Record (PM) – UK*, November 10, sec. NEWS.

Caprio, Gerald, Klingebiel, Daniela, and Noguera, Guillermo 2005. "Banking Crisis Database," in Honohan and Laeven (eds.).

Carpenter, Daniel and Moss, David A. (eds.) 2013. *Preventing Regulatory Capture: Special Interest Influence and How to Limit It.* Cambridge: Cambridge University Press.

Cerny, Philip G. 2005. "Power, Markets and Accountability: The Development of Multi-Level Governance in International Finance," in Baker, Hudson, and Woodward (eds.).

Champ, Bruce, Smith, Bruce D. and Williamson, Stephen D. 1996. "Currency Elasticity and Banking Panics: Theory and Evidence." *Canadian Journal of Economics* 29 (4): 828–864.

Chapman, James 2008. "Protests over the 'Blank Cheque' for Northern Rock." *Daily Mail (London)*, February 20, sec. 1ST.

Chari, V. V. 1989. "Banking Without Deposit Insurance or Bank Panics: Lessons from a Model of the US National Banking System," *Federal Reserve Bank of Minneapolis Quarterly Review* 13(3): 3–19.

Cioffi, John W. and Höpner, Martin 2006. "The Political Paradox of Finance Capitalism: Interests, Preferences, and Center-Left Party Politics in Corporate Governance Reform," *Politics & Society* 34(4): 463–502.

Claessens, Stijn, Kose, M. Ayhan, Laeven, Luc, and Valencia, Fabian (eds.) 2014. *Financial Crises: Causes, Consequences, and Policy Responses*. Washington, DC: International Monetary Fund.

Clark, Nick 2009. "German Government Injects Euro 10bn into Commerzbank; State to Take 25 Per Cent Stake to Preserve Merger Deal with Dresdner Bank." *The Independent (London)*, January 9, sec. BUSINESS.

Clegg, Nick 2009. "Britain Needs Tax Cuts – Not Just a Bank Bailout." *The Independent (London)*, October 9, sec. COMMENT.

Coates, David 2005a. "Paradigms of Explanation," in Coates (ed.).

2005b. *Varieties of Capitalism, Varieties of Approaches*. New York: Palgrave Macmillan.

Cody, Edward 2008. "No Joint European Strategy on Banks; 4 Top Economies Seek World Summit." *The Washington Post*, October 5, sec. A-SECTION.

Comptroller and Auditor General National Audit Office (UK) 2009a. *Maintaining Financial Stability across the United Kingdom's Banking System*. London: National Audit Office. See the appendix.

2009b. *The Nationalisation of Northern Rock*. London: National Audit Office.

2010a. *The Asset Protection Scheme*. London: National Audit Office. See appendices 3 to 7 and glossary.

2010b. *The Creation and Sale of Northern Rock Plc*. London: National Audit Office.

2015. *The Report of the Comptroller and Auditor General to the House of Commons*. London: National Audit Office.

Conaway, Laura 2009. *NPR Planet Money: Geithner's Stress Test*. February 25 (Radio).

Corkery, Aiden 2008. "Shares Plunge as Rescue Plans Fail; Irish Stocks Are Hammered as Bailouts Have Little Impact." *Daily Mail (London)*, October 7.

Crawford, David and Walker, Marcus 2009. "Germany Ignored Regulator's Hypo Warning; Documents Show Market Watchdog Bafin Raised Alarm Bells Six Months before Massive Government Bailout." *The Globe and Mail (Canada)*, May 28, sec. REPORT ON BUSINESS: INTERNATIONAL; CREDIT CRISIS.

Crowe, Christopher and Meade, Ellen E. 2007. "The Evolution of Central Bank Governance around the World," *The Journal of Economic Perspectives* 69–90.

Cukierman, Alex 2008. "Central Bank Independence and Monetary Policymaking Institutions – Past, Present and Future," *European Journal of Political Economy* 24(4): 722–736.

Cukierman, Alex, Web, Steven B., and Neyapti, Bilin 1992. "Measuring the Independence of Central Banks and Its Effect on Policy Outcomes," *The World Bank Economic Review* 6(3): 353–398.

Culpepper, Pepper D. 2010. *Quiet Politics and Business Power: Corporate Control in Europe and Japan*. Cambridge, UK: Cambridge University Press.

Culpepper, Pepper D. and Reinke, Raphael 2014. "Structural Power and Bank Bailouts in the United Kingdom and the United States," *Politics & Society* 42 (4): 427–454.

Cusack, Thomas R., Iversen, Torben, and Soskice, David W. 2007. "Economic Interests and the Origins of Electoral Systems," *American Political Science Review* 101(3): 373.

Cusick, James and Watt, Chris 2009. "Brown's Role Questioned as Government Takes 63 Per Cent Stake in Lloyds; Chief Executive Daniels under Pressure as Treasury Forces Bank to Lend GBP28bn." *Sunday Herald,* March 8, sec. NEWS.

Daily Mail (London) 2008. "Royal Bank of Scotland Goes Begging for E13billion Bail-Out to Cover Losses." *Daily Mail (London),* April 19, sec. IRE.

Darling, Alistair 2012. *Back from the Brink: 1000 Days at Number 11.* London: Atlantic Books Limited.

Deeg, Richard 1999. *Finance Capitalism Unveiled: Banks and the German Political Economy.* Ann Arbor: University of Michigan Press.

Deeg, Richard and Jackson, Gregory 2007. "Towards a More Dynamic Theory of Capitalist Variety," *Socio-Economic Review* 5(1): 149–179.

Deeg, Richard and Lütz, Suzanne 2000. "Internationalization and Financial Federalism: The United States and Germany at the Crossroads?," *Comparative Political Studies* 33(3): 374–405.

Demirgüç-Kunt, Asli and Detragiache, Enrica 1998. "The Determinants of Banking Crises in Developing and Developed Countries," *Staff Papers – International Monetary Fund* 45(1): 81–109.

Demirgüç-Kunt, Asli and Levine, Ross 1999. *Bank-Based and Market-Based Financial Systems: Cross-Country Comparisons.* Washington, DC: World Bank Publications, vol. 2143.

Dempsey, Judy 2008. "Germany Loosens Limit on Executive Pay at Banks That Use Its Bailout Fund." *The New York Times,* October 21, sec. B; BUSINESS/ FINANCIAL DESK.

Devlin, Robert and Ffrench-Davis, Ricardo 1995. "The Great Latin American Debt Crisis: A Decade of Asymmetric Adjustment," *Revista de Economica Politica* 14(3): 117–142.

Dey, Iain 2007. "Barclays and RBS Line Up Fed for Pounds 15bn Credit Line Arranged to Provide 'Short-Term Liquidity' for Banks' American Customers." *The Sunday Telegraph (London),* October 21, sec. CITY.

Dey, Iain and Smith, David 2008. "Fred the Shred in the Line of Fire." *The Sunday Times (London),* April 20, sec. BUSINESS.

Dey, Iain and O'Connell, Dominic 2009. "The Men Who Broke a Bank; Eric Daniels and Sir Victor Blank Took Britain's Safest Bank and Turned It into a Basketcase – and Left the Taxpayer on the Hook Too, Report Dominic O'Connell and Iain Dey." *The Sunday Times (London),* March 8, sec. NEWS.

Diamond, Douglas W. and Dybvig, Philip H. 1983. "Bank Runs, Deposit Insurance, and Liquidity," *The Journal of Political Economy* 401–419.

Dougherty, Carter 2008a. "Authorities Aid Banks in Europe." *The New York Times,* September 30, sec. C; BUSINESS/FINANCIAL DESK.

2008b. "Few Takers so Far as Europeans make Financial Rescue Packages Available." *The New York Times,* October 18, sec. B; BUSINESS/ FINANCIAL DESK.

2009. "U.S. Investor Lacks Allies in German Bank Battle; Financier Threatens Suit if Government Buys Up Hypo Real Estate." *The International Herald Tribune,* April 27, sec. FINANCE.

Doward, Jamie, Stewart, Heather, Bachelor, Lisa, and Smith, David 2007. "Panic? Queue Here: Emergency Loans from the Bank of England. Worried Customers Waiting in Line across the Country to Rescue Their Savings. Pleas for the Country to 'Stay Calm' as Britain Is Finally Caught in the Financial Crisis that Started in Small-Town America with Reckless Lending to People Who Could Not Afford Mortgage Repayments, What Next in the Battle to Keep the Globe Afloat?" *The Observer (England)*, September 16, sec. OBSERVER FOCUS PAGES.

Duke, Simon 2007. "Branson Takes the Lead in Multi-Billion Race to Rescue Rock." *Daily Mail (London)*, November 26, sec. 2ND.

Duncan, Gary and Lewis, Carol 2009. "Nationalisation of Hypo Bank Proposed as the First Move in Radical German Plan to Ease Banks Crisis." *The Times (London)*, April 10, sec. BUSINESS.

Duncan, Hugo 2008. "Shares in B & B Dive on Fears for its Future." *The Evening Standard (London)*, July 4, sec. C.

Duncanson, Hilary 2008. "Connery Backs Bid to Block HBOS Merger." *Press Association Mediapoint*, December 8.

Dyson, Kenneth and Padgett, Stephen 2005. "Introduction: Global, Rhineland or Hybrid Capitalism?," *German Politics* 14(2): 115–124.

Economist 2007a. "Lessons of the Fall: Northern Rock." *The Economist*, October 17.

2007b. "Soft-Touch Regulation." *The Economist*, October 11.

Essen, Yvette 2008. "Banking B & B Charm Offensive to Promote Pounds 400m Rescue." *The Daily Telegraph (London)*, June 9, sec. CITY.

Euromoney 2009. "German Banks Get Stressed Out," June.

European Commission 2001. *Press Statement after the Meeting of Commissioner Monti and State Secretary Koch-Weser on 17.7.2001*. Brussels: European Commission.

2007. *State Aid NN 70/2007 (Ex CP 269/07) – United Kingdom Rescue Aid to Northern Rock*. Brussels: European Commission.

2008. "State Aid C 9/08 (Ex NN 8/08) – Sachsen LB Invitation to Submit Comments Pursuant to Article 88(2) of the EC Treaty," *Official Journal of the European Union* C71 (March 18): 14.

2009a. "Commission Decision of 21 October 2008 on State Aid Measure C 10/08 (Ex NN 7/08) Implemented by Germany for the Restructuring of IKB Deutsche Industriebank AG (Notified under Document C(2008) 6022)," *Official Journal of the European Union* L278 (October 23): 32.

2009b. "Commission Decision of 4 June 2008 on State Aid C 9/08 (Ex NN 8/08, CP 244/07) Implemented by Germany for Sachsen LB (Notified under Document Number C(2008) 2269)," *Official Journal of the European Union* L104 (April 24): 34.

2009c. "Communication from the Commission – the Recapitalisation of Financial Institutions in the Current Financial Crisis: Limitation of Aid to the Minimum Necessary and Safeguards against Undue Distortions of Competition," *Official Journal of the European Union* C10 (May 10): 2.

2009d. *2009/971/EC: Commission Decision of 12 May 2009 on State Aid Which Germany Proposes to Grant towards the Restructuring of WestLB AG (C 43/08*

(Ex N 390/08)) (Notified under Document C(2009) 3900) Text with EEA Relevance. Brussels: European Commission.

2009e. *State Aid N 244/2009 – Commerzbank – Germany*. Brussels: European Commission.

2009f. *State Aid N 264/2009 (Ex-PN 59/2009) – Germany Rescue Aid (Recapitalisation and Risk Shield) to HSH Nordbank AG*. Brussels: European Commission.

2009g. *State Aid No 422/2009 and N 621/2009 – United Kingdom Restructuring of Royal Bank of Scotland Following Its Recapitalisation by the State and Its Participation in the Asset Protection Scheme*. Brussels: European Commission.

2010a. "Commission Decision of 18 July 2011 on State Aid C 15/09 (Ex N 196/09), Which Germany Implemented and Is Planning to Implement for Hypo Real Estate (Notified under Document C(2011) 5157)," *Official Journal of the European Union* L60 (March 1): 1.

2010b. "State Aid C 40/09 (Ex N 555/09) – Additional Aid for WestLB AG Related to Spin-Off of Assets Invitation to Submit Comments Pursuant to Article 108(2) TFEU (Text with EEA Relevance) (2010/C 66/08)," *Official Journal of the European Union* C66 (March 17): 15.

Evans-Pritchard, Ambrose 2008a. "Berlin Rescues IKB to Avoid a 'Banking Tsunami.'" *The Daily Telegraph (London)*, February 14, sec. CITY; GERMAN ECONOMY.

2008b. "Lending; Eurozone Agrees to an Emergency Bailout Plan." *The Daily Telegraph (London)*, October 13, sec. CITY.

Ewing, Jack 2010. "Losses at Landesbank May Bring Changes to Banking in Germany." *The New York Times*, January 12, sec. B; BUSINESS/ FINANCIAL DESK.

Farndon, Lucy 2008. "FSA Wanted British Banks to Buy B & B." *Daily Mail (London)*, July 12.

Farrell, Sean 2008. "Lloyds–HBOS Merger Doubts as Shares Slump; Halifax Stock Plunges 14 Per Cent Amid Speculation that Lloyds TSB Will Renegotiate Offer." *The Independent (London)*, October 1, sec. BUSINESS.

2009. "I Don't Think History Will be Kind to Lloyds' Bosses." *Belfast Telegraph*, March 10.

Fecht, Falko 2004. "On the Stability of Different Financial Systems," *Journal of the European Economic Association* 2(6): 969–1014.

Federal Deposit Insurance Corporation 2013a. "Historical Statistics on Banking," accessed March 7, 2013, http://www2.fdic.gov/hsob/.

2013b. "Statistics on Banking," accessed March 7, 2013, http://www2.fdic.gov/sdi/sob/.

Felix, David 1990. "Latin America's Debt Crisis," *World Policy Journal* 7(4): 733–771.

Financial Services Authority (UK) 2011. *The Failure of the Royal Bank of Scotland: Financial Services Authority Board Report*. London: Financial Services Authority.

Fincher, Christina 2007. "Bank of England Keeps a Stiff Upper Lip." *National Post's Financial Post & FP Investing (Canada)*, August 17, sec. FINANCIAL POST.

Fioretos, Karl Orfeo 2011. *Creative Reconstructions: Multilateralism and European Varieties of Capitalism after 1950*. Ithaca, NY: Cornell University Press.

Fleming, Sam 2008a. "The Bank Unveils the King of all U-Turns." *Daily Mail (London)*, April 22, sec. 1ST.

2008b. "Lenders Hit by £ 17bn Wipeout; Bank Rescue Plan Revealed Green Comes Out Fighting US Bails Out Big Business." *Daily Mail (London)*, October 8.

2009. "EU Will Bring New Lenders to High St." *Daily Mail (London)*, October 28.

Ford, Emily 2011. "Germany to Resurrect Beefed-Up Bank Bailout Fund." *The Times (London)*, December 15, sec. BUSINESS.

Forsyth, Michael 2008. "Bail-Out Questions That Must Be Answered; Michael Forsyth Says the Tories Are Right to Demand More Information about Labour's Blank Cheque." *The Daily Telegraph (London)*, October 25, sec. FEATURES; COMMENT.

Fraser, Ian 2008. "The Bankers' New Clothes; RBS's Refunding Move Is the First Step in UK Banks Waking Up from Their Self-Delusion to the Reality of the Credit Crunch." *Sunday Herald*, April 27, sec. BUSINESS.

Gallagher, Rosemary 2008. "HBOS Merger Reaches Point of No Return." *Scotland on Sunday*, October 19.

Gazette (Montreal) 2008. "Dresdner Rescues $19-Billion SIV, Standard Chartered Bails," February 22, sec. BUSINESS.

Global Banking News 2008. "UK Government, Barclays Fixes Recapitalisation Deals," November 19, 2008.

Globe and Mail (Canada) 2008. "Bayern Gets $47-Billion Lifeline; to Cut 5,600 Jobs," December 2, sec. REPORT ON BUSINESS: INTERNATIONAL; BUSINESS TICKER: INTERNATIONAL: EUROPE: FINANCIAL SERVICES.

Goodhart, C. A. E. 2009. *The Regulatory Response to the Financial Crisis*. Northampton, MA: Edward Elgar Pub.

Goodway, Nick 2008a. "Barclays Rounds Up £ 7.3bn of New Funds." *The Evening Standard (London)*, October 31.

2008b. "RBS Warns of Job Cuts in Spite of Its Bailout." *The Evening Standard (London)*, November 4.

2008c. "UK Banking Has Avoided Worst of Subprime Crisis." *The Evening Standard (London)*, February 29, sec. A.

Gormley, William T. 1979. "A Test of the Revolving Door Hypothesis at the FCC," *American Journal of Political Science* 23(4): 665–683.

Gorton, Gary 1988. "Banking Panics and Business Cycles," *Oxford Economic Papers* 40(4): 751–781.

Gould, Jonathan 2007. "Subprime Woes to Cost Germany's IKB $1-Billion." *The Globe and Mail (Canada)*, September 4, sec. REPORT ON BUSINESS: INTERNATIONAL; FINANCIAL SERVICES.

Gourevitch, Peter Alexis and Shinn, James 2005. *Political Power and Corporate Control: The New Global Politics of Corporate Governance*. Princeton: Princeton University Press.

Governing Council of the European Central Bank 2008. *Recommendations of the Governing Council of the European Central Bank on Government Guarantees for Bank Debt*. Brussels: European Central Bank.

Granlund, Peik 2004. 'Do Bank Exit Regimes Affect Banking Conditions?' in Mayes, David G. (ed.). *Who Pays for Bank Insolvency?* Houndmills, Basingstoke, and Hampshire: Palgrave Macmillan.

Griffiths, Katherine 2009. "'We Came Close to Not Being Able to Get Money from Bank Machines'; Exactly a Year Ago, Britain's Banking System Died and Had to be Shocked Back to Life. Katherine Griffiths Relives the Hour-by-Hour Drama." *The Times (London)*, October 10, sec. BUSINESS.

Griffiths, Katherine and Aldrick, Philip 2008. "Long Line of Suitors But None Was Right for Rock." *The Daily Telegraph (London)*, February 18, sec. CITY.

Grind, Kirsten 2012. *The Lost Bank: The Story of Washington Mutual – The Biggest Bank Failure in American History*. New York: Simon & Schuster.

Group, Julia Werdigier 2008. "Barclays to Get Cash Infusion from Qatar and Abu Dhabi." *The International Herald Tribune*, November 1, sec. FINANCE.

Guardian Unlimited 2008. "HBOS Rights Issue Flops," July 21.

Gup, Benton E. 2010. "Financial Crises and Government Responses: Lessons Learned," in Wright (ed.), p. 48.

Hackethal, Andreas and Schmidt, Reinhard H. 2005. "Structural Change in the German Banking System?" *Working Paper Series: Finance & Accounting, Johann Wolfgang Goethe-Universität Frankfurt Am Main*, no. 147.

Haggard, Stephan 2000a. "The Politics of the Asian Financial Crisis," *Journal of Democracy* 11(2): 130–144.

2000b. *The Political Economy of the Asian Financial Crisis*. Washington, DC: Peterson Institute.

Hall, Peter A. and Soskice, David W. (eds.) 2001. *Varieties of Capitalism: The Institutional Foundations of Comparative Advantage*. New York: Oxford University Press.

Handke, Stefan and Zimmermann, Hubert 2012. "Institutional Change in German Financial Regulation," in Mayntz (ed.), p. 119.

Hardie, Iain and Howarth, David 2009. "Die Krise but Not La Crise? The Financial Crisis and the Transformation of German and French Banking Systems," *Journal of Common Market Studies* 47(5): 1017.

Hardie, Iain and Howarth, David (eds.) 2013. *Market-Based Banking and the International Financial Crisis*. Oxford, UK: Oxford University Press.

Hardie, Iain, Howarth, David, Maxfield, Sylvia, and Verdun, Amy 2011. 'Zysman Thirty Years On. The Political Economy of Finance Revisited.' Unpublished manuscript. Victoria: University of Victoria.

2013. "Banks and the False Dichotomy in the Comparative Political Economy of Finance," *World Politics* 65(4): 691–728.

Hattenstone, Simon 2009. "Saturday: Sorry Is the Hardest Word: £ 500bn of Taxpayers' Money Has Been Spent Bailing Out the Banks – Including RBS, Which This Week Announced Record Losses. Simon Hattenstone Asks Fred Goodwin if He'll be the First Banker to Apologise." *The Guardian (London) – Final Edition*, January 24, sec. GUARDIAN SATURDAY COMMENT PAGES.

Hay, George 2008. "The Devil You Know." *Breakingviews*, November 10.

Heath, Allister, Dunne, Helen, and Burroughes, Tom 2007. "Between a Rock and a Hard Place; as the Credit Crunch Comes to a Head, the World's Leading Financial Institutions Are Beginning to Count the Cost, Say Allister Heath, Helen Dunne and Tom Burroughes." *The Business*, September 15.

Helleiner, Eric, Pagliari, Stefano, and Zimmermann, Hubert (eds.) 2010. *Global Finance in Crisis: The Politics of International Regulatory Change*. New York: Routledge.

HM Treasury 2006. *Memorandum of Understanding between HM Treasury, the Bank of England and the Financial Services Authority*. London: HM Treasury.

Honohan, Patrick and Laeven, Luc (eds.) 2005. *Systemic Financial Crises: Containment and Resolution*. Cambridge and New York: Cambridge University Press.

Hopkins, Kathryn and Treanor, Jill 2009. "Financial: King Reveals Secret HBOS and RBS Bailout: Bank of England Boss Tells of £62bn Emergency Loans: Revelation Prompts City Confusion and Shocks MPs." *The Guardian (London) – Final Edition,* November 25, sec. GUARDIAN FINANCIAL PAGES.

Höpner, Martin 2005. "What Connects Industrial Relations and Corporate Governance? Explaining Institutional Complementarity," *Socio-Economic Review* 3(2): 331–358.

Höpner, Martin, and Lothar Krempel 2004. "The politics of the German company network." *Competition and Change* 8(4): 339–356.

Hosking, Patrick and Costello, Miles 2008. "Bradford & Bingley Arrears Levels and Repossessions Soar." *The Times (London),* August 30, sec. BUSINESS.

Hosking, Patrick and Seib, Christine 2008. "FSA Put Pressure on Top Five Banks to Support Bradford & Bingley Rights Issue." *The Times (London),* June 10, sec. BUSINESS.

Hosking, Patrick, Seib, Christine, and Kennedy, Siobhan 2008. "RBS Will be 'First of Many' UK Banks to Raise Funds from its Shareholders." *The Times (London),* April 22, sec. BUSINESS.

Hutton, Will 2007. "Comment: Any More Mistakes and We Follow the US into Crisis: Our Politicians' Blind Trust in Market Forces Increases the Possibility of a Recession. We Could See the Values of Our Homes Slashed." *The Observer (England),* November 25, sec. OBSERVER COMMENT PAGES.

Inman, Phillip 2007. "City Fears Second Bank Is Heading for Credit Crisis: Northern Rock Points to Other Rescue Fund User: Barclays Shares Hit by Financial Stability Fears." *The Guardian (London) – Final Edition,* November 3, sec. GUARDIAN HOME PAGES.

Investors Chronicle 2007. "FTSE's Fall Accelerates," September 14.

Irish Times 2007. "IKB Repeats Losses Could Hit EUR 700m," September 29, sec. FINANCE; OTHER STORIES.

2009. "Germany Moves to Nationalise Hypo Bank," March 21, sec. FINANCE; BUSINESS NEWS.

2010. "German Guarantees for Hypo Increased," May 29, sec. FINANCE; BUSINESS TODAY.

Iversen, Torben 2005. *Capitalism, Democracy, and Welfare*. New York: Cambridge University Press.

Jabko, Nicolas and Massoc, Elsa 2012. "French capitalism under stress: How Nicolas Sarkozy rescued the banks," *Review of International Political Economy* 19 (4): 562–585.

Jagger, Suzy and Webster, Philip 2009. "Lloyds Banking Group Is Set for an Early Repayment of £2.3bn." *The Times (London)*, June 8, sec. BUSINESS.

Jamieson, Bill and McIntosh, Lindsay 2008. "Still Time to Save 'the Bank.'" *The Scotsman*, October 15.

Johal, Sukhdev, Moran, Michael, and Williams, Karel 2012. "Post-Crisis Financial Regulation in Britain," in Mayntz (ed.), p. 67.

2014. "Power, Politics and the City of London after the Great Financial Crisis," *Government and Opposition* 49(3): 400–425.

Johnson, Simon and Kwak, James 2010. *13 Bankers: The Wall Street Takeover and the Next Financial Meltdown*. New York: Pantheon Books.

Jolly, David 2008. "Commerzbank to Acquire Allianz's Banking Arm for $14 Billion." *The New York Times*, September 1, sec. C; BUSINESS/FINANCIAL DESK.

Kaletsky, Anatole 2007. "Another Black Wednesday Was a Whisker Away." *The Times (London)*, September 20, sec. FEATURES.

Kalinowski, Thomas 2011. "Regulating International Finance and the Evolving Imbalance of Capitalisms since the 1970s: 11/10," *Max-Planck-Institut Für Gesellschaftsforschung Discussion Papers*. Cologne: Max Plank Institute.

Kaminsky, Graciela L. and Pereira, Alfredo 1996. "The Debt Crisis: Lessons of the 1980s for the 1990s," *Journal of Development Economics* 50(1):1–24.

Katzenstein, Peter J. 1978. *Between Power and Plenty: Foreign Economic Policies of Advanced Industrial States*. Madison: University of Wisconsin Press.

Keefer, Philip 2002. "DPI2000 Database of Political Institutions: Changes and Variable Definitions," The World Bank's Development Research Group.

Keefer, Philip and Stasavage, David 2003. "The Limits of Delegation: Veto Players, Central Bank Independence, and the Credibility of Monetary Policy," *The American Political Science Review* 97(3): 407–423.

Kelly, Kate 2009. *Street Fighters: The Last 72 Hours of Bear Stearns, the Toughest Firm on Wall Street*. New York: Portfolio.

Kindleberger, Charles Poor and Aliber, Robert Z. 2011. *Manias, Panics and Crashes: A History of Financial Crises*. Basingstoke: Palgrave Macmillan.

Krugman, Paul 2008. "Gordon Does Good." *The New York Times*, October 13, sec. A; EDITORIAL DESK; OP-ED COLUMNIST.

2009. "Bailouts for Bunglers: Op-ed." *New York Times*.

Laeven, Luc and Valencia, Fabian 2012. *Systemic Banking Crises Database: An Update*. Washington, DC: International Monetary Fund.

Landler, Mark and Bennhold, Katrin 2008. "Bold Pledges from World Leaders, But Investors Await the Details." *The New York Times*, October 13, sec. A; BUSINESS/FINANCIAL DESK.

Langley, Paul 2005. "The Everyday Life of Global Finance: A Neglected 'Level' of Governance," in Baker, Hudson, and Woodward (eds.), p. 85.

Levitin, Michael 2008. "Commerzbank Gets €8.2bn in State Cash." *The Daily Telegraph (London)*, November 4, sec. CITY.

Lichfield, John and Paterson, Tony 2008. "From Iceland to Greece, Europe Marches Out of Step; Leaders Attempt to Show Unity as Market Crisis Raises Threat of New Political Rifts." *The Independent (London)*, October 7, sec. NEWS.

Linklater, Magnus 2008. "Crunch Has Put Paid to Scottish Independence." *The Times (London)*, October 15, sec. FEATURES; SCOTLAND.

Livesey, Ben and Menon, Jon 2007. "British Lender's Shares Plummet; Seven-Year Low. Hundreds Withdraw Savings Despite Assurances." *The Gazette (Montreal)*, September 18, sec. BUSINESS.

Loriaux, Michael Maurice 1997. "The End of Credit Activism in Interventionist States," in Loriaux, Woo-Cumings, Calder, Maxfield, and Pérez (eds.).

Lowenstein, Roger 2000. *When Genius Failed: The Rise and Fall of Long-Term Capital Management*. New York: Random House.

2010. *The End of Wall Street*. New York: Penguin Press.

Lütz, Susanne 2004. "Convergence within National Diversity: The Regulatory State in Finance," *Journal of Public Policy* 24(2): 169–197.

2005. "The Finance Sector in Transition: A Motor for Economic Reform?," *German Politics* 14(2): 140–156.

Lukes, Steven 1974. *Power: A Radical View. Vol. 1*. London: Macmillan.

Lydall, Ross and Jamieson, Bill 2008. "One Rule for Lloyds, One for Everyone Else, Signals Darling." *The Scotsman*, November 19.

Lynch, Russell 2008. "B&B Bank Is Nationalised to Ease Crisis; Government Pledge as It Takes over £41bn in Mortgages a Camera Crew Outside a Bradford & Bingley Branch Yesterday." *Belfast Telegraph*, September 29.

2009. "Taxpayers' Pounds 25bn to Rescue RBS." *Daily Record*, February 27, sec. NEWS.

Lynch, Russell and Christie, Lucy 2008. "HBOS 'Could be Nationalised' if Takeover Bid Fails." *Press Association Mediapoint*, November 15.

Lyons, William 2007. "Branson Poised to Up Bid as Rock Mulls Arnold Plan." *Scotland on Sunday*, December 9.

Macdonell, Hamish 2008. "Darling Rejects Salmond's Claim Bank Could Have Been Saved." *The Scotsman*, September 22.

Macdonell, Hamish and MacMahon, Peter 2008. "Lloyds–HBOS Merger Still Not a Done Deal, Says Top Banker." *The Scotsman*, September 22.

MacNamara, Kelly and Russell Lynch 2009. "Bailout by Bank of England Revealed." *Belfast Telegraph*, November 25.

Maddox, David 2008. "Independent HBOS Fight 'Gaining Pace.'" *The Scotsman*, November 17.

March, James G. and Olsen, Johan P. *Democratic Governance*. New York: Free Press.

Market News International 2008. "Update 4: BOE King: Lloyds–HBOS Merger Cannot Be Undone," November 3.

Martin, Cathie Jo 2005. "Beyond Bone Structure: Historical Institutionalism and the Style of Economic Growth," in Coates (ed.), p. 47.

2006. "Sectional Parties, Divided Business," *Studies in American Political Development* 20(2): 160–184.

Mason, Joseph R. 2010. "The Evolution of the Reconstruction Finance Corporation as a Lender of Last Resort in the Great Depression," in Wright (ed.), p. 70.

Mason, Rowena 2009. "New German Law Paves Way for State Ownership of Banks." *The Daily Telegraph (London)*, February 19, sec. CITY.

Massie, Allan 2008. "The Bail-Out That Crushes SNP's Dream." *Daily Mail (London)*, October 15.

Mayntz, Renate (ed.) 2012a. *Crisis and Control: Institutional Change in Financial Market Regulation.* Frankfurt: Campus Verlag, Vol. Bd. 75.

2012b. "Institutional Change in the Regulation of Financial Markets: Questions and Answers," in Mayntz (ed.).

McArdle, Helen 2011. "Brown: Financial Crisis of 2008 Was Just the Beginning." *The Herald (Glasgow),* May 17, sec. HS-NEWS.

McCarty, Nolan, Poole, Keith T., and Rosenthal, Howard. 2013 *Political Bubbles: Financial Crises and the Failure of American Democracy.* Princeton: Princeton University Press.

McConnell, Ian 2007. "No Bailout for Lenders – King; Bank of England Governor Raises Hopes That Interest Rates Have Peaked – for Now." *The Herald (Glasgow),* September 13, sec. BUSINESS.

2008. "Government Stake in Royal Confirmed at 57.9 Per Cent; Bank's Investors Reject Capital-Raising." *The Herald (Glasgow),* November 29, sec. BUSINESS.

McCusker, Peter 2008. "Barclays in No Bonuses' Move to Pacify Investors." *The Journal (Newcastle, UK),* November 19.

McDonough, Tony 2007. "Northern Rock Had to Be Bailed Out, Says Darling; Market Watch Comment." *Daily Post (Liverpool),* November 28, sec. BUSINESS.

2008. "No End in Prospect for the Northern Rock Nightmare; Tony McDonough Reviews the Collapse of Northern Rock, and Asks What the Future Holds in Association with Rensburg Sheppards." *Daily Post (Liverpool),* January 2, sec. BUSINESS.

McIntosh, Lindsay 2008a. "Cracks Begin to Show in HBOS Buy-Out." *The Scotsman,* October 1.

2008b. "RBS Shares Plummet as Partner Bank Is Nationalised." *The Scotsman,* September 30.

McRae, Hamish 2007. "When It Comes to Finance, Nationalised Companies Seem to be Doing the Best." *The Independent (London),* November 28, sec. COMMENT.

Menz, Georg 2005 *Varieties of Capitalism and Europeanization: National Response Strategies to the Single European Market.* Oxford: Oxford University Press.

Minsky, Hyman P. 1982. *Can 'It' Happen Again? Essays on Instability and Finance.* Armonk, NY: M.E. Sharpe.

Mitchell, Christopher W. 2016. "The Structure of Financial Markets and the Form of State Bailouts, 1974–2009." *Business and Politics* 18 (2): 97–122.

Moir, Jane 2008. "Shareholders Won't Give Barclays Easy Ride; But They're Expected to Vote for the Bank's Fund-Raising." *The Business Times Singapore,* November 20.

Moran, Michael and Payne, Anthony 2014. "Introduction: Neglecting, Rediscovering and Thinking Again about Power in Finance," *Government and Opposition* 49(3): 331–341.

Morris, Nigel 2008. "Branson Rebuffed as Darling Nationalises Northern Rock." *The Independent (London),* February 18, sec. NEWS.

Neligan, Miles 2007. "Rock Proves Hard Place for PM." *Birmingham Post,* December 19, sec. BUSINESS.

Northedge, Richard 2008. "Barclays Goes East to Raise Funds But Leaves Its Existing Shareholders Fuming." *The Independent on Sunday,* November 9.

Observer 2010. "The Weekend Brown Saved the Banks from the Abyss: The 'Long Weekend' when Britain Went to the Brink: The Prime Minister's Leadership Qualities Were to the Fore on the Weekend in October 2008 when Financial Calamity Was So Close." *The Observer (England),* February 21, sec. OBSERVER IN FOCUS PAGES.

Olson, Mancur 1982. *The Rise and Decline of Nations: Economic Growth, Stagflation, and Social Rigidities.* New Haven: Yale University Press.

Pagano, Marco and Volpin, Paolo F. 2005. "The Political Economy of Corporate Governance," *The American Economic Review* 95(4): 1005.

Pagano, Margareta 2008. "New Beowulf Takes a Swipe at the City's Over-paid Dragons." *The Independent – Business & Money,* May 4, sec. BUSINESS.

Panitch, Leo and Gindin, Sam 2005. "Euro-Capitalism and American Empire," in Coates (ed.), p. 139.

Paulson, Henry M. 2010. *On the Brink: Inside the Race to Stop the Collapse of the Global Financial System.* New York: Business Plus.

Pearlstein, Steven 2015. "Court Tells Government It Was Wrong to Seize AIG, But Awards No Money to Billionaire Ex-CEO." *Washington Post,* June 15.

Peev, Gerri 2009. "Scottish Banks' Secret GBP 62bn Bailout." *The Scotsman,* November 25.

Perotti, Enrico C. and von Thadden, Ernst-Ludwig 2006. "The Political Economy of Corporate Control and Labor Rents," *The Journal of Political Economy* 114(1): 145–174.

Piattoni, Simona 2009. "Multi-Level Governance: A Historical and Conceptual Analysis," *Journal of European Integration* 31(2): 163–180.

Polanyi, Karl 1944. *The Great Transformation.* New York and Toronto: Farrar & Rinehart, Inc.

Polillo, Simone and Guillén, Mauro F. 2005. "Globalization Pressures and the State: The Worldwide Spread of Central Bank Independence," *The American Journal of Sociology* 110(6): 1764–1802.

Porter, Andrew, Randall, Jeff, Winnett, Robert, and Kirkup, James 2008. "Day of Reckoning; Darling's Pounds 50bn Bank Bail-Out No Guarantee for Savers RBS Chiefs Forced to Quit." *The Daily Telegraph (London),* October 8, sec. NEWS.

Pratley, Nils 2007. "Financial: Viewpoint: By Rights Rock Should Come Clean." *The Guardian (London) – Final Edition,* November 21, sec. GUARDIAN FINANCIAL PAGES.

2008. "Financial: Viewpoint: King's Saved the Banks But Will He Save Homebuyers?" *The Guardian (London) – Final Edition,* April 22, sec. GUARDIAN FINANCIAL PAGES.

Prynn, Jonathan 2008. "(1) Brown Orders Merger Bid to Save Hailfax (2) It's an Amazing Deal for Lloyds TSB; Lloyds TSB in Talks to Create a Super-Bank." *The Evening Standard (London),* September 17.

Radelet, Steven and Sachs, Jeffrey D. 1998. "The East Asian Financial Crisis: Diagnosis, Remedies, Prospects," *Brookings Papers on Economic Activity* 1998(1): 1–90.

Rayner, Gordon 2008. "The Pounds 37bn Deal with So Much Riding on It; Gordon Rayner Examines the Agreement and Its Implications for the Public, Government and Financial World." *The Daily Telegraph (London)*, October 14, sec. NEWS; THE DEAL.

Rees, William 2009. "Brown Cannot Shirk the Blame for Lloyds; the Prime Minister and the Two Top Men Have Ruined a Good Bank by a Failure of Due Diligence." *The Times (London)*, March 9, sec. FEATURES.

Reid, Margaret I. 1982. *The Secondary Banking Crisis, 1973–75: Its Causes and Course*. London: Macmillan.

Reinhart, Carmen M. and Rogoff, Kenneth S. 2009. *This Time Is Different: Eight Centuries of Financial Folly*. Princeton: Princeton University Press.

Remmer, Karen L. 1990. "Democracy and Economic Crisis: The Latin American Experience," *World Politics* 42(3): 315–335.

1991. "The Political Impact of Economic Crisis in Latin America in the 1980s," *The American Political Science Review* 85(3): 777–800.

Risk, Hamish 2010. "Capital Markets: Merkel Flexes Her Muscles." *Euromoney*, October.

Roe, Mark J. 2003. *Political Determinants of Corporate Governance: Political Context, Corporate Impact*. Oxford: Oxford University Press.

Rosa, Jean-Jacques and Pérard, Edouard 2010. "When to Privatize? When to Nationalize? A Competition for Ownership Approach," *Kyklos* 63(1): 110–132.

Rosas, Guillermo 2006. "Bagehot or Bailout? An Analysis of Government Responses to Banking Crises," *American Journal of Political Science* 50(1): 175–191.

2009. *Curbing Bailouts: Bank Crises and Democratic Accountability in Comparative Perspective*. Ann Arbor: University of Michigan Press.

Rosas, Guillermo and Jensen, Nathan M. 2010. "After the Storm: The Long-Run Impact of Bank Bailouts," in Wright (ed.), p. 108.

Roth, Michael 1994, "'Too-Big-to-Fail' and the Stability of the Banking System: Some Insights from Foreign Countries," *Business Economics* 29: 43–43.

Royo, Sebastián 2013. "How Did the Spanish Financial System Survive the First Stage of the Global Crisis?" *Governance* 26(4): 631–656.

Russell, Jonathan, Griffiths, Katherine, and Aldrick, Philip 2008. "Fury as 'Thieving' Chancellor Nationalises Northern Rock." *The Daily Telegraph (London)*, February 18, sec. CITY.

Satyanath, Shanker 2006. *Globalization, Politics, and Financial Turmoil: Asia's Banking Crisis*. New York: Cambridge University Press.

Scally, Derek 2008. "Banks to Pay Dearly for German Bailout." *The Irish Times*, October 14, sec. FINANCE; GLOBAL BANKING CRISIS.

2009a. "German 'Bad Bank' Sees the First Step in Revolution." *The Irish Times*, May 16, sec. FINANCE; BUSINESS NEWS.

2009b. "German Move to Establish 'Bad Bank.'" *The Irish Times*, April 22, sec. FINANCE; BUSINESS NEWS.

2009c. "German MPs Grapple with Dublin Bank's Financial Woes." *The Irish Times*, August 7, sec. FINANCE; BUSINESS AGENDA.

2009d. "German Property Lender HRE Agrees Nationalisation Amid Angry Scenes." *The Irish Times,* October 6, sec. FINANCE; BUSINESS TODAY.

2009e. "Hypo Shareholders to Consider EUR 321m State Takeover." *The Irish Times,* April 18, sec. FINANCE; BUSINESS NEWS.

2009f. "Shares in Hypo Jump 70% as Merkel Approves Draft Expropriation Bill." *The Irish Times,* February 19, sec. FINANCE; BUSINESS TODAY.

2009g. "Top Banker Said Depfa Crisis Nearly Collapsed System." *The Irish Times,* July 8, sec. FINANCE; BUSINESS NEWS.

2010. "German Banks Agree to Radical Overhaul." *The Irish Times,* September 29, sec. FINANCE; BUSINESS TODAY.

Scherer, Ron 2007. "US Debt Jolts World Markets." *Christian Science Monitor,* August 17.

Schneider, Martin and Tornell, Aaron 2004. "Balance Sheet Effects, Bailout Guarantees and Financial Crises," *The Review of Economic Studies* 71(3): 883–913.

Scotsman 2008. "What HBOS–Lloyds Deal Means to Scotland," September 19.

Seager, Ashley, Elliott, Larry, and Treanor, Jill 2008. "Financial: Banking Crisis: Bank Governor Insists Bail-Out Will Not be a Bottomless Pit: Credit Line Expected to be Tapped for £50bn: Sub-Prime Securities Will Not Be Accepted." *The Guardian (London) – Final Edition,* April 22, sec. GUARDIAN FINANCIAL PAGES.

Seib, Christine 2007. "Banks Seek Secret Loans after Rock Ruin." *The Times (London),* October 3, sec. BUSINESS.

Seib, Christine and Andrews, Amanda 2008. "'Our Shares Are Worthless' Say the Rock's Furious Investors." *The Times (London),* February 18, sec. BUSINESS.

Settle, Michael 2008a. "Banking on a New Era; Giants 'Nationalised' in Taxpayers' GBP37bn Bailout; Bonus Culture Hit as Bosses Go without Payoffs; Shares Up 8 Per Cent as City Reacts to Momentous Day." *The Herald (Glasgow),* October 14, sec. NEWS.

2008b. "No Golden Goodbyes as Chiefs' Heads Roll in Bank Rescue Plan; Michael Settle Examines Exactly What the Bailout Will Mean for the Struggling Organisations Involved." *The Herald (Glasgow),* October 14, sec. NEWS.

Sharp, Tim 2009. "Lloyds Secures 87 Per Cent Take-Up in Rights Issue to Raise GBP4bn; Boost from First Bank to Repay Government." *The Herald (Glasgow),* June 9, sec. BUSINESS.

Shonfield, Andrew 1965. *Modern Capitalism: The Changing Balance of Public and Private Power.* New York: Oxford University Press.

Slater, Steve and Marques, Clara Ferreira 2008. "Olivant Quits Northern Rock Rescue Race." *National Post's Financial Post & FP Investing (Canada),* February 5, sec. FINANCIAL POST.

Smith, David 2007. "Hammer Blow for the Boom." *The Sunday Times (London),* September 16, sec. FEATURES; NEWS.

Smyth, Jamie 2008. "German Finance Minister Dismisses Proposed Pan-European Rescue Fund." *The Irish Times,* October 3, sec. FINANCE; GLOBAL FINANCIAL CRISIS.

Sonderfonds Finanzmarktstabilisierung 2011. "Massnahmen Aktuell," Deutsche Bundesbank, http://www.soffin.de/de/soffin/leistungen/massnahmen-aktuell/index.html, accessed April 30, 2011.

Sorkin, Andrew Ross 2009. *Too Big to Fail: The Inside Story of How Wall Street and Washington Fought to Save the Financial System from Crisis – and Themselves.* New York: Viking.

2011. *Too Big to Fail: The Inside Story of How Wall Street and Washington Fought to Save the Financial System – and Themselves.* New York: Penguin Group.

Stewart, Heather 2008. "Business & Media: Business: Inside Story: A High Price to Save the Banks: For a Long Time, Bank Governor Mervyn King Tried to Hold the Line on 'Moral Hazard' But, as the Credit Crisis Deepens, He Has Had to Admit Defeat – and Take on Unwanted Assets to Get the Market Moving." *The Observer (England)*, April 20, sec. OBSERVER BUSINESS PAGES.

Stewart, Heather and Connon, Heather 2007. "Fears Grow for British Economy as Panic over Northern Rock Spreads: Experts Warn That a Decade-Long Borrowing Binge Has Left Britain Dangerously Exposed to the Fallout from the Global Liquidity Crisis." *The Observer (England)*, September 16, sec. OBSERVER BUSINESS PAGES.

Stiglitz, Joseph E. 2010. *Freefall: America, Free Markets, and the Sinking of the World Economy*. New York: W.W. Norton & Co.

Streeck, Wolfgang 2010. "E Pluribus Unum? Varieties and Commonalities of Capitalism: 10/12," *Max-Planck-Institut Für Gesellschaftsforschung Discussion Papers*. Cologne: Max Plank Institute.

Sunday Telegraph (London) 2008. "State Ownership of Banks Should be Strictly Temporary," October 12, sec. FEATURES; LEADING ARTICLE.

Sunday Times (London) 2008. "Europe's Banks Face More Pain, Too," September 14, sec. BUSINESS; BUSINESS.

Swagel, Phillip 2009. "The Financial Crisis: An Inside View," *Brookings Papers on Economic Activity* 2009(1): 1–63.

Tabb, William K. 1998. "The East Asian Financial Crisis," *Monthly Review* 50 (2): 24–38.

Telegraph, 2012. "Former RBS Chief Executive Fred Goodwin Stripped of His Knighthood; Fred Goodwin, the Disgraced Former Royal Bank of Scotland Chief Executive, Has Been Stripped of His Knighthood," February 1.

Teteryatnikova, Mariya 2009. "Resilience of the Interbank Network to Shocks and Optimal Bail-Out Strategy: Advantages of 'Tiered' Banking Systems," Working Paper. Italy: European University Institute.

Thomas, Nathalie and Rosemary Gallagher 2009. "The Lehman's Legacy: Has Banking's Dragon Finally been Tamed?" *Scotland on Sunday*, September 13.

Thompson, Sarah 2007. "Banks and Insurers Pace Market Retreat." *The International Herald Tribune*, November 27, sec. FINANCE.

Tift, Duncan 2008. "False HBOS Rumour Puts Markets into a Tailspin." *Birmingham Post*, March 20, sec. BUSINESS.

Tift, Duncan and Cranage, John 2008. "Darling Was Right to Act on Rock, Say Top Bosses." *Birmingham Post*, February 19, sec. BUSINESS.

Tinning, William 2008. "Pressure on Darling as Germany Guarantees All Savings." *The Herald (Glasgow)*, October 6, sec. NEWS.

Total Securitization 2009. "German Lender Center of Bailout Battle," November 20.

Treanor, Jill 2008. "Front: HBOS Rescue in Jeopardy: Plunge in Embattled Lender's Shares Leaves Lloyds Paying Billions Too Much." *The Guardian (London) – Final Edition,* October 1, sec. GUARDIAN HOME PAGES.

2009a. "Financial: Sheikh Exits Barclays with £ 1.4bn Profit: Share Sale Undermines Bank's Non-State Bailout: Taxpayer Sitting on £5bn Loss in RBS and Lloyds." *The Guardian (London) – Final Edition,* June 3, sec. GUARDIAN FINANCIAL PAGES.

2009b. "National: Banking Crisis: Taxpayer May End Up with 95% of RBS after Record Loss Revealed: Chancellor Admits Risks Being Taken as Bank Chief Says 20,000 Jobs under Threat." *The Guardian (London) – Final Edition,* February 27, sec. GUARDIAN HOME PAGES.

Treanor, Jill and Elliott, Larry 2008. "Banking Crisis: War Games, Champagne and Frantic Efforts to Save HBOS: PM and Bank of England Intervene to Head Off Another Banking Debacle." *The Guardian (London) – Final Edition,* September 18, sec. GUARDIAN HOME PAGES.

Treanor, Jill, Gow, David, Traynor, Ian, and Watt, Nicholas 2008. "Front: Brown Bail-Out under Threat as Bank Seeks Better Deal: Shares Plunge as Recession Bites: Highest Jobless Rise in 17 Years: Lloyds Wants Easier Repayment: PM Calls for New Economic Rules." *The Guardian (London) – Final Edition,* October 16, sec. GUARDIAN HOME PAGES.

Tsingou, Eleni 2010. "Regulatory Reactions to the Global Credit Crisis: Analysing a Policy Community under Stress," in Helleiner, Pagliari, and Zimmermann (eds.), p. 21.

Tyler, Richard 2008. "Brown Is Urged to Guarantee Deposits; Banking Crisis the Contagion Spreads; Pressure on Prime Minister Grows as Germany Bails Out Bank." *The Daily Telegraph (London),* October 6, sec. CITY.

Underhill, Geoffrey R. D. and Blom, Jasper 2012. "The International Financial Architecture: Plus Ça Change…?" in Mayntz (ed.).

US Congress House Committee on Financial Services 2011. *The Final Report of the Financial Crisis Inquiry Commission: Hearing before the Committee on Financial Services, U.S. House of Representatives, One Hundred Twelfth Congress, First Session, February 16, 2011.* Washington: US Government Publishing Office.

US Department of the Treasury 2013. *Troubled Asset Relief Program (TARP) Monthly Report to Congress – December 2012.* Washington, DC: United States Department of the Treasury.

Verdier, Daniel 2002. *Moving Money: Banking and Finance in the Industrialized World.* Cambridge, UK: Cambridge University Press.

Walker, Bruce 2009. "Fred Sued for Pounds 9bn; Furious Rbs Investors Vow Court Action." *Sunday Mail,* October 11, sec. NEWS.

Walker, Marcus 2009. "Germany Weighs Hypo Seizure." *Wall Street Journal Abstracts,* January 28.

Walker, Marcus, Munoz, Sara Schaefer, and Gauthier-Villars, David 2008. "Bailout Price Tags Raise the Question: How? As World Markets Rise, Economists Fret over Cost to Taxpayers and Governments." *The Globe and Mail (Canada)*, October 14, sec. REPORT ON BUSINESS: INTERNATIONAL; GLOBAL FINANCIAL CRISIS: EUROPEAN PLANS.

Waples, John 2008. "The Six Days That Almost Broke the Bank." *The Sunday Times (London)*, June 8, sec. BUSINESS.

Warner, Jeremy 2008a. "Bear Fire Sale Marks Start of Capitulation." *The Independent (London)*, March 18, sec. BUSINESS.

2008b. "With HBOS under Renewed Attack, Forced Takeover May be the Solution." *The Independent (London)*, September 17, sec. BUSINESS.

Watkins, Simon, Buckingham, Lisa, and Atkinson, Dan 2007. "Subprime Panic on the High St; Special Report after the Northern Rock Debacle, Barclays Could Now be Facing Meltdown as Shares Crash 9% in One Day." *Mail on Sunday (London)*, November 11, sec. C1.

Weaver, R. Kent and Rockman, Bert A. 1993. "Assessing the Effects of Institutions," in Rockman, Bert A. and Weaver, R. Kent (eds.) *Do Institutions Matter? Government Capabilities in the United States and Abroad*. Washington, DC: The Brookings Institution.

Weber, Beat and Schmitz, Stefan W. 2011. "Varieties of Helping Capitalism: Politico-economic Determinants of Bank Rescue Packages in the EU during the Recent Crisis," *Socio-Economic Review* 9(4): 638–669.

Weber, Max and Kalberg, Stephen 1930[2001]. *The Protestant Ethic and the Spirit of Capitalism*. London: Fitzroy Dearborn.

Wessel, David 2010. *In Fed We Trust: Ben Bernanke's War on the Great Panic*. New York: Three Rivers Press.

West, Karl 2008. "BoE Move Boosts Finance Shares." *Daily Mail (London)*, October 4.

Whitfield, Paul 2009. "Germany Launches Hypo Takeover." *Daily Deal/The Deal*, April 20.

Wighton, David 2012. "'Your Guy Mervyn Has a High Pain Threshold'; Northern Rock Was Heading for Collapse, But as Britain's Economy Was Struck by Panic, There Was Only Inertia at the Bank. David Wighton Reports." *The Times (London)*, March 13, sec. NEWS.

Wilson, Peter 2007. "UK Laws Tied My Hands, Says Embattled Bank of England Governor." *The Australian*, September 21, sec. FINANCE.

Winnett, Robert 2008. "Business; Bank Is Blown Away." *The Daily Telegraph (London)*, September 18, sec. NEWS.

Wolf, Martin 2010. *Fixing Global Finance*. Baltimore: Johns Hopkins University Press.

2014. *The Shifts and the Shocks: What We've Learned – and Have Still to Learn – from the Financial Crisis*. London and New York: Allen Lane.

Woll, Cornelia 2014. *The Power of Inaction: Bank Bailouts in Comparison*. Ithaca, NY: Cornell University Press.

Woo, Wing Thye, Jeffrey Sachs, and Klaus Schwab 2000. *The Asian Financial Crisis: Lessons for a Resilient Asia*. Cambridge, MA: MIT Press.

Wookey, Jethro 2008. "Pfandbrief: The Sincerest Form of Flattery." *Euromoney*, November.

World Bank 2012a. "WBI Governance & Anti-Corruption," http://web.worldbank.org/WBSITE/EXTERNAL/WBI/EXTWBIGOVANTCOR/0,menuPK:1740542~pagePK:64168427~piPK:64168435~theSitePK:1740530,00.html, accessed March 19, 2012.

2012b. "World Development Indicators," http://data.worldbank.org/data-catalog/world-development-indicators, accessed July 23, 2012.

Wright, Robert E. (ed.) 2010a. *Bailouts: Public Money, Private Profit*. New York: Columbia University Press.

2010b. "Hybrid Failures and Bailouts: Social Costs, Private Profits," in Wright (ed.), p. 18.

Yeyati, Eduardo Levy, Micco, Alejandro, Panizza, Ugo, Detragiache, Enrica, and Repetto, Andrea 2007. "A Reappraisal of State-Owned Banks [with Comments]," *Economia* 7(2): 209–259.

Young, Alf 2008. "Warning: Light-Fingered Opportunists Are Operating in this B & B AlfYoung on Tuesday." *The Herald (Glasgow)*, June 3, sec. BUSINESS.

Zimmermann, Hubert 2010. "Varieties of Global Financial Governance? British and German Approaches to Financial Market Regulation," in Helleiner, Pagliari, and Zimmermann (eds.), p. 121.

Zysman, John 1983. *Governments, Markets, and Growth: Financial Systems and the Politics of Industrial Change*. Ithaca, NY: Cornell University Press.

Index

For EU product safety concerns, contact us at Calle de José Abascal, 56–1°, 28003 Madrid, Spain or eugpsr@cambridge.org.

www.ingramcontent.com/pod-product-compliance
Lightning Source LLC
LaVergne TN
LVHW011522200926
848484LV00001B/116
* 9 7 8 1 1 0 7 1 5 9 2 3 5 *